FE 19

Calais, Boulogne and The North

Calais, Boulogne and The North

AN EAT AND SLEEP GUIDE
New French Entrée 19

PATRICIA FENN

Quiller Press

First published 1999 by
Quiller Press Ltd, 46 Lillie Road, London, SW6 1TN

Copyright 1999 © Patricia Fenn

ISBN 1 899163 50 6

Illustrations by Ken Howard and Emma McLeod
Jacket by Claire Davies
Area Maps by Helen Humphries
Designed by Jo Lee
Printed by Biddles Ltd

CONTENTS

RAISONS D'ÊTRE

This is emphatically a new guide. Not a reprint, not a rehash. There have been so many changes since 1994, when the last book on The North was published, that a completely fresh view was demanded. So perhaps I am getting off to a bad start by virtually repeating here in the first place what I wrote in FE12, the last book on the North of France. That is because the raisons d'être for the series is one of the few things that are not new. So old readers please ignore, prospective new readers please read on...

The French Entrée series is designed to fill a gap. Rough Guide it is not, Luxury Guide it is not either. It does have components of both, however, with a good deal in the middle. The assumption is that most of us need horses for courses - the luxury hotel for the anniversary, the Michelin star for the gastro-gorge, the rustic gem for the end-of-the-month, the regional cooking to boast about back home, the convenient overnighter just off the autoroute, the seaside guesthouse for the buckets 'n' spades. In France of course.

Do not buy this guide if all you need is a quick symbolised reference book. Here is plenty of flesh on the bones. You may or may not be interested to know what colour the napkins are, what the relationship is between the chef and the hostess, where the locals eat, which menu is best value, or which bedroom has the best view. You may or not be concerned with the markets, the churches, the shops, the walks, the picnic spots, historical happenings, apocryphal tales, all which take up considerable space in French Entrées, but it's up to you to pick out the details that matter to *you*. My aim is to paint the picture but not to limit the range to one set of preferences or income groups. I describe, *you* get to choose.

INTRODUCTION

TO CALAIS, BOULOGNE AND THE NORTH

There were headaches attached to defining the area to be covered by this book. FE12 covered a vast area of The North, extending to the Ardennes and down to the Somme. Previous books had stretched down to Paris. By now I know my own limitations and realised that a choice had to be made. Either I struggled on single-handed or I involved another writer to share the territory. If I chose the first option, the book was going to take so long to research that some of it would be out of date before it was published (and I would be swearing I would never write another); if I allocated part of the area to someone else, the result would probably be patchy and I would lose some of the personal detailed knowledge that gives flavour, substance and, I hope, authority.

A third alternative occurred. Looking through my files of readers letters, it is obvious that the area they are primarily concerned with is quite compact. Some do explore further inland from the coast, and good luck to them because there is much to see in the tourist-neglected hinterland. But the vast majority use a guide on this area to help them choose somewhere to eat or sleep just across the Channel. They do not spend a fortnight here, but rather a long weekend or even a day; the less time they have to spend in the car the better.

So it appears that French Entrée has turned full circle. The first books, 17 years ago, were written to introduce the Brits to the pleasures that lay so near, but previously so far. I remember that many were nervous of driving on the wrong side of the road or having to speak a strange lingo. It's hard to believe now that second holidays, short breaks abroad, were something new. The area covered then was immediately round the Channel ports. This subsequently expanded to one hundred kms inland, and that is exactly the same area in this latest book. Restricting the limits has enabled me to spend the same amount of time researching a smaller area more intensively, so that I can safely say that I know virtually every village in its confines and every restaurant and hotel. I have been able to add details, like good walks, good excursions and good attractions, for which there was previously neither time nor space. I hope it will make a better book.

Because the area is smaller, it is definitely not less interesting nor varied. I continue to be amazed at the variety on offer. Look at the one-offs: **Cassel**, a hilltop fortress in the middle of the Flanders plain, and it's hard to believe that not so very far away is the sophisticated **Le Touquet-Paris-Plage**, all 1930s nostalgia. Look at the old ramparted town of **Montreuil** in its new guise as a gastro-centre, with Michelin stars competing with rustic contenders. Look at **St Valéry**, at the vast estuary of the Somme, oozing history and salty charm, then consider **Arras**, with one of the biggest and most beautiful squares in Europe at its heart, and several others besides. **St Omer** is unique, with its rivers, canals, locks, market gardens and misty moistness, **Berques** is a pleasant surprise, like a mini Bruges, **Hesdin** too has water running through it's centre, a charming town well worth a visit, and **Rue** deserves better recognition for its historical connections and lack of tourists. Even familiar **Boulogne** keeps some surprises up its sleeve for those who have never climbed up to the old town. I still discover something new on every visit. This time it was **Gravelines**, which I had never got around to before. Fascinating and, like all the others mentioned, completely different from anywhere else.

The scenery too is greatly under-estimated. It may not be the Alps but it's certainly not all flat, as so many sceptics claim. Only a few kms drive from Boulogne are the delightful Boulonais hills, green and unspoiled, sheltering time-warped villages and a degree of rusticity that is rare in England's over-crowded acres. The estuary of the Somme is vast and magnificent, with the opalescent light that has delighted artists for many years and which gave the area its name the Côte d'Opale. There are forests and many rivers, with strange monosyllabic names like the Slack, the Hem, and the Aa. The valleys of the Course, the Canche and the Authie are all demanding to be explored.

As for the beaches they are incomparable. They stretch the entire way from the Belgian border to the Somme, broken at the two Caps, Gris and Nez, by high chalk cliffs, but otherwise offering miles of firm sand and dunes.

Sadly this gateway to France has predictably been the scene of centuries of bloody conflicts. War and territorial acquisitions, with the aggression and tragedies that accompany them, have always been part of the area's heritage. The bloodshed in this century among the Flanders poppies and the cornfields of the Somme and the subsequent alien occupation of the whole region are a contemporary reminder of its vulnerability. For those who are remotely interested in the past there are plenty of memorials.

ENTRÉE TO THE ENTRÉES

SYMBOLS

This is a chatty book, not a concise set of symbols. That said, there are times when symbols come in useful as space-saving shorthand. Here is the French Entrée code:

Hotels and restaurants are categorised in three groups. H is obviously Hotel, and R restaurant. In three cases there will be 'Ch d'H', which stands for Chambres d'Hôtes, or bed and breakfast. (As we now have a full-blown bed and breakfast guide in the series, they have been generally excluded from the other guides, but these three are exceptional for various reasons.) Next in line will be L for Luxury, M for Medium and S for Simple.

The L Group

If you are planning a celebration (or are plain rich) this is the group to look for, and you will find great value, compared with prices for similar standards back home. I find myself apologising when I have to write that a top of the range French hotel room costs 700f, but the equivalent (at time of going to press) £70 odd doesn't go far for two persons' accommodation on this side of the Channel. Luxuries might include marble bathrooms with power showers and fleecy bathrobes hanging behind the door, a swimming pool, tennis courts, spacious 'parcs' dotted with recliners, elegant public rooms, and immaculate service. There will certainly be a complementary smart restaurant. Expect to pay between 600 and 1,000f for a double room and 50-75f for breakfast. The latter sum is actually better value than some of the cheaper *petits déjeuners* in the other categories, because the orange juice will be freshly squeezed, the croissants will be home-baked not dry and leathery, the preserves will be in pots not foil, the butter will be *doux*, and it will probably include a buffet style choice of eggs, ham, fish, yoghurts, cereals and fruit, from which you can fill up until dinner time.

There are some bargains too amongst L restaurants. The economic necessity of seeing bums on chairs for every meal means that chefs will offer rock-bottom priced menus for the less popular meals like lunch and mid-week dinners. There are several Michelin-starred nominations in the guide where you can eat like a lord on a three course 130f menu. The most expensive is the only two-starred restaurant, Marc Meurin in Béthune, where the cheapest evening menu clocks in at 260f, but even here there is a lunchtime not-to-be missed menu at 180f.

Compare these prices with a two-star Michelin restaurant in the U.K. and you will immediately understand why it makes good sense to do your celebrating in France. Head here if you want your meal to be a memorable one, with chefs realising that if they want to hang on to hard-earned, fiercely competitive awards, standards must never never slip. At long last the more enlightened French cooks are beginning to admit that there is something new under the sun and that traditional French cuisine is not the only one. It is in this category that you will taste new flavours and combinations, with influences from all over the world, not just la Belle France. Beware the wine prices. They are often higher than at home and can transform a bargain into a financial crisis. On the other hand, you are more likely to be able to buy a glass of decent wine here, rather than a whole bottle, an important consideration at lunchtime, with driving in mind.

The M Group

The most numerous group in both hotels and restaurants. The hotels are nearly all owner-managed, and will have upgraded their rooms to make sure that they are all en suite. They will be well-equipped, with English television channels, good bathrooms, and plenty of extras. The chain hotels would come into this group but you will not find them here. I know that they can be useful at times when all that is required is a convenient bed for the night, but my reasoning is that I personally would not choose them for any other reason, they are more or less predictably the same, and that readers can perfectly well find them for themselves, without any help from me. Old readers will know by now that this is a totally subjective guide and I am allowed prejudices.

M restaurants range from brasseries to comfortable bourgeois establishments, archetypally French with their tapestry chairs and velvet curtains, full of *hommes d'affaires* at lunchtime and families on Sundays. Chefs sometimes aspire to Michelin accolades, not quite there yet. These are the ones to spot while you can still afford them. Some are chosen because they are in especially attractive sites, overlooking water perhaps. Fish restaurants will probably come in this category, because fresh fish, however simply cooked, is basically expensive and cannot be included in the S group. Prices for the cheapest menu will be around 80-140f.

The S Group

The S hotels and restaurants are the ones that give me most pleasure and most pain. If I discover a really good one, like the Restaurant de la Gare at Les Attaques or le Cerisier at Laventie, I am mightily chuffed and enjoy the readers' letters congratulating me. On the other hand, these are the ones that so easily go wrong. They change hands more frequently than the others do, and the *patron/chefs* seem to have more marital disasters, leading to disruption in the kitchen and *accueil* as well as in the home. Understandably corners are cut to keep prices down, and sometimes this shows, disastrously. The S hotels are even more worrying than the S restaurants because you can forgive an indifferent meal but a bad night's sleep is not easily forgotten. There aren't many of them in the guide; use them by all means but read my caveats before you commit yourself. They will cost between 175 and 220f for a double room, and breakfast (don't expect too much) will be around 35f.

S restaurants are another proposition. I use them frequently at lunchtime when, in order to appreciate properly my forthcoming evening meal, all I want is a plate of cheese with a salad, or *terrine*, or *crudités*, or an omelette, or a bowl of mussels. For those of sterner stuff the *plat du jour* is the dish to head for. It will change every day, to cater for the locals who eat at their favourite restaurant every lunchtime. Around 40f will buy a three course *menu fixe*. Bistros and brasseries feature here, so all tastes and pockets are catered for. As a general rule I would caution against spending a large sum in a S restaurant. The kitchens just do not have the scope nor the chef the expertise to do justice to the more expensive menus, which can shoot up to the 180f mark and are based on the like of bought-in *foie gras*. Desserts are often a disappointment - crème caramel, commercial ice cream, chocolate mousse and indifferent apple tart is about the range.

There is a new category introduced this time. '**Otherwise...**' indicates those establishments which do not qualify for inclusion in the main headings but are worth a mention. It may be that I have inadvertently missed them on my round-ups (not often I am happy to say), or that a reader has recommended them too late for inspection, or that their claim to distinction is an unusually attractive site, or more frequently that there is nothing better in that particularly area.

'**Cl.**' is short for closed and refers to weekly and annual closing days. Ignore these at your peril. There can be nothing more frustrating than arriving after a long drive, with a hearty appetite and thirst, to find the door firmly barred and the whole establishment so shuttered and uncaring that you wonder if it's lost and gone forever. By far the most popular closing days are Sunday dinner and Monday all day; some entries are in the Otherwise section solely because they are the only restaurants open on the dread Sun. Mon.

'**o.o.s.**' means out of season. 'Season' is loosely interpreted as Easter to November, but if in doubt it is always best to check first, because it could refer only to July and August.

So, to translate a typical entry, 'Cl. Sun. p.m.; Mon; Thurs. o.o.s., 15/7-14/8, fêtes' would indicate that the place is closed every Sunday evening, all day Monday, Thursday out of season, from 15th July to 14th August, and on fête days (list opposite).

M is the symbol for Market.

The arrow symbol ➤ indicates a specially recommended entry. A list of arrows and the reasons for their selection is on p.10.

NEW refers to the hotels and restaurants that have been chosen since the publication of the last book (FE12) on the area, published in 1994.

TIPS FOR BEGINNERS

French Public Holidays
New Year's Day
Easter Sunday and Monday
Labour Day, 1st May
VE Day, 8th May
Ascension Day
Whit Sunday and Monday
France's National Day, 14th July
The Assumption, 15th August
All Saints' Day, 1st November
Armistice Day, 11th November
Christmas Day

Many is the now older and wiser traveller to France who has ignored the above fêtes and been forced to sleep in the car. Check that they are not part of your holiday; if they are book well ahead for both bed and board. The same applies to Sunday lunch when generations of French families settle down soon after mid-day to enjoy an orgy of eating, drinking, conversation and baby-worship that can easily last till teatime. Don't imagine you can squeeze in for a second sitting. There is no such thing.

And don't rely on eating at lunchtime after 1.30 in any case. *"Finis"* is a word that the waiters really enjoy.

If your French is non-existent, make use of the local tourist bureaux, usually prominently lodged in the best building in the town centre, who will make the booking for you. Pick up local maps and advice while you're at it.

Shopping Hours

Most shops close for a lengthy lunch break at 12.30. Don't bank on them re-opening for a couple of hours. Some supermarkets stay open, but by no means all, and it is sometimes impossible to buy even petrol during the sacred lunch-time. On the plus side it is a joy to find shops open until 7 in the evening. Ingredients for the evening meal, and particularly freshly baked bread, are shopped for in the late afternoon. How sensible.

A list of the main local supermarkets and their opening hours is on p. 24.

Another hazard is the Monday closing. There is no absolute rule about this but many smaller shops stay shuttered all day on Monday as well as Sunday.

Some on the other hand open up after lunch. If you're thinking of adding an extra day to the weekend, make it Friday, when you will be able to shop and eat.

Markets too snap shut for lunch. Most of them pack up for the day then. (See list on p. 23.)

What to buy

Every year there are fewer items to bring home that are not available in this country; it is just a question of comparing prices now. Best buy of course is wine and beer. See some suggestions where to buy under 'Calais' and throughout the book where applicable. A list of hypermarkets and their closing times are on p. 24.

I always stock up on pure Arabica coffee, which is better and considerably cheaper in France, as is top-quality chocolate. You save a bit on preserves like Bon Maman jams, and with the exchange rate so favourable an average weekly shopping list would undoubtedly cost less in France than in England. It's all a question of how much you want to lug around. I would prefer to spend the time in the markets, finding seasonal produce, like mushrooms, or olives, or asparagus, or strawberries, which may not be any cheaper but are a whole lot fresher than I can buy back home. Cheeses are definitely on my list, just because it is a pleasure to have so much variety and such high quality. *Saucissons* are a good buy for summer lunches or picnics. Don't be tempted to buy any more bread, however delicious, than you can consume immediately it will go stale very quickly simply because it doesn't have any preservatives incorporated.

Maps and Guides

I must stress that the maps on pages 27-28 are intended only as indications of the location of the entries. They should be used in conjunction with the appropriate Michelin map, 236. I find the French Michelins a pleasure to use, so reliable and all-encompassing are they. Navigating even the delightfully rural white roads with their help is a doddle.

The red Michelin book, quite apart from all it's other virtues, has excellent town maps. Gault Millau gives more specific detail and is better for spotting newcomers, but you do have to understand French and it is useless for the S grades. It's expensive too. The Logis de France do a useful guide to their chain of hotels, including the name of the *patron* (in Michelin you have to be a rosette-holder before this accolade is granted). You can buy this at the French Government Tourist Office at 178 Piccadilly, London W1, the source of all manner of helpful advice and literature before you set off. There are two French guides, whose red badges are worth looking out for in the windows of their favoured establishments: *Le Petit Futé*, from which I have stolen some winners, and *Le Routier*, which is best for S choices.

I of course magpie any guide I can get my hands on and shamelessly filch their contents if I think they're going to be of any use. The best guide of all is always word of mouth, or a car park full of French cars.

Breakfast

An increasingly sore point, as more and more hotels cash in. 50f is about the norm nowadays for a hunk of baguette, an indifferent croissant, jam and butter in tin foil, coffee and long-life milk, and if you're lucky(!) bottled orange juice. The only alternative is to get out of bed and find a good café.

ARROWS

➤ The arrows are to direct you towards the bullseyes. These are the trusted and true. The attributes for which they receive the arrow accolade are: good value, extra good food, good welcome and even good situations. The stars have all of these, but the arrows all have at least one to make them stand out from the crowd.

Sometimes arrows have to be deleted because readers have not agreed with my judgement, or I have revisited and been disappointed, or perhaps simply because there is just not enough information available to warrant certainty. If you have any views, and are good enough to pass them on to me, they will be put in the pool of wisdom and re-cycled in time for the next edition.

Obviously the standards by which the S establishments are judged are very different from the Ls. When reviewing the latter it is quite justifiable to be extremely picky. You are paying for nothing but the best, and second best is not acceptable.

The fact that there are rather a lot of arrows in this relatively small area is an indication of the amount of time spent there and information collated over the years, both by myself and by faithful readers. I view them all with great affection for not having let me down.

Aire sur la Lys: *Auberge de la Treille d'Or* (R)S. Simple good value. *Les Trois Mousquetaires* (HR)M-L. Comfortable hotel within easy reach of port, excellent cooking.

Arques: *La Grande Ste. Cathérine* (HR)S. Good value, good welcome.

Arras: *L'Univers* (HR)M. Good position in interesting town. *Les Trois Luppars* (H)S. Good value, good situation. *La Faisanderie* (R)M-L. Excellent cooking.

Les Attaques: *Restaurant de la Gare* (R)S. Consistent good value.

Attin: *Au Bon Acceuil* (R)S-M. Excellent value, popular choice.

Auchy-les-Hesdin: *Auberge de la Monastère* (HR)S-M. Cheerful good value.

Bergues: *Le Berguenard* (R)M-S. New and interesting. *Le Pont Tournant* (R)S-M. Good value.

Béthune: *Marc Meurin* (HR)L. Best cooking in the book. Comfortable rooms.

Beussent: *Chez Barsby* (Ch d'H)L. Superb new *chambres d'hôtes*.

Blendêques: *Le St. Sébastien* (HR)S. Good value.

Bollezeelle: *St Louis* (HR)M. Convenient, welcoming.

Bournonville: *Le Moulin* (R)S. Quantity.

Boulogne: *Chez Jules* (R)M-S. Best brasserie. *La Coquillette* (R)S. Good value, best Italian.

Calais: *Le Channel* (R)M. Consistent good value. Very popular. *Aquar'Aile* (R)M. Best fish. *L'Histoire Ancienne* (R)M. Good value bistro. *La Pleïade* (R)M. Interesting cooking. *Le Grand Bleu* (R)M. Good value fish

Cassel: *l'Estaminet T'Kastell* (R)S. Delightful eccentricity.

Dèsvres: *Agriculture* (R)S. Home cooking.

Dunkerque: (Tétéghem) *La Meunerie* (R)L. Best cooking in le Nord.

Favières: *Le Clé des Champs* (R)M. Unusually good cooking.

Hallines: *Hostellerie St. Hubert* (HR)M. Stylish, peaceful.

Hardelot: *Hotel du Parc* (H)L, *Orangerie* (R)L. Casual luxury.

Hazebrouck: *Le Gambrinus* (H)S. Simple value, welcome.

Hesdin: *La Brêteche* (R)M. Good cooking, good value.

Hesdin-l'Abaye: *Hotel Cléry* (HR)M. Comfortable hotel, well situated.

Huby-St-Leu: *La Garenne* (R)M. Definitely different.

Laventie: *Le Cerisier* (R)M-S. Outstanding cooking at bargain prices.

La Madelaine-sous-Montreuil: *La Grenouillère* (R)L. Outstanding cooking.

Maintenay: *Le Moulin* (R)S. Rustic charm.

Molinghem: *Le Buffet* (R)M. Good cooking.

Montreuil: *Château de Montreuil* (HR)L. Old favourite, luxurious, superb cooking.

Hotel de France (H)M. Lots of character.

Le Clos des Capucins (H)S (R)M. Affordable hotel, good cooking.

Le Coquempot (R)M. Excellent value, good welcome.

Quend: *Le Fiacre* (HR)M. Inexpensive luxury.

St Josse: *Auberge du Moulinel* (R)M-S. Outstanding cooking and value.

Saulchoy: *Val d'Authie* (R)S-M. Great value.

Le Touquet: *Le Westminster* (HR)L. Unabashed luxury.

Flavio (R)L. Consistently high standards.

Wimereux: *l'Atlantic* (H)M-S (R)M-L. Prime site, excellent fish.

L'Epicure (R)M. Interesting cooking

La Goîlette (Ch d'H)M. Outstanding chambres d'hôte.

Wimille: *La Brocante* (R)L Skilful and innovative cooking.

GETTING THERE

The area is generously served with cross-Channel transport facilities. The choice between conventional ferry, tunnel or Hoverspeed must be a personal one. Each has its advantages and I am happy to mix and match. It would be futile to try and list the prices, since they vary so much from week to week, with special offers, especially on the ferries, making the prospect of a quick hopover extremely tempting.

For those passengers who have already had a long car journey to Kent, need the opportunity to stretch legs, gulp some fresh air and enjoy a leisurely meal the answer will be to choose the P&O Stena Line ferries. The ships have been regularly improved throughout the years and I can recommend their facilities as comfortable, going on luxurious, especially if you make the extra small investment for Club Class, which guarantees peace and quiet along with the free coffee and newspapers. Their journey time is around 75 minutes, with frequent crossings. Booking number is 0990 980980. If you like to feel French the moment you leave Dover try SeaFrance 0990 711711.

The tunnel is perhaps the most hassle-free, the quickest (journey time around 35 minutes) but the least agreeable. If your priority is to get there quickly, if you suffer from seasickness (but not claustrophobia) this is the one to go for, especially if your main reason for travelling is to visit the Cité Europe which is immediately at the mouth of the tunnel. Departures are very frequent. You don't have to book but it is always prudent to do so. If you arrive early or late for your reservation, they will allow you to take the most convenient train, subject to availability. Many people allow an extra half-hour to visit the duty free shop, which along with the cafés and other shops is the most agreeable of the three outlets. Le Shuttle: 0990 353535.

Hoverspeed has its fans, me among them, because of its speed - 45 minutes and French port Boulogne. Given fair weather, it is a very smooth and comfortable crossing, though you have to forego the fresh air. The obvious disadvantage is that The Seacat does not enjoy extremely rough weather, and is sometimes cancelled if the forecast looks too dire. Not for those with delicate stomachs but otherwise a good choice. Hoverspeed 0990 240241.

FOOD AND DRINK

This is farming land. Rich and fertile soil yields gratifying crops, fat pigs and cows munch contentedly, lambs graze on the salt marshes Hearty appetites pay little attention to *nouvelle cuisine*. The air is often chilly and damp, a problem eased by the consumption of substantial peasant food. This is not a region known for its sophisticated gastronomy, but for traditional home-cooked fare that has changed little over the centuries.

As in most regions of France, *la chasse* is a preoccupation. Particularly in the Somme area you can be sure to find dishes that have evolved from a surplus of hare, venison, wild boar, pigeon and wild duck. Look for *civet de lièvre* (jugged hare), *civets de chevreuil* (venison casserole), *terrine de sanglier* (terrine of wild boar), *suprêmes de pigeon* (pigeon breasts) and *pâté de canard* (wild duck pâté, a speciality of the Amiens region).

The North is the principal fish-supplying area for the whole of France. The Channel fishing fleet bring into Boulogne, Étaples and Dunkerque sole, plaice, bass, turbot and herring for commendably swift distribution country-wide. Cockles and scallops are the speciality of Le Crotoy at the mouth of the Somme, mussels, shrimps and prawns abound and are sold direct from the boats or the fishermen's homes. That appalling combination of mussels and chips spills over from Belgium. Both *moules* and *frites* are excellent but one at a time please. *Caudiers de pichons* is the local equivalent of the southern *bouillabaisse,* and all the better for being composed of cold water fish.

The rivers of the area teem with trout, which is to be found on every valley menu along the Authie, the Canche, the Course and the Somme. It has been the speciality of the Auberge d'Inxent for several generations of owners. The lakes - *étangs* - of the Upper Somme are a fisherman's paradise; he can be sure of a supper of carp, tench or eel. *Pâté d'anguilles* is a favourite way of serving the eel in restaurants and smoked eel, to my mind, is superior to smoked salmon.

The salt marshes around the river estuaries are prime grazing grounds for the lamb that end up on the tables as *gigôts de pré salé*. Unbeatable flavour. The dark rich soil of the market gardens - the *hortillonages* - of the area around St. Omer and Amiens produces superb vegetables. Thick soups make warming winter fare and *la soupe des maraîchers* or *la soupe des hortillons* is composed of whatever veg are available - cabbage, leeks, potatoes are staples, but peas and lettuce get used too in summer, along with plenty of herbs. *La soupe de potiron* features in autumn, made from pumpkin, flavoured with onion and leeks, enriched with cream.

14

Perhaps the regional dish most likely to be encountered is the *flamiche*, nowadays most likely to come in the form of an open flan or pie, filled with vegetables. And very good too it can be. Its origins were the leftovers from the bread-making, which used to be baked in the oven at the precise moment when the wood started catching fire. *Flamiche > flamme > flame*. It is not hard to see the resemblance to the Mediterranean staple, pizza, where the dough base is topped with tomatoes and olives instead of these more homely Northern vegetables.

Ficelles you are certain to encounter. Basically they are pancakes, stacked with fillings between the layers. Cheese and ham are the most common ingredients, lubricated with a cheesy sauce. Cut like a cake, eaten with a salad, they make a very satisfactory lunch dish.

Picardy produces 25% of France's potatoes. That's a lot when you think of the *frîtes* alone. The cultivation of the potato was introduced into France by a native of the eastern Somme area, Parmentier, and ever since 1785 many classic potato dishes bear his name, as in potage *Parmentier*. Dishes peculiar to this region include *pommes en coquettes*, indicating the use of plenty of cloves of garlic, or *en magomiaux* which is not as you might think courtesy of the Magimix but fried in lard, with onions, basted in cider. *Bigalan* is a traditional recipe used by every baker in St. Valéry; sliced potatoes flavoured with onion are baked in shortcrust pastry.

Ploughman's lunches have plenty of local cheeses to choose from. *Maroilles* is probably the most famous and probably the strongest. A little goes a long way, especially if you bring it home in a hot car. If you have never tried it before, make sure you buy a good specimen from a reliable *maître fromager* like Philippe Olivier in Boulogne. You will also find it used in dishes like *flamiche au maroilles* or *poulet au maroilles*. The name Maroilles comes from the Abbey which used to make it 1,000 years ago, but you may find it under other names like *Craquignon* or *Marolles* - and its by-products, with other flavours added, become *Sorbais*, *Mignons, Quarts* or *Baguette Laonnaise* according to the area in which they are produced.

Most of the cheeses of the North have robust flavours, to say the least. *Trappiste, Dauphin, Roller* and *Gris de Lille* are other varieties to look out for in the markets. The latter is also known as *Vieux Ponant* (Old Stinker), which says it all.

The Somme is an important centre for the production of sugar from locally grown beet. Sugar keeps out the cold, and Northerners have sweet teeth. In every Grand'Rue *pâtissiers* and *chocolatiers* will have pride of place. Specialities include *le crotelloy* (from Le Crotoy), *biscuit de Doullens*, and *tuile Amienoise*, an almond enriched biscuit curled like a roof tile (*tuile*) from Amiens. Amiens is famous too for another almond-based delicacy, the *macaron*, whose original (and best) recipe is fiercely contested between fifteen *pâtissiers*. The one thing they agree upon is the town in which it originated.

For important occasions, like weddings, funerals and communion there has to be a gateau *battu*. It's a bit boring really - just butter, eggs, flour and sugar, well-beaten (*battu*).

Crêpes are found all over France, but *landimolles* only in Picardy. They add a little fresh cream to lighten the batter, and more than a drop of *genièvre*. Lard takes the place of butter, so the whole confection is cholesterol-ridden.

No wine is grown in the area, but the excellent beer helps to compensate. The nearer you get to the Belgian border, the higher the consumption. It can be more expensive than wine and - watch out drivers - far more alcoholic, but not to be missed. Rich Flemish *carbonades* (stews) and *potées* (thick soups) utilise the beer for cooking where wine-growing regions would slurp in the wine. Beer is also used in the preparation of *Maroilles* which is washed in beer every ten days throughout its four-month maturing.

Juniper berries make the clean-tasting *genièvre*, gulped down as a *digestif,* for which the little town of Houlle in the Pas de Calais is renowned. They crop up again to flavour cabbage and pork combinations.

And to round off this substantial fare? Try a *bistouille*. Coffee is laced with whatever alcohol comes to hand. Keeps out the cold anyway.

THE GOOD BEACH GUIDE

Among the many reasons for visiting this area - to shop, to eat, to stock up on wine, to embark on a journey elsewhere - rarely does one consider the beaches. Perhaps that is because they share our hostile weather, but look at any beach in southern England on a fine day and you will see a far higher people-to-space ratio than would ever occur in northern France. The fine sand stretches for the entire area covered by this book, from the Belgian border all the way to the mouth of the Somme, 200 km of coastline as well-endowed with dunes, rocks, bays and resorts as any in Europe.

From north to south, here is the range:

Just inside the border, 10 km N of Dunkerque, lies **Bray-Dunes**. As its name implies, sand is its *raison d'être*. There are literally hundreds of kms of the stuff, spilling over into villages. There was once a great port here but in 1777 it was engulfed in a sandstorm that left only the clocktower of its church protruding. Its final demise came in 1943 when the Germans blew it up.

A century or so ago a philanthropic M. Bray bought up the entire area and established a summer seaside refuge for the workers of Dunkerque. Subsequently its fortunes declined and shabbiness set in. There are some signs of smartening-up, with an accent on sporting activities and family amusements, and enticements to '*les jeunes*', like a summer rock festival.

I can't say I find it appealing in August when the population jumps from a peaceful 4,700 to a frenetic 100,000, nor in winter, when the sand flies into the hair and eyes, but pick a fine day and enjoy a walk along the magnificent firm beach, or along the prom (plenty of beach cafés). There is also a marked 14 km walk which continues inland to Zuydecoote, where the original port became silted up.

Mâlo-les-Bains
Dunkerque's best beach, to the east of the town. It takes its name from an entrepreneur, one Gaspard Mâlo, who a century ago bought up 600 hectares of sand and built some of the characteristic villas in the Anglo-Normand style. overlooking the fine beach. They are sadly faded and jaded now and probably in danger of being pulled down to make room for yet more boring apartments. This is a family-orientated resort, and a top residential area, with plenty of shops and restaurants to choose from and ideal bucket 'n' spade territory.

Petit Port-St.-Philippe and Grand Port-St.-Philippe

Both these twin towns at the mouth of the river Aa boast magnificent beaches, where the sand is so firm that they double up as football pitches. For a taste of the briny you can't beat a walk out along the breakwater at GPF. I recommend this duo, which few Brits seem to have discovered. Plenty of good fish restaurants near the fishing boats lend plenty of atmosphere.

Calais' firm sands offer a rarely appreciated opportunity to walk off that prolonged lunch, or to snatch air and exercise after a long car drive. Backed by dunes, they extend to the rows of wooden beach huts at **Blériot-Plage**, named after the aviator who in 1909 made the first cross-Channel flight from here.

Next comes **Sangatte**, nearest beach to the tunnel exit, and then, between the sheltering arms of the two Caps, Blanc Nez and Gris Nez, the village of **Wissant**, a prosperous port long before Calais but swallowed up in 1738 by drifting sand. Now the 12 km beach is firm and good for walking, great for shrimpers and rock climbers, probably one of the best along the coast. There are plenty of hotels and restaurants set back in the town centre.

This is the most attractive stretch of the whole littoral, with the coast road winding up above dramatic chalk cliffs; there are fine prospects on one side across the 19 miles of water to the rival cliffs in Dover and on the other the rolling Boulonnais hills. Great for walkers. The cliff paths are well indicated, dipping down to the cleft in the rocks that is **Escalles**. The interesting and sheltered beach here is approached by a lane from the main road. Refreshment available in the village.

Audresselles and **Ambleteuse** come next, the former with the remains of an old fort to clamber over, the latter a picturesque fishing village with a somewhat bizarre beach, scattered with huge flat-topped boulders. You can buy mussels and shellfish from the houses of the fishermen here, or consume a platter in one of the cafés.

Wimereux is better known and deservedly so. It would certainly be one of my favourite places to stay, near to the ports, with some of the best restaurants, a splendid b. and b., a prom for promenading, and a beach for beachcombing. The sands are firm and extensive - just so long as the tide is not high, when they disappear altogether and the waves tend to splash over the *digue*.

Boulogne's eastern beaches are spoiled by the ugly profile of the docks, but on the other side of the port are the beaches used by the Boulonnais at weekends -

Portel and **Equihen-Plage**, each with bars and cafés.

Deep pine woods and fabulous beaches run all the way to Étaples, the fishing port at the mouth of the Canche. This is prime camping territory - lots of space, lots of shade, lots of sand. **Hardelot-Plage** is the best-known resort along this stretch. It's a modern, custom-built community, well equipped with seasonal cafes and holiday shops, geared towards summer villas and apartments and consequently a bit dead out of season, apart from the golfers.

An even newer resort is **Sainte Cécile-Plage**; the beach, one of the best, is ideal for riding along (stables nearby) but again it's all a bit desolate when the sun doesn't shine.

Le Touquet on the other hand keeps going year-round, with an abundance of shops, markets, hotels, restaurants and entertainment. The beach is unbeatable - miles of firm sands in three directions, left, right and centre too when the tide recedes seemingly for ever. Fractious would be the child who was not happy here, with the options of paddling, castle-constructing, shellfish-capturing and even enlisting in the beach clubs for juvenile exercises, trampolining and gymnastics. Conscience-free parents can get in some sun-worshipping secure in the knowledge that their offspring are fully and contentedly occupied. Le Touquet believes in fun for all ages. The more adventurous might like to have a go at wind-sailing (*char-à-vent*), popular all along this coast. Instruction courses are available on the beach, along with windsurfing and dinghy sailing classes.

Situated on the wide promenade is the answer to unkind weather. Aqualud boasts an *ambiance tropicale* regardless of what the temperature is like outside. It's a huge fun-filled experience of getting wet at the seaside without involving the sea. Waves aplenty, along with slides, chutes and whirlpools. See p.167 for more details.

Next comes **Stella-Plage** and **Merlimont** - more dunes, more windsailing and inland, Bagatelle, the pioneer of all French 'attraction parks', featuring the biggest toboggan ride in Europe.

The air in next-door **Berck-Plage** was discovered to be particularly rich in iodine, and the winter particularly mild, so a hundred years ago it became established as a medical centre specialising in diseases of the bone. You can still see adult prams with leg extensions being pushed along the prom but nowadays it has become a family resort, big, brash and busy. If you like a lively holiday, amusement-arcaded, pin-machined, souvenir-shopped, ice-cream-licking, *frites* galore, this is for you. There are 15 km of fine blond sand, ideal for the sand-yachting competitions for which the resort is known.

If noise and bustle is not what you are looking for, try the reverse. You will have to share the lovely 13 km walk along the north bank of the estuary of the river Authie from the dunes of Bec-de-Perroquet to Pont-à-Cailloux only with the birds.

Between the estuaries of the Authie and the Somme is 25 km of sandy shoreline. **Fort Mahon Plage** is a recently developed resort, a bit characterless but excellent for windsailing because it is never short of wind, and well equipped with beach-gear shops and restaurants. The road swings away from the coast southwards, to make room for the nature reserve of Marquenterre (see p.134). A detour to admire the 300 species of birds that drop in here is highly recommended.

On the north bank of the magnificent estuary of the Somme is the resort claiming to have the only south-facing beach in the North of France - **Le Crotoy**. In fact only a section of it faces south because it curves round the mouth of the estuary, but it's a very fine beach whichever aspect you choose, if perhaps a bit more bracing than its Mediterranean competitors. The town has lots of character, with brightly coloured fishing boats pulled up on the beach and a medley of fish restaurants serving Sunday lunchers massive *plâteaux de fruits de mer*. A good choice for an excursion on many counts.

At the very end of the region covered by this book comes perhaps my favourite beach of all. **Sainte Valéry-sur-Somme** has many charms - a peaceful mediaeval ramparted *haute ville*, great historic interest, lovely walks along the river, a funny little steam train that puffs around the bay, and, most distinctive of all, the vast sands of the Somme estuary. At low water, accompanied by a guide, you can walk across to Le Crotoy, if you have two hours to spare. When the tide takes over the sand disappears and you are left with sparkling water and swooping gulls. There is, however, still a tiny secret beach at the very end of the promenade, too insignificant to be rated as a big attraction, but a charming place for a paddle and a picnic.

GOLF COURSES

Plenty to choose from. Here are some of the best:

Le Touquet Golf Club, Ave du Golf, 62520 Le Touquet,
(0)3.21.06.28.00; fax (0)3.21.06.28.01.
2 x 18 holes: Forest Course and Sea Course.
1 x 9 holes: Manor Course.

Hardelot Golf Club, Ave.du Golf, 62152 Hardelot.
(0)3.21.83.73.10; fax (0)3.21.83.24.33.
2 x 18 holes: Dunes Course and Pines Course.

AA St Omer Golf Club, Chemin des bois, Acquin-Westbecourt, 62380
Lumbres. (0)3.21.38.59.90; fax (0)3.21.93.02.47.
1 x 18 holes.
1 x 9 holes.
Unusually good restaurant, open to non-players too.

Nampont Golf Club, Maison Forte, 80120 Nampont St Martin.
(0)3.22.29.92.90; fax (0)3.22.29.97.54.
2 x 18 holes: Les Cygnes and Le Belvedere.

Dunkerque Golf Club, Fort-Vallieres, 59380 Coudekerque-Branche.
(0)3.28.61.07.43; fax (0)3.28.60.05.93.
1 x 18 holes

Wimereux Golf Club, Rte. d'Ambleteuse, 62930 Wimereux.
(0)3.21.32.43.20; fax.(0)3.21.33.62.21.
1 x 18 holes

Arras Golf Club, rue Briquet Taillandier, 62223 Anzin St. Aubin.
(0)3.21.50.24.24; fax (0)3.21.50.29.71.
1 x 18 holes.

MARKETS

Weekly markets are important days in Frenchmen's lives. Here is the chance not only to buy the best seasonal produce around, but also to catch up with friends and neighbours and enjoy a good gossip. Unlike so many of our markets (of which there are depressingly fewer every year), the produce has not fallen off a lorry or been rejected by reputable shops. The French housewife would never stand for that. Do not imagine that by buying market vegetables you will be getting the cheapest, but rest assured that you will be getting the freshest. Farmers wives have risen at dawn to pick whichever crops are likely to beat the other stallholders. Sometimes they have only a bunch of herbs or a kilo of wild mushrooms to offer, or one rabbit or two chickens. Their tomatoes will not be identical, their potatoes will still have dirt on them, their artichokes will be knobbly, but they will have travelled the shortest possible distance from earth to shopping basket. Above all else their produce will be seasonal and if there is a seasonal glut the customer will benefit. If you've ever pined to buy not one small bunch but armfuls of asparagus, go in May and do just that.

There is more to marketing than bringing home some trophies, however. Wander around and feast all the senses on the colour, noise, smells and yes indeed the feel of the harvest. Altogether different from a session in Sainsburys.

I am talking specifically about the edible produce. I am not at all happy about the recent additions to the market, like raucous videos, cheap plastic in whatever form, nasty nylon clothes. They are the exception to what I said above. They might well be cheaper than those from a shop and they might well have fallen off a *camion*.

Here is a list of some of the more important markets in the area. They all pack up at lunchtime:

Aire sur la Lys: Friday: Grand'Place and Place Notre Dame.
Amiens: Sat. and Wed. main market; Tues. and Sat. covered *halles*.
Ardres: Thursday on the fairground.
Arras: Sat. and Wed.: Place des Héros and Place de la Vacquerie; Thurs.: Place Marc Lanvin; Sun.: Place Verlaine.
Berck: Tue. Fri. and Sun.: Place de la Mairie in Berck Ville; Wed. and Sat. Place de l'Église in Berck Plage.
Béthune: Mon.: Grand'Place and Place Lamartine; Fri.: Place Lamartine.
Boulogne: Sat. and Wed.: Place Dalton.
Calais: Sat. and Wed.: Place d'Armes; Sat. Thurs. and Sun.: Z.U.P. du Beau Marais.
Camiers: Mon.: Place Communale.
Dèsvres: Tue.: Grand'Place.
Étaples: Tue. and Fri.: Place de la Mairie.
Fauquembergues: Thurs.: Grande Place.
Frévent: Tue.: Place du Marché
Fruges: Sat.: Place du G. de Gaulle.
Guines: Fr.: Place Foch.
Hesdin: Thurs.: Place d'Armes, bd. Richelieu.
Licques: Mon.: Place Christiane Collette Evrard.
Marquise: Thurs.: Grand'Place Louis le Senecha
Montreuil: Sat.: Grande Place.
St Omer: Sat.: Place Foch.
Samer: Mon.: Grand'Place Foch.
Sangatte: Fri.: Place de la Mairie, Blériot.
Le Touquet: Sat. and Thurs.: Marché Couvert year-round; from 19th May to September, Mon. Thurs. and Sat.
Wimereux: Tue. and Fri.: place Albert 1er.
Wissant: Wed.: Rue Gambetta.

HYPERMARKET AND SUPERMARKET OPENING HOURS

Cité Europe at Coquelles, near Calais. Shops open Mon.-Thurs.: 10 a.m.-8 p.m., Fri.: 10 a.m.-9 p.m., Sat.: 9 a.m.-10 p.m., cl. Sun.

Carrefour hypermarket: Mon. to Fri.: 9 a.m.-10 p.m., Sat.: 8.30 a.m.-10 p.m.

Auchan, also near Boulogne: Mon.-Sat.: 8.30 a.m.-10 p.m.

Sundays: PG supermarkets are open from 9 a.m.-1 p.m.; most food and wine shops open until around 12.30. Calais beer and wine cash-and-carrys are also open on Sunday.

A Calais advice line deals with enquiries 9.30 a.m.-4.30 p.m. from Mon. to Sat. on 0181-348.0503.

WHAT NEXT?

I have been very conscious that the updating of the French Entrée series has been slow and frustrating, largely because of the detail and nature of the contents. It has therefore been decided to concentrate the guides to the more northerly areas (after all the essence of the original concept) in order to enable me to update each book every two years and to re-write completely each one every three years.

Under my jurisdiction will be *Brittany* (to be updated or re-written next year), *Normandy*, (re-written last in 1997) and *The North*.

I have co-opted a well-known and experienced travel writer, Michael Leech, to tackle *Champagne, Ardennes*. Laurence Phillips is re-writing *Paris* and will also combine it with other Eurostar destinations, Lille and Brussels, to be published later in the year. The intrepid Rosemary Gower-Jones has taken over *Chambres d'Hôtes* in France in its entirety.

There is a "new look" but the format will remain the same and I will be Series Editor. In each case the author will have visited personally every entry, and no payment has been received from hoteliers and restaurants. We continue to value the contribution made by readers, who write to share their experiences and views, favourable or otherwise, and help to make each edition even better than the last! The address to send reports is

Quiller Press Ltd., 46 Lillie Road, London SW6 1TN.

We hope that our efforts will greatly add to your enjoyment of La Belle France.

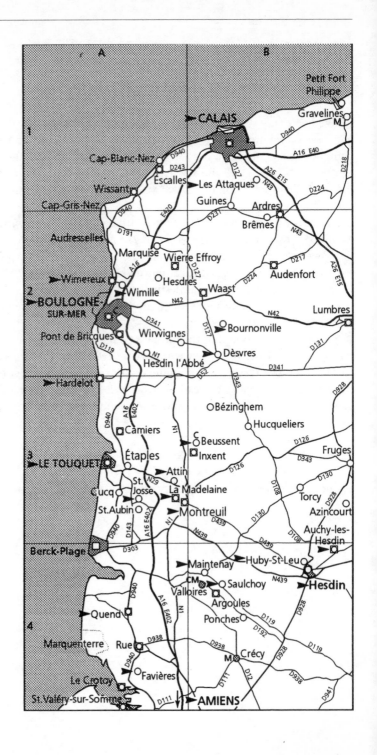

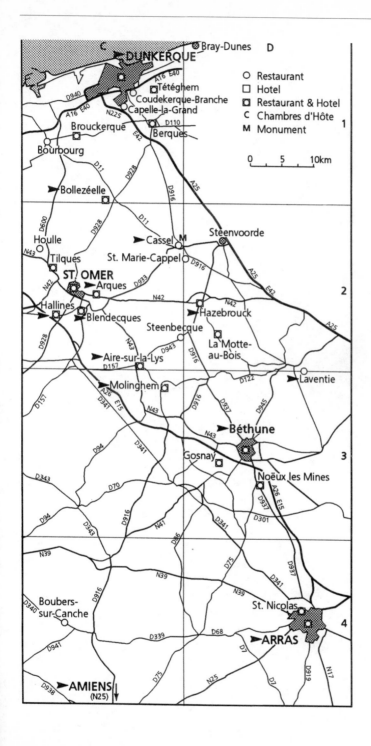

O Restaurant
□ Hotel
◙ Restaurant & Hotel
C Chambres d'Hôte
M Monument

0   5   10km

CALAIS, BOULOGNE AND THE NORTH

AIRE-SUR-LA-LYS 62120 Pas-de-Calais.
19 km SE of St. Omer, 58 km SE of Calais
M Fri.

I don't believe that many visitors to that British favourite, Les Trois Mousquetaires, ever get round to exploring Aire. They just lap up the comfort then set off down the RN23 again, back to Calais or on to pastures new and rather warmer. Big mistake. There's a lot more than they ever imagined about this sizeable town, built at the confluence of four rivers, the Lys, the Melde, the Laquette and the Mardyck. It also stands at the junction of four canals, so there's a lot of wetness around.

Its centre of course, especially on Fridays, is the vast market square. Here is the imposing Hotel de Ville, now cleverly converted in modern but sympathetic style, to house a library, boutiques and some children's play areas. It's majestic belfry carries a restored carillon; Corinthian pilasters and a carved double-headed eagle amid battle standards all add to its importance. At right angles, on the corner of the rue d'Arras, is a gem, the Renaissance Hotel du Bailliage, built in brick and stone very early in the 17th century. Two sides are arcaded with Doric columns; above them even more delicate Ionic columns divide the façade into bays. I enjoy the details, particularly the statuary - look for St. James, St. Anthony, the theological virtues of faith, hope and charity, the cardinal virtues of temperance - strength, prudence and fortitude - and the elements of earth - air, fire and water.

Wherever you choose to stroll in the town, if you use your eyes (look up as well as down and across) you cannot fail to discover buildings that are two, three and even four hundred years old. One stroll should lead along the rue St. Pierre to the vast collegiate church, with its Gothic tower, finished only in the 18th century. It houses a statue of the Virgin, with a delightful story attached.

In 1213 Ferrand of Portugal was besieging Aire and the starving citizens prayed to the Virgin's statue in this church for salvation and, more urgently,

29

bread. Miraculously the bread appeared and the virgin earned her title Notre-Dame-de-Panetière. She has since had an adventurous life but triumphed over all adversities. Come the Revolution and she was a prime target for destruction as an object of superstition, but a baker's boy claimed he wanted to use her as firewood and kept her hidden till the danger was past. In 1944, when bombs set the sanctuary of the church alight, Notre-Dame-de-Panetière was smashed to matchwood and it looked as though her end had come at last; but the citizens were not prepared to lose their protectrice so readily; they collected every splinter and put them together again, so that she can still be seen today, standing on a gilded carving of the moon.

The Bailliage has been put to good use - it is now a very helpful tourist office. Pick up a variety of leaflets, including an interesting circuit of the valley of the Lys.

I particularly recommend Aire to anyone with Scottish connections. Legend has it that the town was founded by Lyderic, prompted by his Scottish wife, the princess Chrymild. See for yourself if they don't both look Scottish - their giant effigies are still on occasion paraded through the streets and Lyderic has a fine ginger beard.

➤ **Auberge de la Treille d'Or (R)S**
67 rue d'Arras (0)3.21.39.02.62 Cl. Sun. p.m.; Mon.
One street back from the Grande Place in an old building that they say was a 19C coaching inn. The façade has a trail of golden grapes painted on it, to justify the name.

Here is the kind of old-fashioned family-run business offering the old-fashioned value that it's getting harder and harder to find. M. and Mme Tourais are welcoming and cosy and a bit old-fashioned themselves - all to the good.

The dining room is net-curtained, cosy, and yes old-fashioned. Jacky Tourais specialises in meat, so if you fancy a *filet, tournedos* or *fauxfilet,* this is the place to head for because the prices are very reasonable. He also likes to show what he can do, so more ambitious items are on the speciality menu - braised ham with spinach and champagne sauce, *profiteroles* stuffed with kidneys in a cream and calvados sauce and served with green apples. Fish also features - poached turbot poached *aux deux sauces et aux deux couleurs,* simply cooked sea bass, or skate *en habit vert.* A hefty starter is his *soupe de poissons,* with all the trimmings, for 40f. Other starters are just as interesting as the *entrées.*

Every day there is a *suggestion du jour* at 45f and, except at weekends, a menu at 70f, e.g. *tourte fermière chaude aux herbes* followed by fillets of red mullet, oven-roast and served with seafood sauce. Then cheese or dessert. Other menus at 109, 150 or 225f are all astonishing value.

"We had an excellent four-course meal. The total bill for two, including aperitifs and wine, was 257f. The quality and presentation of the food was excellent and we were made most welcome." Lynne and John Goode.

An arrow for way above average cooking, nice hosts and unpretentious value.

➤ Les Trois Mousquetaires (HR)M-L
Château du Fort de la Rédoute (0)3.21.39.01.11; fax (0)3.21.39.50.10

It was with audible sighs of relief that we turned off the *nationale* into the imposing gates and saw before us journey's end, the well-manicured, turreted, balconied, pinnacled and beamed Château de la Rédoute. I noted in the last edition how smart it was looking, as though the red bricks had been reddened, the white stone blanco-ed, and the wood freshly creosoted, with the pond water weed-free, and the spotless swans lined up beside the decorative ducks. That is still the case. Les Trois Mousquetaires is prospering.

The car park revealed a solitary French car among the GB upmarket models. How strange it must be to be the solitary Frenchman in your own country.

In the reception area, little has changed; it's still lots of dark oak, a bit feudal-style, but there seemed to be more suitcases to fall over by the desk, where its nice receptionist was clearly overworked, answering the phone, welcoming new guests, dealing with bills and even carrying bags herself. No sign of the Venet family until I spotted Philippe (more of him every year), busy in his office. He looked all wrong without his chef's whites on and I have the feeling that he's happier when he's wearing them rather than a suit.

Two bad hotel choices running and a dank and drizzling day made the prospects of the luxury of the Musketeers all the more appealing. We sank into a leather armchair and ordered two stiff ones. I must admit that even with them at hand the thought did occur to me that we could have relaxed better in a cosy bar or lounge rather than the frenetic reception area and all those suitcases.

However, there was nothing to spoil our enjoyment of the comfortable rooms and efficient bathroom. The rooms have been decorated elaborately, with complicated pelmets and coronas over the bed, a bit fussy but spacious and well equipped. No chance of re-visiting the other 30 rooms or two apartments, since, as is the norm, they were all full; ours cost 600f as do the majority; there are smaller rooms at 480f and two with shower for 250f. Suites are 850f. In the annexe there are two more rooms at 330 or 430f.

Fresh from a restorative bath, we skipped the thought of an *apéritif* since no-one else had settled in the reception area and proceeded into the large dining room, past the glass-walled kitchen, where several chefs, but not Philippe, were hard at it.

The décor is nothing special - greyish and brownish - so that nothing detracts from the food. The 120f menu is still extraordinarily good. I remembered of old the three home-made *terrines* - duck with Grand Marnier and oranges, country-style with onions and beer, or ham with pistachios and juniper, and was pleased to find them still featuring. Husband enjoyed his chicken liver and diced bacon salad with chicory, then Licques chicken, simply roasted with garlic and potatoes with bacon, but I was a bit disappointed in my stuffed courgette flowers. I had imagined them crisply deep-fat fried, but these were stodgy. My flambéed trout with pink peppercorns was perfect though and, chosen from the 17 desserts, my Agen cup with puréed prune sauce and Armagnac and Husband's warm blueberry tart were both top-notch.

Coffee came with to-die-for home-made chocolates; they and the *amuses gueules* that had preceded the meal had shown the skill of serious talent in the kitchen. Madame Venet Mark II, the bijou Caroline, was very much in evidence to serve and to smile.

The Mousquetaires and I go back a long way and perhaps that is the trouble. It is not very helpful to compare present with past but I have to say that I do feel a certain nostalgia for the time when there were just four bedrooms, the restaurant was clearly Philippe's be-all and end-all, Madame Venet presided benignly, and the serving wenches came in flowery cotton dresses and mop caps (I'm not kidding and not so long ago either). I am not alone. The piles of fan mail do seem to have tailed off recently - the higher prices lead to higher expectations. Here is one letter selected from the more recent tendency:

"This is the first time I have totally disagreed with your assessment. The rooms were nothing to write home about and dinner was overpriced, appallingly slow in the delivery and served with a complete lack of charm by a surly young waitress. The final straw was when they arrived in the middle of dinner requiring us (yes requiring!) to fill in our breakfast order. When we said we wouldn't require breakfast as we were leaving at 7 a.m., we were told that it was impossible as reception would not be open.

Hugely disappointed and suggest you need to revisit. Apart from anything, it was more like being in Surrey on Sea than France. (Name withheld in case he ever wants to go back!)

So... The arrow stays, but only precariously. I still think that this is a rare example of luxury in this area and that the food is good. Perhaps the easy custom is spoiling the atmosphere; in which case, with more examples, the arrow will be diverted in the next update.

AMIENS 80000 Somme
100 km from Boulogne

The new autoroute, the A16, now connects both Calais and Boulogne directly to Amiens, making this ancient capital of Picardy all the more accessible and an even more desirable candidate for a short break. To be sitting in a café in the *parvis*, looking up at one of the world's greatest cathedrals, the largest in France, less than two hours from arrival at the channel ports, is an opportunity not to be ignored.

Amiens' list of assets is a long one: - its setting in a unique watery landscape far removed from traffic fret, the charming new St. Leu development which, yes, really does hint of Venice, the good shops, the abundance of restaurants, the university animation and of course, No.1 star, Notre Dame.

First impressions are of the cathedral's sheer size. Two Parisien Notre Dames would fit inside comfortably. Built on a spur above the river, providing a sensational backcloth from St. Leu, it splendidly dominates the city. Anyone remotely interested should buy a good guidebook to discover some of its wonders but, just to whet the appetite:

Trade in cloth, particularly in velvets, which are still produced in Amiens, was at its peak in the 13th century and provided the funds to build this testimony of faith and refuge from suffering for an age beset with plague and war. It is barely credible that its elegant and intricate form should have been completed in less than fifty years, between 1220 and 1269, resulting in an unparalleled unity of style. The vaulted nave, supported by a score of delicate pillars, soars away into neck-cricking distance. You won't find finer craftsmanship anywhere in the world than in the choir, where the 110 stalls are carved with 4,000 figures illustrating familiar biblical scenes translated into the life-style of the 16th-century Amienois. Unfortunately too many visitors have weakened the fabric and visiting hours have to be limited. It was open from 2.30 to 5p.m. when I was last there, but check.

The most popular statues, reproduced freely on postcards and posters, are the youthful gilded Virgin, smiling, slightly flirtatious, with the infant Jesus nonchalantly perched on her hip, and the cherub known as The Weeping Angel. He looks down on the tomb of an archbishop known for his love of children and certainly looks sad; however, I tested the legend that if a Christian looked at him steadily for five minutes, the tears would begin to flow down his chubby cheeks. Alas, no trace of moisture manifested itself from the statue - the only eyes that watered were mine.

In winter you will have plenty of space to appreciate such details and to soak up the peace and beauty of the cathedral; in summer arrange at least one visit outside coach hours, and allow more time than you think you might need to absorb her benefices. Walk round the whole building to understand the scale and cross the road to sit on the steps opposite to study the west porches, with their army of elongated figures. Look for St. Firmin, the Spanish evangelist who became Amiens' first bishop, on the left porch, and find him again above the stalls in the south aisle, pictured against a 15th-century Amiens, whose cathedral, belfry and ramparts are all recognisable.

To add authority to my own enthusiasm I would quote Ruskin: "This apse of Amiens is not only the best but the very first thing done perfectly in its manner by northern Christendom."

The cathedral has miraculously survived the devastation of two world wars, when 60% of the venerable city was lost. The ancient ramparts are now replaced by a busy ring road. But it is still an interesting and animated centre economically, intellectually and artistically and those important buildings, like the Hotel de Ville and the Law Courts that were spared in the destruction, have been recently cleaned and restored. The Musée de Picardie in the rue de la République ((0)3.22.97.14.00, N.B. cl. Mons) is a fine neo-classic building, inaugurated by Napoleon III in 1868. It is one of France's outstanding museums, both for its paintings (El Greco, Ribera, Fragonard, Boucher, Tiepolo, Guardi etc.), murals (Puvis de Chavannes) and sculptures from the Middle Ages to the 19th century. It also has a fine archeological collection.

Markets:

Behind the Hotel de Ville are the market *halles*, in a modern building. If you're looking for an occupation for a cold wet day, head right here, because there is plenty of colour and variety to cheer the spirit. The fish stalls in particular are an education. Open for Tuesday to Saturday from 9 to 5 and on Sunday from 9 till noon. On Saturday and Wednesday mornings there are more stalls functioning in the square outside, representing one of the most important markets in the Somme. Saturday too is the day when the market gardeners from the hortillonages set up their stands along the Quai Parmentier and on a fine day it's a very agreeable stroll along the banks of the glittering river checking out what is freshest and best

Once a year, in June, the market is held as it was in the past; the market gardeners progress down the river, dressed in full mediaeval garb, in high-powered boats full of freshly collected vegetables.

Every second Sunday there is a flea market on the Quai Parmentier. Haggling expected.

Shopping

Easy - just one long street, partly pedestrianised, stretching from the station to the modern glass edifice, the Maison de Culture. The landmark at the station end is the unmissable (some may say unfortunately) Perret Tower, the sole survivor of a plan to rebuild the district around the station after WW2. Its main claim to distinction was that it was the highest building in Europe at the time.

Turn your back on it hastily and walk down the rue de Noyon to the green be-fountained square of the Place Réné Goblet. The street-name then changes to rue des Trois Cailloux, pleasantly pedestrianised and lined with shops, past the wide Place Gambetts, a good place to stop for a coffee.

St Leu

Threaded by canals, the quarter of St Leu was created in the Middle Ages, when water brought power to the various mills operated by weavers, dyers, tanners and flour millers. As the industries faded away, so did the the area, the canals became clogged, the warehouses crumbled, the houses deteriorated, until it became a disgraceful slum, peopled with drop-outs. Even ten years ago it was unwise to walk alone here and certainly not after dark.

The restoration programme begun then and still continuing today has been thorough and imaginative and now this is the most attractive area of the whole city. The old cottages have been rescued and painted in bright colours, antique dealers and boutiques have moved into the charismatic buildings and restaurants and bars abound. An intelligent move was to site the new science faculty of the university here, bringing constant animation to the area and regular custom to its bars. The cobbled Quai Bélu is the busiest and perhaps the most attractive of the renovated streets, and is literally lined with restaurants to suit all tastes and pockets. The Passage Bélu leads to the antique dealers' gallery. In a maze of ancient streets, look for the rue de Metz l'Evêque for another successful restoration programme. Bordering the area, the Pont du Cange is the oldest bridge in Amiens, where vestiges of the ramparts may be seen and battlements still indicate the old tower. From May to September on the first Saturday of the month, you can join a tour of the quarter at night, starting at 10pm.

Les Hortillonages.

No visit to Amiens during the summer months would be complete without experiencing the Hortillonages, a unique waterworld as strange as anything dreamt up by Walt Disney. From mid April to the end of September you can take a boat trip from the chemin du Halagé (marked off the bvd. de, Beauville), a 50 minutes' meander in one of the typical low, high-powered punts that give you a duck's eye view of some of the 300 hectares of gardens that stretch into the very heart of the built-up area of the city. They are bisected by 55 kms of *rieux* (small canals), and the larger navigable canals, all irrigated by the rivers Somme and Avre, and can only be discovered from a boat or by walking along the towpath.

Hortillon was the name given by Caesar's soldiers to the men who tended these gardens then to feed the troops and there were vegetable plots here even in pre-Roman times. Today the *hortillons* still get about in the distinctive flat-bottomed tarred boats - *bâteaux à cornet*.

The black rich soil of the gardens is banked above the waterline. Most of them sport neat rows of bumper leeks, cabbages and caulis - three crops a year they can produce - but there are flowers too and on a September visit it was the colour that struck me most. I had been expecting a wishy-washy watercolour effect of gentle greys and greens - but no, there was a positive riot of not only autumn leaves and scarlet creepers but of gaudy dahlias, mammoth artificial-seeming sunflowers, marigolds, asters, golden rod, not to mention purple cabbages, crimson tomatoes; rosy apples on the trees were as shiny and profuse as those in a nurseryman's catalogue. On most plots stands some kind of shelter, from micro-hut to keep the fishing gear in to dolls-house bungalows, often with attendant gnomes.

I thoroughly recommend a relaxing interlude spent here, preferably on a sunny day, when the water sparkles as you drift stealthily in intense quietness amongst the water lillies, poplars and willows, disturbing a variety of wildfowl.

HOTELS
•••

Amiens has a good range of hotels and restaurants, but none outstanding and no arrows. The **Prieuré**, the potential star because of its prime position alongside the cathedral and its venerable building, is currently out of the running because the road outside has collapsed and is impassable and the annexe to the hotel is propped up on iron supports. In any case, reports recently have been of unsympathetic welcome and slipping standards. But keep an eye on the situation, because a three-star, well-run Prieuré hotel is just what Amiens needs. Meanwhile I have to break my rule of not including chain hotels.

What it does have, however, is a highly attractive scheme, in which the first three of my chosen hotels participate. That is two nights for the price of one, arriving any Friday or Saturday throughout the year. Book at least eight days ahead, mentioning the *"Bon Weekend en Ville"* scheme. Confirm in writing or fax. So you effectively halve the price, making these hotels look very cheap indeed.

Grand Hotel de l'Univers (H)M
2 rue de Noyon. (0)3.22.91.52.51. fax. (0)3.2292.81.66. cl.

Described as a *grande maison bourgeoise* the Univers stands, grey and solid, on the main street; some of the rooms overlook a small park and these are the ones to ask for. M. Noyeau is still the owner/manager but since Best Western have become involved a considerable amount of redecoration and re-arrangement has gone on; mercifully they have retained the big central well, which allows light and airiness into the whole hotel. All 41 bedrooms are now bright and cheerful, with good bathrooms. 305-500f is good value, especially for two nights.

Relais Mercure (H)M
17 place au Feurre. (0)3.22.91.86.57.

This is the old Postillion, which used to be a readers' favourite, partly because of its picturesque old building and partly because of its favoured position just to the west of the cathedral. The Mercure group had taken over so recently before my visit that the paint was hardly dry on the walls. Much of the character of the old coaching inn has been lost in the modernisation and in the contemporary décor but old beams and rafters have been retained wherever feasible. A whole new wing has been arranged across the courtyard, making 47 rooms in all, and a lift has been installed. The bar at the entrance is much more comfortable and no longer attracts the ebullient *jeunes* which used to make life a misery for those of us who sleep lightly and are allergic to pop music. So some good, some not so good. Perhaps the prices of 460 and 480f are a touch high. Until you stay two nights that is.

Le Prieuré, Amiens

"Keep an eye on the situation"

Alsace Lorraine. (H)S
18 rue de la Molière. (0)3.22.91.35.71.

The general instructions "near the station" are not very helpful, especially if you are arriving by car, because of the one-way system and narrow lanes. Listen to one who found out the hard way:- approaching from the north (via *autoroute* or *nationale*), cross over the bridge, proceed up the bld Alsace Lorraine following signs to the *gare* and take the second turning to the left, into the rue de la Vallée, then second left and second left again into the rue de la Molière, where the hotel is on the left and parking is wherever you can find a space.

The hotel is a tall and narrow white-painted building in an unappealing area. The smartly painted navy-blue door is the first clue of the inherent stylishness. The decoration has been achieved in impeccable taste - lots of white, via curtains, walls and paint, softened with antique furniture, mostly pine, large 19C gilt mirrors and plenty of pretty lamps. There is a refreshing glimpse of a green courtyard beyond the entrance hall and a little breakfast room to the right where a scantily clad lady frolics on a swing beside a villainous looking suitor, in an old stucco-framed engraving.

The 13 rooms are all light and elegant, with decorative fabric bedheads and - oh joy! - effective lights. Bathrooms are modern but only three have baths. 350f. The owners are pleasant and helpful, though I can't forgive one disgraceful lapse. On a freezing windy afternoon, just as darkness was falling, I returned to the hotel to get some writing-up achieved, to find the front door firmly locked. I sat on the doorstep for two miserable hours before the owners returned. And no-one put any money in my hat.

This is a good example of getting what you pay for. Three-star upwards have 24-hour reception, lifts, bars and garages. Two stars like the Alsace Lorraine do not. In cheerless winter weather it is often worth paying for comforts like an armchair in a warm lounge and a stiff drink.

Hotel Victor Hugo (H)S
2 rue de l'Oratoire. (0)3.22.91.57.91. fax. (0)3.22.92.74.02.

For those whose dates do not include a weekend, or who want to stay only one night, and are looking for a bargain, this is it. Strategically placed in a quiet central street, with friendly owners, the rooms cost a mere 180f, with showers; family rooms are available for another 20f. They are simply but adequately furnished and soothingly decorated in cool white.

RESTAURANTS
....

Dozens to choose from, but serious gourmets will have to drive out just south of the city on the route Nationale to Dury, where l'Aubergade is the sole Michelin star.

Les Marissons (R)M
Pont de la Dodane (0)3.22.92.96.66. cl Sat lunch; Sun; 2/1-9/1

Amiens' superlative - the prettiest, the fullest, the smartest, the most expensive, the best-known-restaurant.

The setting qualifies for that 'i' word - idyllic it has to be - in the St. Leu area on an island separating a canal and a stream crossed by a bridge, with all the lights of the bars on the Quai Bélu sparkling in the water, and with that superlative back-drop - the floodlit cathedral.

In the garden fairy lights twinkle in the trees and in summer this is the place to book a table - a superlative aspect. It's pretty nice inside too. In the 15th century this was a boatshed, believe it or not. The character remains, the wood shavings do not. M. Benoit has chosen the colours of Picardy to decorate his charming restaurant - yellow walls, blue chairs, yellow cloths and curtains which are wisely left undrawn to take in the view of the looming Notre Dame. Old rafters, fresh flowers (and some plastic ones too), soft lighting, all make for a soothing ambiance. A stuffed swan tucked in the eaves and puppets (known in Amiens as *cabotans*) by reception make talking points.

We made a huge mistake by straying from the 160f menu and eating *à la carte*, resulting in a ridiculously high bill. I should know better, but neither of the choices on the menu - chicken which we had eaten for lunch, nor the *rascasse,* not my favourite fish, appealed. There was even a 110f version - soup, salmon and apple tart - which would have been adequate if not exciting, but I wanted to test out the chef's capabilities. My smoked eel with cider vinegar and honey was rich and tangy, the scallops with wild mushrooms were cooked to perfection, and husband's salt-marsh lamb came with some unusual vegetables - *crosnes de Marquenterre* - a kind of salsify - but, with one of the cheapest bottles of wine, they cost nearly £90, which spoiled the taste somewhat.

It could have been worse. My passion for scallops could have led me to order *La Kermesse de le St Jacques,* involving six courses featuring the delectable bi-valve and costing a cool £295f a head. Even I might find that a bit much *scallops carpaccio, tarama, crostillant, avec chou vert à la flan de bière* and *aux fromages.*

Couronne R(M)
64 rue St Leu (0)3.22.91.88.57.cl. Sun. pm Sat. 2/1/ - 10/1 and 14/7 - 14/8
Strangely enough Amiens has few straightforward, traditional, un-quirky restaurants but this is one. Untrendy, solid, respectable, reliable, popular with the *hommes d'affaires* (which is always a recommendation) and excellent value. Michelin awards a red *Repas* for its 92f menu, which is three substantial courses of dishes like *gigôt d'agneau* and *sole bonne femme.*

The address is St Leu, but you will find La Couronne in the main traffic-way, not in the touristy tarted-up *quartier.* You don't come here for the décor but for the food.

Amiens has an amazing supply of themed restaurants, some of them very good, many of them along the Quai Bélu. At no. 45, *Le Porc St Leu* (0)3.22.80.00.73 you can sample more pork products than you would imagine possible. *Boudins, saucissons, pates, terrines,* liver, chops, steaks, *rillettes,* roasts, grills, even an omelette stuffed with pork. Menus start at 95f. It's a pretty little restaurant with red check cloths and a tiny rear garden and, like all these restaurant suggestions, it has covetable tables outside overlooking the river. A few doors along is **La Pataterie**, where, surprise surprise, the theme is potatoes. The baked spud is a newcomer to France and does not appear in classical French cuisine, but they seem to have taken it to their hearts. Here there is a choice of about fifteen fillings, from the simple cream and chives for 28f to the ubiquitous St Jacques at 85f. **La Lanfouste** is at no. 33. (0)3.22.91.37.62, supplying the fishy element. All sorts, and especially its namesake, on menus from 88f.

At the end of the quay nearest Les Marissons there's a noisy 'British pub' and at the other there's that rare French species, a wine bar; it's called **La Queue de Vache**, which was the old name for the quay when cows were watered at the riverside here. Along with the glass of wine you can order cheese, quiches and light snacks - a very useful alternative to normal French tucker.

La Soupe à Cailloux (R)S
16 rue des Bondes (0)3.22.91.92.70 cl Mon. o.o.s.

Still in St Leau but across the bridge is this little grey-painted bistro, with simple wooden tables and floor, popular with students. If it has a speciality it is in eclectic dishes - *soupe au pistou, travers de porc* and *tarte au rhubarbe.* Menus start at 69f.

Not all the themed restaurants are in St Leu. One of the best is:

Les Bouchées Doubles (R)M
11 bis rue Gresset (0)3.22.92.14.32. cl. Sun. pm.

Almost opposite the Hotel de Ville, a cheerful pink and red brasserie catering for Amiens' carnivores. Great hunks of red meat, like the *piece bouchées doubles,* are high quality and cooked just the way you like it. Eat *à la carte* for around 160f. Good atmosphere. Recommended.

Le Bouchon (R)M-S
10 rue Alexandre Fatton. (0)3.22.92.14.32. cl. Sun. pm.

Not to be confused with the above, this is a cosy bistro with a décor of old tin plaques, near the Tour Perron, where chef Laurent Lefèvre offers some of the best cooking in Amiens. His touch is half way between Parisian bistro and

Lyons brasserie-classic, with subtle refinements. Excellent value are dishes like roast duck cooked with truffles, a terrine of pike and tails of langoustines with *morilles* on the 115f menu. There is a cheaper version at 65f.

Le T'Chiot Zinc (R)S
18 rue de Noyon (0)3.22.91.43.79 cl. Sun. and Mon. lunch.
Pronounced like a sneeze, this narrow bistro in the main street is one of Amiens' most popular eateries. Outside on the pavement is a whole sucking pig rotating on the spit. There are five rooms altogether, with customers packed in wherever a space occurs. The patron/chef steers round the tables, shaking all the regulars' hands. Waiters never dawdle, the pace is frenetic, so don't come here for an intimate quiet evening.

The value is great - the cheapest oysters in town are to be found here - 63f for a dozen No.3 Claires. A gigantic *plateau de fruits de mer* features a whole lobster at 340f for two people. The 98f menu includes wine and substantial appetisers. Chunks of garlicky *tête de veau* were plonked down almost before we were seated. Plenty of Picard specialities on the menu like *ficelle, flamiche, caqhuse* (I asked the waiter to explain what the latter involved but he was in such a hurry I only gathered that it involved pork and didn't sound very nice).

My *carpaccio* of salmon overflowed the plate and was good and juicy and husband's egg mayonnaise was a perfectly unfussy specimen; we were all in favour until the next course - sucking pig for him, *moules* for me turned out to be dry and over-cooked. In retrospect I suspect that might have been because, finding the pace too hectic, we asked for a ten minute respite between courses, during which our meal was probably kept warm. I'm not going to damn Le Zinc on this one experience because the vibes were good, even if you do risk indigestion.

Brasserie Jules (R)M
Bld. Alsace Lorraine. (0)3.22 71.18.40. cl. Sun.p.m.
A new brasserie near the station in the Centre Commerciale and the nearest eaterie if you are staying at the Hotel Alsace and Lorraine. The quality of the raw ingredients here - fish especially - is very high and service and settings are efficient and comfortable. Light and airy for a brasserie; a reliable choice. Menus from 105f.

> ARDRES 62610 Pas-de-Calais.
> 17 km SE of Calais
> **M** Thurs.

Occupied by the English for seventeen years during the Hundred Years War, and the connection has endured. Generations of English travellers have used it for a first and last staging post, especially before the autoroute bypassed the little town. The Grand Hotel Clément, once a simple family-run auberge known for its fine cooking, was a favourite cross-Channel bolthole.

The triangle of the steeply sloping, cobbled Place d'Armes, surrounded with venerable houses, roofs awry, is as charming as ever, worn grey steps still lead up to the Carmelite chapel which dates from the 17th century, avenues of lime trees lend distinctive character.

The Clément has seen many changes. It fell into a sorry state, and for several years English folk using old guidebooks were disappointed that their old faithful was no longer delivering the promised goods. Now it has been bought by the owners of the Relais (see below). They are systematically doing the place up, but there is a huge amount of work and expense to be tackled and it is still far from recommendable. Ten bedrooms have been refurbished (230f with shower, 335f with bath) and another seven will be ready eventually. Menus are from 83f. I found it all very gloomy, but the potential is huge. Watch this space.

La Chaumière (H)S
67 ave. Rouville (0)3.21.35.41.24

A safe bet if you are looking for a small hotel, with parking, garden, and English-speaking *patron*. M. Jean Délérance is an efficient thoughtful host. His twelve bedrooms are all different, good-sized, pristine, all with bath or shower. They cost a very reasonable 190-290f. No restaurant but several within walking distance the Relais or the Francois 1er are the ones M. Délérance recommends.

Here is a somewhat less enthusiastic view: *"Smaller room this time and I don't think I'd call it faultless - no savonette or bathmat. And the radio was on at breakfast time (but quite quiet and not dreadful music). But there are lots of nice things - very pleasant guv'nor, and a good breakfast with offers of more coffee, jam, bread etc."* Ron Salmon.

Le Relais (HR)S
(0)3.21.35.42.00 Cl. Tues.

A very pretty black-and-white building in a leafy square; as its name implies,

Le Relais

once a staging post on the route from the Channel to the south. The entrance has tiled floor, cane furniture, fireplace and well-stocked bar, presided over by blonde Madame Rivelou. In summer there is sitting and drinking available in the rear garden and car parking is easy in the courtyard.

Simple smallish rooms cost 210f with shower and 240f with bath. This would make a cheap overnight base for a family in the two *familiale* rooms - 330f for four people.

It has always been the food rather than the rooms that have drawn customers to the Relais. Good straightforward cooking, generous helpings on menus that start at 83f.

"The big dining room was substantially full and there wasn't a French person there. Pretty good though poêle descargots, gigôt d'agneau à la Bretonne (superb quality lamb), good cheeses followed by sorbet". Ron Salmon.

La Bonne Auberge (HR)S
Route de Guines, Brêmes (0)3.21.35.41.09 Cl. Sun. p.m.

1 km W of Ardres on a sharp bend on the D231.

Madame Desmulle shouts laughter. She doesn't just giggle, she explodes, and that's most of the time.

One thing that makes her hoot is the fact that her regular guests don't want her to change a thing. Another is that she's going to. Her seven minuscule bedrooms up in the roof, all flowery, cosy, very rustic, very cheap, have pleased generations of British just as they are, but they lack one thing that a younger generation demands and that is a bathroom apiece. Hitherto guests have accepted the snag of padding down the corridor, when the cost of a double room is 150f. **150f!** Madame Desmulle shrieks at the idea. So, there is going to be a huge programme of reconstruction, which will end up with en suite rooms and a considerably higher rate. I just pray that 'improvement' will not mean removing the character.

The food has always been a good reason for patronising l'Auberge. The dining room is bigger than you'd think, and there's another huge room behind, catering for all manner of celebrations. Items are pink napery, lots of plants, red velvet, big clock, artificial flowers, old gramophone and a photo of Diana. Outside is a big garden where breakfast is willingly (with lots of laffs) served in summer.

Menus start at 68f (*flamiche*, trout, dessert) and go all the way up to140f, which rather grandly aspires to *foie gras* and turbot. I'd go for the ones in between which settle for more homely dishes like *gigôt dagneau*.

If things had been a bit more settled there would have been no reason to remove the arrow, but until the dust has settled I fear it will have to go. I look forward to revisiting the new-style Auberge and no doubt having a few more good laughs.

ARGOULES 80120 Pas-de-Calais.
10 km W of Nempont-St. Firmin, 39 km SE of Boulogne

One of the prettiest villages along the valley of the Authie. A 300-year-old lime tree provides much of the character, shading the central green, and artists still find inspiration from the nearby abbey and Gothic church.

The gardens of the Abbey of Valloires are famous and are looking particularly good at the moment, after very necessary tidying and re-planting, and hundreds of garden enthusiasts visit every week to feast their eyes on the colours.

Les Jardins de Valloires
(0)3.22.23.53.55 for information
7 hectares of botanical gardens, planted with 4,000 varieties. Open to the public. See also FE15 *Gardens of France* by Barbara Abbs.

You can stay here in the Abbey and wake up in the morning to this splendid prospect. Rooms are available in what were once Cistercian monks' cells, but very spacious cells they must have been. They are now furnished with antiques and have a bathroom apiece, so although life here may still be contemplative it is certainly not Spartan. The rest of the abbey is still very shabby and houses a school. See *Chambres d'Hôtes* for full details.

Le Gros Tilleul (HR)M

Place du Château (0)3.22.29.91.00; fax (0)3.22.23.91.64 Cl. Sun. p.m.; Mon.; 19/12-1/2

Named after the giant lime tree, le Gros Tilleul has a long history. It used to be a renowned restaurant with a popular 'character' *patron*, then went through a painful period of deterioration. Now the whole valley seems to be prospering again and Marie Christine and Patrick Beuge are making major investments in the old inn. They have installed a swimming pool behind the hotel and equipped all the bedrooms, several of them brand new, with bathrooms, mini-bars and colour televisions. I find the older rooms very dark, set as they are in the roof, with tiny windows, and I cannot claim that the modern furnishing is what I would have chosen for an old country inn, but downstairs retains the rustic feel, with a comforting log fire burning in the restaurant on chilly evenings. Room rates are 350f, 380f and 450f.

Menus 70f mid-week, 97f, 190f.

Le Coq en Pâte (R)M

(0)3.22.29.92.09

Unrecognisable as the potentially attractive but disgracefully dilapidated old café which, with similar *patronne*, the Coq en Pâte used to be. Now this is a smart restaurant, with designer black chintz fabric and rose-coloured walls. Service in the pretty rear garden is particularly agreeable. I thought the menus a touch pricey at 90f for merely *terrine*, omelette and ice cream, or 120f upwards, but there's no denying it's a very attractive set-up, with sophisticated service and superior cooking.

> ARQUES 62510 Pas-de-Calais.
> 2 km S of St. Omer by rue d'Arras

There is a distinctly villagey feel to Arques, making it quite separate in identity from its neighbour St. Omer, although the two run into one another. There's plenty to see and do around here, making it a good alternative to staying in St. Omer.

The Neufossé canal links up here with the rivers Aa and Lys and little streams flow at random in front of the 17C château to the public gardens (good for picnics) and into the lakes there. The town is probably best-known for its glass-making and visitors can take a tour of the Verrerie Cristallerie d'Arques (see St. Omer, p. 00) and pick up some bargains in the shop there. Another very different tour is to the amazing hydraulic lift, the *ascenseur des Fontinettes* (apply to the grandiose 19C Town Hall for details). It's certainly another aspect for those who think they know the Pas-de-Calais inside out to see the huge barges pulled up by the locks here and to realise what a remarkable achievement this engineering triumph was in the 19th century. And still is for that matter. Another diversion, always worthwhile in my book, is to take in the Tuesday market.

▶ **La Grande Ste Cathérine** (HR)S-M
51 rue Adrien d'Anvers (0)3.21.38.03.73; fax (0)3.21.38.17.39. Cl. Sat. lunch o.o.s., 26/12-30/12

I hoped last time that an arrow would be feasible here and the mail has indicated that indeed it would. Readers have unanimously enjoyed this 17C ex-coaching house in the main street. Penny, the wife of *patron* Julien Hemery, is English, so there will be no language problems here. There is a distinctly English pub feel to the mahogany and brass bar area, popular with both guests and locals.

The twelve bedrooms are well equipped, with private bathroom apiece, and cost 200-300f. This would be a good family idea, since there are suitable rooms available and lots of space at the rear in a large garden, practical not only for summer barbecues and candle-lit dinners but also for letting off juvenile steam. Very soothing to find a sizeable 'parc' like this in the middle of the traffic fret.

The cooking, served in the panelled dining room, is surprisingly sophisticated, with a variety of house specialities, like a *feuilleté de crabe, au coulis de crustaces*. The 110f menu includes good wine, a complimentary Kir, *amuse-bouche* and coffee, and then for example, an onion tart spiced with smoked bacon, steak *au poivre* or *suggestion du marin* served with *sauce Duglèré* (tomato). Then a fresh fruit flan, or a dark chocolate *marquise*. Excellent all-inclusive value which it would be hard to beat.

"Sunday lunch was at the Grande Ste Cathérine with Penny Hemery. Once again she treated us royally and was delighted when we presented her with a copy of your Entrée. Many of our members have since returned individually and it has become a firm favourite for us". Ian Skelton.

The arrow is for all-round good value.

ARRAS 62000 Pas-de-Calais.
112 km SE of Calais **M** Sat., Wed.: Place des Héros and Place de la Vacquerie; Thurs.: Place Marc Lanvin; Sun.: Place Verlaine

---

No way could I leave out Arras from this book which is about the best of the north. Certainly if I had to choose an out of season weekend break away from the coast, it would be right here. So, although it just misses my 100 km limit, as with Amiens, the boundaries were bent a trifle to squeeze in this unique town. After all, access is easy and quick, with the autoroute so near and the other guideline of an hour's drive can just be met.

Park near the huge Abbaye St. Vaast - the largest abbey in France - and you can walk through three squares, each one opening out of the last like a layered Russian doll, except that in this case they get bigger, culminating in the explosion of the Grand'Place, which must be one of the largest in Europe and is certainly the most striking. Its surrounding arcaded Flemish houses, with their ornamented stepped gables, red brick, old stone, create an intensely satisfying total harmony. So perfect is their design that the suspicion that one has stumbled into a stage-setting might well occur, and indeed the apparatus of a film crew lay sprawling on the cobbles on my last visit.

In fact an artful deception has been practised, in that most of these houses are not the 17th and 18th century originals they would seem, but a reconstruction from the rubble that was all that was left of the great squares after the 80% destruction of the First World War. The extent of the damage of four years bombardment can be seen in the (badly-displayed) photographs in the foyer of the impressive Flemish-Gothic Town Hall in the Place des Héros.

This is the normal home of the monumental giants, Jacqueline and Colas, who come out for an airing whenever there is the slightest excuse, like fête days or sports triumphs, when they are paraded throughout the town, providing great photo-opportunities. Built originally in 1891, they were destroyed in WW1, reconstructed, destroyed again in WW2, then rebuilt in the 1980s, a commendable statement of municipal confidence in the overriding and continuing attraction of the best of things past.

The photos illustrate how only a very few of the old Flemish houses still stood, their gables sometimes lurching drunkenly towards the hole left by their neighbours. It would make sad viewing had the renaissance been less thorough and successful.

Don't miss a guided visit to the underground tunnels, from the Town Hall (every day except Christmas Day and New Years Day, weekdays 10-noon and 2-6, Sundays and fêtes 10-noon, 3.00-6.30 [to allow for extra lunch time of course!]) These tunnels, excavated from the chalk, have a fascinating and lengthy history. Dug originally in the 10th-12th centuries, they were abandoned until the prosperous 17th and 18th-century wine merchants needed somewhere to store the wine and cloth waiting to be shipped to England. There are twenty miles of tunnels altogether, some of them connected to private houses. (Don't worry - the tour, which lasts half an hour, covers only half a mile.)

The tunnels have been put to many good uses over the years. In the 18th century when the thriving town was over-populated, they were used for housing the surplus population, and often thereafter for refuge. Arras has the doubtful distinction of being the home of Robespierre, who was particularly hard on his fellow-citizens during the Terror, so the underground labyrinth was the obvious hiding place. In more recent times 2,400 soldiers were billeted here in WW1 and photographs of their living and sleeping quarters bring the extraordinary story vividly to life as no mere account can do.

From the ridiculous subterranean to the sublime heights. Take the lift up to the belfry, 250f above ground level (including 33 steep and winding steps, unsuitable for those short of agility or breath) for a not-to-be-missed-on-any-account eagle's eye view of the town. It's a good idea to make this excursion early in your visit to get an idea of the layout and interrelation of the squares. This vantage point is the give-away for the pseudo antiquity of the houses far below. Their weathered façades might look ancient enough but the new roofs are definitely 20th century.

So vast are Arras squares that even the extensive markets that take place on Saturdays and (to a lesser extent) Wednesdays fail to fill them. This is probably the best market in the North and a visit contrived on one of these days is well worthwhile. The stallholders, with their bright umbrellas, offer a huge range of goodies, from the heaps of seasonal vegetables to nasty plastic toys.

Among Arras' other claims to fame are the *bleu d'Arras* - blue and white porcelain, originally made in the 18th century, on sale in many shops in the town today and on display in the museum housed in the Abbaye St. Vaast. On show in the abbey's cloisters and refectory are the tapestries which gave the town its name - arras - the weaving of which brought the prosperity that caused houses on the squares to be built for their rich merchant owners. Walk round the *places*, looking for the heraldic signs of the local craft guilds and of the ruling families of the time.

Shopping

The market, of course, is the obvious place to stock up on local specialities from the farmers' wives, with their half-dozen eggs, two cheeses and a bunch of herbs. The place des Héros is lined with little shops, some dedicated to food, some to clothes, some to antiques, but there are two that are quite outstanding. At no. 39 is Le Gout du Vrai, where Jean-Claude Leclercq carries on his family's tradition as *Maître Fromager* and purveyor of irresistible *charcuterie*, prepared dishes (think picnic) and comestibles in jars, tins and boxes (bring home for popular presents). He puts the caves beneath his establishment to excellent use by using them to store his huge range of cheeses, both local and national. In his brochure he writes that the art of *'affiner'*, which two generations of his family have mastered, consists of numerous careful treatments to the cheeses. First they are washed in water, then in beer, then in alcohol, turned frequently and brushed, in order to give them even more flavour and perfume(!) "This perseverance in our work," he writes, "confers on the cheeses Le Gout de Vrai (the genuine taste)."

The other shop worthy of special mention is for the sweet-toothed. Yannick Déléstrez at no. 50 on the other side of the place des Héros, has a wickedly tempting selection of all things naughty but nice - hand-made chocolates and pastries both sweet and savoury.

For clothes shopping the main area to head for is the rues Gambetta, and St. Aubert, where the department stores are to be found.

HOTELS
••

NEW ➤ Univers (HR)M
3 pl. Croix Rouge (0)3.21.71.34.01; fax (0)3.21.71.41.42

What a pleasure it is to see this old favourite alive and well again, after several years decline. A restored 18C Jesuit monastery in a quiet square in the centre of town, within walking distance of the great squares, is a good recipe for an unusually attractive hotel.

The new owners have spared little expense in bringing the shabby old building back to life. I particularly like what they have done to the dining

Grand Hotel de L'Univers

room - exposed and cleaned the old brick, which is now a lovely blond colour, and chosen a yellow and green colour scheme, so that all is light and bright. The bedrooms have all been redecorated too, but in fact apart from renewing the fabrics, there was little else necessary here because the building's character - big windows, high ceilings, more light - provides the décor. None of them is particularly spacious, and the first one that we were shown was so midget-sized that there we had to climb over suitcases to get out of bed. Up in the attics, it was very dark too and although the price was modest 350f we could not face the claustrophobia and changed to a first-floor beauty, 600f well spent.

Menus start at 99f and increase to 260f, with the bonus of good carafe wine. 37 rooms from 350-600f.

So the arrow is awarded with some reservations. Plus points are the beauty of the building, its convenient location and the certainty of a quiet night. Less commendable are the cheaper rooms and the lack of any owner-management presence. It was a touch impersonal. The haves outweigh the have-nots.

> **Les 3 Luppars** (H)S
49 Grande Place (0)3.21.07.41.41; fax (0)3.21.24.24.80
Even more central, slap bang on the Grande Place, and no complaints of lack of personal touch here. Hostess Viviane de Troy merits many commendations from readers who have had problems solved, advice given, and general hands-on care from the *patronne*. De Troy is a famous local name, thanks to the exceptional wine cellar accumulated by Jean de Troy, father of the present incumbent. Son Robert is said to be one of the best-informed *sommeliers* in France, and is only too happy to take any interested party down to his magnificent caves below the hotel (and with any luck, sell them some wine).

Les Trois Luppars is always pointed out by the tour guides as the oldest house in the square. It has that distinction because it was fortunate to survive the terrible bombardment that destroyed its neighbours, but for many years it looked as though systematic neglect and decay would finish off what the war had failed to do. In 1990 the de Troys bravely embarked on a lengthy and costly restoration of the derelict building. Ask Madame to show you her photographs of the state it was in, in order to appreciate the scale of the task they were taking on. With no state grant, the façade still had to be restored meticulously in keeping with its historical importance. The three luppars after which the hotel is named (luppar is the mediaeval word for leopard) are to be found on the original plaque.

Behind the little rear courtyard is another old building owned by the de Troys, with the original mediaeval shutters in one room. The two buildings muster 42 bedrooms between them, quite modern in character, and functional, with different attributes, sizes and prices - so be specific when you book. A sauna is a new attraction.

Breakfast was another big bonus, with yoghurt, fruit and cereals supplementing the usual French fare; the butter came in pots and the jams were Bon Maman and not foil-wrapped smears.

Here is one reader's experience: "*There was a gigantic funfair in the square outside the hotel and the noise was shattering, but Madame showed us to a quiet room on the 1st floor - 200f with toilet and shower, and we didn't hear a thing. We actually joined in the fun in the square later in the evening. The breakfast was wonderful"*. Patricia Thompson.

42 rooms with prices ranging from 200-300f. ***Madame de Troy has offered French Entrée readers a discount on their first night's stay. Show her a copy of the book and she will knock 10% off the bill.***

An historic little hotel, with modest prices, in a prime site, with delightful owners, merits an arrow.

RESTAURANTS
· ·

➤ **La Faisanderie** (R)L-M
45 Grande Place (0)3.21.48.20.75; fax (0)3.21.50.89.18 Cl. Sun. p.m.; Mon., school holidays and 3 first weeks of August

Last time I wrote glowingly about The Pheasantry, I had to add a stop-press margin note: "inexplicably lost Michelin star". Even more inexplicably that Michelin star has not to date been replaced, since Jean-Pierre is cooking better than ever. He is undoubtedly one of the best chefs in the North of France. Perhaps this is a good time to pay him a visit because he is obviously trying extra hard and the prices are extra keen. What other restaurant of this calibre offers a 92f menu every day of the week except Sundays?

La Faisanderie.

Here are a few examples of what you can expect for this modest sum: For starters: *le Gratin de Poissons*. Now fish gratin can mean anything from some tinned tuna topped with packet cheese to Jean Pierre's version, which uses whatever fish is best and freshest in the market that morning, topped with a delicate creamy, cheese infused topping. *Terrine Maison* - sad to say I have eaten (or rather left on my plate) a wafer thin slice of something from the local delicatessen, via a spell in the fridge, on many a menu of this price. Here the punchy juicy *terrine* is served with a selection of *crudités* for good measure.

Main courses (still at 92f mark you) include a melt-in-the-mouth *confit* of duck or a reliable opportunity to try *Potje fleisch*, a traditional Flemish casserole which can be positively disgusting in less skilled hands.

On my most recent visit we went mad and chose the 145f menu. Stuffed crab and sea bass with thyme for me, snails with Ricard and best end of lamb for him. Then both cheese board (and an excellent one too) and skilful dessert. This menu is also available with wines included at 210f.

The setting is as delectable as the food. The cellars of one of the 17C houses in the Grand'Place, all cool grey vaults and columns, great atmosphere. Service is smooth, smiling and highly professional and the wine list an education.

Don't miss this one.

La Rapière (R)S-M
44 Grand'Place (0)3.21.55.09.92; fax (0)3.21.22.24.29 Cl. Sun. p.m.

Across the other side of the square is a restaurant very popular with readers, which I dropped in the last edition after a disappointing report. After another look I think it should be reinstated.

The decor is perhaps a touch odd in this elegant 17C building, with wonderful caves underneath (reserved, alas, for business diners) - it's all rustic and folksy - but that does make for a cosy atmosphere.

The cooking is determinedly traditional, with some regional touches like a *flan au maroilles*. Good value for quantity and quality on menus at 82f (not fête days), 115f, 130f and 170f.

Otherwise:
La Coupole d'Arras
26 bld. de Strasbourg (0)3.21.71.88.44

My favourite kind of brasserie where the waiters wear long white pinnies and black waistcoats and there are potted palms in jardinières, art deco mirrors, café curtains, and red plush banquettes. So far so good, but the food is only so-so. I include it because it is the only restaurant I could find that is willing to feed travellers on a Sunday night. Advice here is keep it simple.

NEW Chez Annie

14 rue Paul Doumer (0)3.21.23.13.51 Cl. Sun. and weekday evenings
Ideal for a lunchtime blow-out at minimum expense, with maximum entertainment. 200 metres behind the belfry, so ideally situated for recovery after climbing all those steps. There are a fair number of steps here too up to the mezzanine floor, which has the best view of all the activity downstairs in the bar. Very much an 'in' place with the locals. Cuisine can best be described as '*familiale*' and none the worse for that. *Plat du jour* costs 41f, copious menu 65f.

Looks highly promising, reports please.

ST NICOLAS 62223 Pas-de-Calais.
2 km N of Arras

Almost a suburb of Arras. Useful to know if driving in town centres make you nervous, since it is just off the autoroute.

Le Régent (HR)M

rue A. France (0)3.21.71.51.09; fax (0)3.21.07.87.56 Cl. Sat. lunch and Sun. p.m.
No response whatsoever from readers on this one, since I awarded an arrow for "cheap comfortable accommodation, excellent cooking and a convenient location", so perhaps the arrow should be suspended, but I would very much like to hear of any confirmation that this is all good news.

The 11 rooms still cost only 220-350f, and the food is as good as ever. Arras businessmen still find it worth their while to drive out here in their lunch time to stoke up. The dining room, elegant and light, opens out on to a pleasant terrace where drinks are served and thence slopes down to the river Avre. Menus, copious and mostly traditional dishes, start at 135f.

> **LES ATTAQUES** 62730 Pas-de-Calais.
> 9 km SE of Calais

A mere 9 km and it's goodbye Calais sprawl and hello Canal-land. The inherent flatness is enlivened by the occasional barge, locks, bridges and towpaths. You can drive all the way back into the heart of the port by using the minor road at the side of Les Attaques bridge; it's a touch bumpy and probably ten minutes slower, but free from traffic rage. It amuses me to see the three parallel routes, the frenzied autoroute, the old lorry-ridden *nationale,* and my favoured lane, by sparkling water all the way, light years away from the alternatives.

There's not much more to Les Attaques than a few houses, a *Mairie,* an old station and:

▶ **Restaurant de la Gare** (R)S
rte d'Andres (0)3.21.82.22.28 Cl. for dinner except on Fri. and Sat. Otherwise lunch only Cl. Mon. o.o.s.

As its name implies, near the station, an insignificant little building, unremarkable until you look at the size of its car park, which is often overflowing with cars (French ones of course). Nowadays there are a few GB plates too because this is probably the restaurant that has won more friends over the FE years than any other. Readers return for a special treat, or schedule a meal there in their journey elsewhere, and then write to me to say nothing has changed.

This includes the two large rooms (another for local festivities at the rear), with flowery wallpaper, tiled floor and an overall beige impression. Locals prop up the bar and chat to nice Madame Rambaut. On the shelves is a fine array of cups from the Les Attaques football team. It's the scene that used to be familiar in every French village, but is now giving way to fast-food caffs.

Francis Rambaut is a butcher by trade, so this is primarily the place to find home-made *terrines, foie gras, rillettes, saucissons* and of course steaks, chops and offal.

The locals were all tucking into the *menu conseillé* (which has to be different every day because so many of them eat nowhere else). For 58f they got *galantine de veau, saucisse et sa garniture* and *tarte maison.* On the more expensive menus - 88f and 140f - the smoked salmon and the *foie gras* are both home-prepared and the steaks change from *entrecôte* to fillet. Husband had just a steak and I had my usual - a hunk of juicy *terrine* and an unexpectedly huge portion of *crudités.* Madame thinks it's a bit strange to want them served together, but humours me.

Francis is looking very prosperous these days - bearded and portly - and I am delighted if this is the case because here is one restaurant I would hate to lose. The Mayor feels the same way - he was eating there on our last visit and higher praise and stronger validation for a restaurant's worth it would be hard to find.

An arrow for consistent good value.

"What a clever discovery. Despite hitting a local wedding we had a reasonably promptly served Sunday lunch. The one point we would make is that there didn't seem to be a menu on Sunday below 85f, fair value though it was. We think it must be the closest restaurant to England which leaves one in no doubt one is in France". J. E Clarke.

ATTIN 62170 Montreuil. Pas-de-Calais.
3 km N of Montreuil

➤ **Au Bon Accueil** (R)M-S
52 rte Nationale 39 (0)3.21.06.04.21 Cl. Sun. p.m.; Mon.; Wed. p.m. o.o.s. 23/2-9/3; 17/8-7/9

The *accueil* is as *bon* as ever from Jacques Delvoye and the cooking as toothsome from his wife Denise. Nothing but praise from readers, all delighted with the value on offer here.

One look at the number of French cars parked imaginatively on the bend of the *nationale* outside the villa-like restaurant and you know you can't go far wrong. It's a big dining room, decorated in country garden mode, and always busy, so book if a Sunday lunch is what you have in mind.

The dishes on the menus look simple enough but there is always a touch of imagination to liven up the predictable, and the ingredients are always obviously fresh. *Menu Express* at 78f offers two courses and wine, *Menu Opale* adds another course, *Menu Emeraude* at 142f gets more sophisticated, and *Menu Mer* at 173f allows you three fish dishes, dessert but no wine. The prices jump to a minimum of 137f on Sundays and fêtes.

"I liked the welcome from M. Delvoye and the lovely pink and green bright dining room. We began with three different fish dishes shared between us: a fresh crab mayonnaise, smoked salmon (particularly good) and a gâteau of salmon with a sauce nantua. All three were excellent, as were the home made bread rolls which were replaced regularly. Then a most unusual scallop dish: the hard shell was surrounded by pastry which you cut away to take off the lid and there nestling

inside were the fresh scallops on a julienne of fresh vegetables. The hollandaise was served separately and we poured it over the scallops in the shell. A pear and blackcurrant sorbet rounded off a very good value lunch. I liked several of the touches, including a suggestion of three wines by the glass, one with each course, for 78f." Roger Davies.

The Arrow remains intact.

AUCHY-LES-HESDIN 62770 Pas-de-Calais.

4 km NE of Hesdin on the D94

Dominating this rather unattractive village (excepting the church) are the grey paper mills, on whose site once stood the monastery that gave its name to the hotel. The dead and wounded from Agincourt, only a few miles away, were brought here to be tended by the monks.

▶ **Auberge de la Monastère** (HR)M-S
(0)3.21.04.84.54; fax (0)3.21.49.39.17 R Cl. Mon.; HR Cl. end Sept-11/11

This is supposed to be a completely re-written book, and so it is, with this exception: I made the mistake of reading what I had written in FE 12, and after a recent follow-up visit found that little had changed about the character of the hotel and its ebullient owner, so I have little useful to add or change. Will faithful readers please therefore forgive me if I reproduce almost exactly the original text.

Go and read the Livre d'Or. It says it all: "hospitality, conviviality, generosity". M. Marécaux loves his work and it shows. The book repeats itself: - "We shall return". His clients come back and back and tell their friends, who come back and back too, so that you should certainly book to make sure of a reservation. Featuring in Wish You Were Here of course did no harm at all.

In October M. Marécaux was worried that he had no rooms left for New Years Eve. 200 guests join in the revels then, some of them farmed out to neighbouring hotels. I wonder why he needed rooms - who goes to bed?

N.Y.E. apart, evenings chez Marécaux are likely to run and run. His proudest boast is that he has played with Acker Bilk, so a session at the piano or the clarinet is a very likely outcome on a Saturday or Sunday, given the slightest encouragement. Clients come as much for the atmosphere as for the bed and board.

The dining room is long and green and gold and red, with flagged floors,

LE MONASTÈRE, AUCHY - LÈS - HESDIN

beams and a raised log fire at one end. It looks at it's best in the evenings, when the candles are lit and an air of expectancy hangs over the place as before a theatrical experience, as this often turns out to be.

In spite of all his gregariousness, *M. le patron* still finds time to take his cooking seriously. His 125f *menu Terroir* features the dishes of his beloved region, which he promotes so tirelessly, and generously include plenty of expensive ingredients like monkfish and scallops, guinea fowl and duck. If you choose to stay demi-pension you get special treatment: "I don't show them the menu - I just ask them what they want".

The long-suffering Mme Marécaux, who is as nice as her husband, looks after as much of the front-of-house as he will allow her to do. No doubt she had a hand in choosing the furnishing for the new bedrooms, which are 350f, with a view over the big rear garden and the courtyard, complete with aviary. The older rooms, more simply equipped and furnished, cost 280f.

"We can only say that the addition of the new bedrooms has been extremely tastefully carried out and little expense has been spared on the furnishing of the rooms, which were absolutely spotless. We enjoyed an excellent meal."

The arrow clearly deserves to stay for cheerful good value.

AUDENFORT 62890 Pas-de-Calais.
20 kms SE of Calais by N43 to Ardres then D224 towards Licques,
then D217. The mill is signed to the right

Even shorter and much prettier, but perhaps not so easy to find is the D127 to Guines - a delightful route all along the canal, and then the D215 to Licques. This takes a mere 20 minutes from port to mill.

Moulin d'Audenfort.
(0)3.21.00.13.16. fax. (0)3.21.00.14.79.
Closing times to be decided - check.

This discovery, made very late, after the book had gone to the publishers, is the one that has pleased me most. Remember you read it here first.

The c.v. of the mill looked too good to be true. The report that reached me suggested that here, a stone's throw from the Channel ports, was a romantic 17C mill on the river Hem, recently acquired and run by a charming family. There aren't many of them around so I set off hotfoot to investigate in a somewhat sceptical mood, confident that I had scoured every village in the Pas-de-Calais, followed up every lead, networked my moles. How could this one have slipped through if it was any good?

I discovered the answer was that it probably was *not* any good until the Vanmackelbergs took over in the summer of '98 and tackled the formidable task of restoring and re-decorating the old inn, which had laid empty for two years. The previous owner, had come to a sticky end (don't ask) and the mud still stubbornly stuck for some time after his departure. There's nothing like a good scandal to amuse the locals and deter the visitors. Another deterrent, no doubt, is that the mill is not on any main road, nor on the way to anywhere, nor in any village, so there is no passing trade.

"The river runs *through* the house" I was told. Well, on the tempestuous January night we stayed there, it very nearly did. There had been torrential rain for weeks and the river was more churned up cocoa than limpid green. Overflowing its banks it tried to climb up the hill past our parked car; it attacked the foundations of the mill, pounding at the lock in a fury of impatient waves. The noise from our bedroom was more like the M25 than country-calm but we slept like babes, comforted by Madame's assurance than an '*inondation*' was impossible.

The water does indeed flow through the lounge in a basin housing the ancient mill machinery. "Normally," says Madame, " the water is crystal and you can gaze down upon the trout." The cumbersome old workings make a unique focal point to the room, with sheaves of wheat on their platform emphasising the rusticity.

There is also a little bar here, an open fire, lots of squashy armchairs and settees and board games set out invitingly. All very cosy and '*familiale*', which is just the atmosphere that the family are trying to create.

Next door is even nicer. Here a huge log fire burns continuously on a raised hearth, girded by a club fender and surrounded by deep chintzy sofas. On such a foul day it was such a joy to sink down here with a cup of tea that plans of driving anywhere else for dinner grew less and less attractive, till we asked Madame if she could possibly feed us, lacking the advance reservation she usually requests. "*Bien sur,*" she assured us - "Duck, steak *au poivre* or venison?"

A hot bath and a freshen-up in the pretty bedroom whose windows overlooked on two sides the furious river, worked wonders and we sallied down to the dining-room-cum-lounge - beams, yellow cloths, tiled floors, yellow striped curtains, one brick wall - accepting that on such a night nobody else would venture out and we would eat alone. Unusually we were confident that here we would never feel bored nor a nuisance. In fact after nine o'clock a party of seven dripping refugees, some English locals and some French, arrived and asked if they could eat. They were served cheerfully by the whole family, including a hitherto unseen 18-year-old daughter.

The formula is four courses for 100f, sometimes with choices, sometimes not. We ate excellent scallops with leeks in a cream sauce, then magret of duck for Him and venison fillet for me. The cheeseboard was perfect - five cheeses all in prime condition, and the *tarte aux pommes* was as good as they come. Excellent value.

There are thirteen rooms altogether, all with bathrooms, some in the mill itself, some in the adjoining miller's house (where three rooms have terraces on which to enjoy summer breakfasts), and some in a right-angle annexe that runs between the garden and the river, so that you can lie in bed and fish from your window. They are all simply but comfortably furnished and cost 300f including breakfast for two.

The Vanmackelbergs are playing it cool in these early days waiting to see exactly what are their guests' preferences - more luxury, which would involve higher prices, or keeping the mill just the way it is. A programme of improvements will go on anyway - the thin carpets will be the next to go. The overgrown garden has been bravely tackled and is a potential delight, running along by the side of the river. Breakfast will be served wherever seems appropriate - in the garden, on the terrace overlooking the lock or in the conservatory, where grapes festoon the glass roofs and the daughter has stencilled grape designs on the walls. They aim to please.

Make no mistake - this is more of a b. and b. flavour than smart hotel - and don't go expecting perfection. The fact that the bed linen does not always match, the bath panels are not yet fixed and the towels are a bit sparse is easily forgiven in the light of the welcome and the charm. The river is the décor. If we liked it, which we emphatically did, in such appalling conditions, I must squander that 'i' word. It has to be absolutely idyllic when the sun shines.

Walkers will be particularly happy here - there is a series of indicated rambles, some taking an hour, some half a day, around the mill, some following the Hem, some cutting across the attractive farmland.

I fear the inevitable of course. With the advantages of proximity to the ports and the utter delight of the rural setting, the *moulin* cannot remain a secret for long. I am pleased for the Vanmackelbergs, but sorry for those of us who would like to keep their hotel all to ourselves. I had a severe battle as to whether to spill the beans or not, but realised that reticence would be a lost cause here - someone is going to cotton on very soon. I hope the French will continue to dilute the British preponderence that I dread. The family are well aware that they may end up like the Chateau Tilques or increasingly Les Trois Mousquetaires - British ghettoes - and are trying to encourage *les autres*. My advice of course is Go Soon.

The arrow is for unique setting, good food, lovely family.

AUDRESSELLES 62164 Pas-de-Calais.
13 km N of Boulogne

A strange beach, with sand in between great flat-topped rocks. Ideal for picnic tables. There's lots of character in this relatively unspoiled fishing village, where crabs and mussels are for sale from many of the low, whitewashed, Flemish-style cottages and there seem to be more boats pulled up in the streets than on the beach.

No special eating recommendation here, but there are several modest café-restaurants in the centre, with tables outside, where a platter of the local molluscs and crustaceans should go down well.

AZINCOURT Pas-de-Calais.
15 km NE of Hesdin

No matter from which direction you approach the village which we know as Agincourt, you could hardly fail to gather that something momentous happened here once upon a time. Fluttering banners, coats of arms in red and gold and heraldic devices suspended at the roadside see to that. There is a museum too, with a video presentation of the battle when in 1415 Henry V and Charles VI met in the combat that was to lead to 10,000 of the French nobility being slain or captured. Not an event for the locals to celebrate you might think. No, but the tourist money's good.

You can follow one of the signed trails around the battlefield, but it takes a considerable stretch of imagination to picture the noise, the excitement, the colour, the action of that misty October day when our king covered himself in glory. 6,000 French soldiers are buried here in a grave pit beneath the roadside calvary near the site of battle, now a blank ploughed field. It was here at the crossroads where Henry delivered his rousing speech upon St. Crispin's Eve.

NEW Restaurant le Charles VI (R)S-M
12 rue Charles VI (0)3.21.41.53.00

The grandfather and grandmother of Armand Boulet owned a somewhat run-down café here. Purpose-built this year next door is their grandson's brand new restaurant, all peachified. Its glowing paint may seem a touch incongruous in such a setting, on a corner near the battlefield, but it's certainly a cheerful sight in this refreshment-free zone. There are some nice touches, like portraying the grandparents to the right of the entrance to the new restaurant and decorating the chairs with engravings of archers. French or English I wonder?

"Gersende Boulet was quite coincidentally baptised with a medieval first name which has its origins in Provence. Her husband Armand is the son of the mayor of Azincourt and a well-travelled and experienced chef. The quality of the food is excellent and very reasonably priced, with menus (including drinks) starting at 80f during the week and go as high as 155f. at weekends. The carte is changed daily. Ambiance chic but very friendly and relaxed." D. H.

> **BERCK-PLAGE** 62600 Pas-de-Calais.
> 17 km S of Le Touquet, 29 km S of Boulogne
> **M** Wed., Sat.

Otherwise:

The whole town of Berck is an otherwise in my book, because, frankly, I just can't take it. I hate the sprawl you have to drive through to get to the front, and once on the front I can't wait to get away again from all the nasty souvenir shops and burger bars. The one natural asset that it is impossible not to admire is the vast stretch of sand, but even this I find intimidating in its scale and busyness.

The resort originated as a centre for invalids, who benefited from the unusual deposits of ozone in the air. There are still a number of medical establishments operating in the town, and strange adult prams can be seen being pushed along the prom.

Just in case anyone disagrees with me in my distaste for the place - a windsurfer or sand-racer perhaps - there are two hotel possibilities, both personally inspected (never let it be said I shirk the cause of duty). **Hotel de la Banque**, 43 rue de la Division Léclerc (0)3.21.09.01.09, currently being re-furbished, 230f with bath, and **l'Entonnoir**, 31 Ave Francis Tattegrain (0)3.21.09.12.13, 200f. Both are within easy toddler-reach of the beach, and both are good value.

> **BERGUES** 59380 Nord.
> 9 km S of Dunkerque

One of the most interesting little towns in Flanders, well worth exploring. Walk along the quiet quays beside the river Colme, across the iron bridges, through winding cobbled streets, admire the stepped gables, double-storied slender windows and carved stone heads on the weathered 18th and 19th century houses and you cannot fail to be reminded of Bruges. The bad news is that much of this historic town was destroyed in 1940; the good news is that it was so sympathetically restored that you would hardly know.

Bergues can be quite confusing to navigate because, as an aerial map clearly illustrates, it is built in the shape of a ring, with the inner circle formed by the rue Carnot, the rue Faidherbe and the rue Nationale enclosing the Eglise St. Martin, with several squares opening off one another. If you have time to spare

- and it would be well spent - ask at the Tourist Office in the Place de la République for a list of suggested walks, in and outside the gates. I append one below.

The centrepiece, in the main square, is the famous 16C belfry, set ablaze in 1940 and dynamited by the Germans in 1944. The reconstruction - a slightly simplified version - uses the same yellow sandstone; the Lion of Flanders looks down from the inverted onion dome and the carillon of fifty bells in the octagonal wooden campanile punctuates the day with some of the most tuneful and prolonged chimes in all Flanders. I timed the one that rang on the hour and it lasted all of ten minutes. Those prepared to climb 199 steps to the belfry's summit, 117ft high, will be rewarded with a fine view of the surrounding countryside, netted with rivers and canals.

No prizes for guessing that the military architect responsible for the town's fortification was the ubiquitous Vaubon. Four gates pierce the ramparts. The Porte de Hondschoote was built after the treaty of Aix-la-Chapelle in 1667, which gave Bergues to France. Vauban utilised branches of the river Colme to build a crown-shaped complex of bastions - the Couronne d'Hondschoote, surrounded by deep moats full of fish. Its layout can only be appreciated by looking at a map. The Porte de Cassel to the south is from the same date, its triangular pediment decorated with the sun emblem of Louis XIV. The other gates, Bieur and Beckerstor, date from the Middle Ages.

Vauban might be gratified to know that his fortifications were used by the French troops in the defence of Dunkerque and only fell when the Germans used 20th-century methods - dive-bombing and flame-throwing - to breach them.

This many-faceted little town can add some important art treasures to it's other attractions. The pride of the Musée Municipale's collection is Georges de la Tour's Hurdy-Gurdy Player, one of two versions. Pieter Breughel, Cuyp and Jordaens are also represented.

The one thing surprisingly lacking is that the huge place de la République, with important belfry, lacks a good central brasserie. It's one of the few Flemish towns that do not boast a Taverne Flamande. The cafés that surround the *place* are pretty dismal plastic and pop. But there are compensations.

Bergues - walk. Takes about an hour, but it is always possible to cut it short, and double back into the town centre. Notice all the wonderful names:

Start at the belfry, for the rampart walk behind the sports hall, between the Tour des Couleuvriniers and the Tour des Faux-Monnayeurs. Climb the stairs of the latter, follow the ramp that runs along the rue Pierre Decroo, to the Bastion St. Pierre. Go down stairs and follow the vaulted path to the Place Charles de Croocq. Through the park up to the flight of steps and take the lane behind, the rue Neuve des Capucins. At the end go down the steps at the Porte d'Hondschoote. Pass by the Maison des Ingenieurs du Roy, cross over canal near the lock gate, turn right and follow the rampart up to the Porte du Quai. Through gate, along the quay up to the Porte du Port. Cross over the canal again and take footpath to the Caserne Leclaire. If you have the energy, climb to top of the Porte de Bierne for a good view. Walk on top of ramp up to the Poudrière du Moulin and back to the belfry via the Porte de Cassel. Drink beer in the *place*.

Unfortunately the hotel scene in Bergue is not good. One reader had a very unhappy experience at a former entry, le Tonnelier.

Otherwise:

Le Commerce (H)S
(0)3.28.68.60.37

A pretty little hotel near the church, spotlessly clean. 14 simple rooms, with showers, cost from 150-350f.

The restaurant scene is another matter:

NEW ➤ Le Berguenard (R)M-S
1 rue Faidherbe (0)3.28.68.65.00 Cl. Sun. p.m.; Mon.

Emanuel de Langhe is a *traiteur* as well as a *restaurateur* and I always find this a good sign - it means that everything is home-made. The money has gone here where it does most good - in the cooking and not in the décor. Le Berguenard is a simple little restaurant in a side street, with nothing pretentious about its table settings, or, for that matter, about the food, which relies on good ingredients carefully prepared. Fish is Emanuel's speciality and his 135f menu should be enough for fish-lovers to make a detour to Bergues especially to eat here. A *panaché* of sole and salmon was anointed with a sweet garlic sauce, and served with rice that had been cooked in flavoursome stock, and a fillet of brill came with a lime sauce. Passion-fruit mousse was a perfect finish to the meal. There is a 125f version, again featuring fish for its first course - layers of sea trout in flaky pastry - followed by veal chop with chicory, on a bed of creamy mashed potatoes, and a gourmet option at 170f.

You should book - Le Berguenard is not only small, it is relatively new and everyone wants to try it. Once they do they go back.

Le Cornet d'Or (R)L
26 rue Espagnole (0)3.28.68.66.27 Cl. Sun. p.m. and Mon.

Chalk and cheese from the previous entry. Le Cornet is a serious, rather grand restaurant serving serious, rather grand food. Jean-Claude Tasserit's talents have been widely recognised since I first wrote about him, and his Michelin star has brought him well-deserved prosperity. His clients from Dunkerque and *environs* keep tables occupied but nevertheless he manages to produce a 120f mid-week menu, which is remarkable value. Others at 158f and 220f.

On an earlier visit I enjoyed asparagus and wild mushrooms cooked in cream and sole stuffed with *langoustines,* both superb and arrow-worthy. The fact that there is no arrow to this edition is not because I know that his cooking is any less praiseworthy but because the restaurant was closed when I tried to visit (and it wasn't Sunday or Monday). Nothing on the file to help me, so we must wait and see. Pity.

LE CORNET D'OR, BERGUES,

➤ **Le Pont Tournant** (R)S-M
Bierne-par-Bergues (0)3.28.68.61.66 Cl. Sat.

Outside the town walls, set back from the D916. More confusing to find now that there is a new roundabout. Hard to explain, but don't despair if you find yourself doing a U-turn to get there. Ask anyone, because everyone knows Le Pont Tournant.

It overlooks the canal, so would be particularly agreeable in fine weather. Not that most of its businessmen clients care - they are very happy munching away indoors in the fug. Technically the large dining room is divided into *fumeurs* and *non-fumeurs*, but, this being France, check the habits of your neighbours before you sit down. Most of them will be regulars - Le Pont is celebrating its 30th anniversary and should know by now how to please them.

The décor will be recognisable as that of many such a French establishment where food comes first - mock beams, speckled tiled floor, *rustique* chairs, amber glass windows - but that's not important. You come here to please the tastebuds rather than the eye.

The menus at first sight look rather dull but in fact produce a good deal more than first impressions might reveal. Look no further than the cheapest one at 65f if you want just a two-course lunch - the *plat du jour* and dessert. For more choice head for the 92f version, for substantial portions of *terrine* (dish left on table) with *crudités*, then perhaps a Flemish speciality like *Potje fleisch* if you have a good appetite, then cheese and dessert. There is also a generous buffet, from which you can help yourself to cold dishes and the famous fruit tarts.

Good honest cooking at good honest prices and arrowed accordingly.

"Excellent food, excellent service. An ideal place to have our last meal of the holiday before making for the Tunnel. 3 hours of undiluted pleasure." Lesley Bayliss.

BÉTHUNE 62400 Pas-de-Calais.
34 km N of Arras, 40 km SW of Lille, 65 km SE of Calais
M Mon., Fri.

I asked two shopkeepers if the carillon in the belfry always struck so eccentrically - I noted it was always on the hour, usually on the half-hour, sometimes on the quarter hour and sometimes in between. They both said they were so used to it they never listened. That's a shame because it's a delightful little jingle that cheers up the large cobbled central square, and warms the hearts of the customers sitting outside the numerous cafés - I counted nine - that surround it. How praiseworthy that the citizens do not allow a little problem like the chill northern climate prevent them enjoying al fresco conviviality.

The belfry too is worth noticing - 14th century, the oldest in the Pas-de-Calais. And so are the eccentric buildings, particularly on the north side of the *place,* where they are so narrow that there cannot be more than one room on each floor. Their style is a mixture of Flemish and art deco, all spiky, gabled, balconied and carved, some wood, some stone. In fact none of them are the originals. After the devastation of WW1 the entire square was rebuilt. Béthune has had more than it's fair share of destruction. The Germans, who occupied it during the last war, fired the entire kilometre between the *place* and the station as a parting gesture of hatred.

Otherwise:

Vieux Beffroi (HR)M
48 Grand'Place (0)3.21.68.15.00; fax (0)3.21.56.66.12

This old hotel centre-stage on the square is now part of a complex of three hotels, virtually taking over the town's accommodation. The 65 rooms range from 200-350f. Menus from 75f.

NEW ROOMS

➤ Marc Meurin (HR)L
15 pl. de la République (0)3.21.68.88.88; fax (0)3.21.56.37.15 Cl. Sun. p.m. Mon. except fêtes; first fortnight in August

Béthune might not be the most obvious place to find the top-rated chef in the whole of the North of France. Its proximity to Lille no doubt helps. But wherever Marc Meurin cooked, a meal in his restaurant would undoubtedly *mérite le détour.* I asked him what was the difference between one and two star (Michelin) cuisine, but I'd come to the wrong man. M. Meurin has never strained every fibre to join the exclusive club of just seventy chefs in the whole of this cuisine-obsessed country that can boast the second *macaron.* He just loves his job and happens to be very good at it. When he heard that he had been promoted in April 1998, it was a total surprise. He had neither striven nor hoped for the honour. So his reply was that nothing had changed. He cooked as he had always done (superbly). I realised, after eating chez Meurin recently, that I didn't really need to ask the question. My tastebuds told me all I needed to know. Here was an intensity of flavour, an attention to detail, a passion for fresh ingredients, a flair for combining subtle taste affinities that I had never found in the best one-star establishments.

His restaurant is tucked away in a quiet leafy square not far from the town centre in an elegant turn-of-the-century house. The reception area, presided over by blonde Madame Meurin, is charming, with red and white *toile de jouy* wallpaper. The colour scheme is repeated all over the house; in the three small dining rooms (tables well apart, atmosphere intimate); fresh white paint relieves the dramatic red walls. Red and white curtains, red and white striped high-backed chairs, red and white porcelain table settings, red and white fresh flowers and ruby candles may sound over the top, but believe me the impression is far from that, so clever has been the balance. The only touches of downright grandeur are the glittering chandelier and the sweeping staircase.

Marc Meurin is a hands-on chef. He is to be found in the kitchen, not toadying up to his clients or appearing on television. He did find time, after all his customers had been served, to come and chat with me but otherwise his is the hand that stirs the sauce. He leaves the socialising to his efficient *maître d'h*, M. Caron, whom I soon discovered had learned his near-perfect English working at my local, the Angel at Midhurst. After a spell with Raymond Blanc, he realised his dream of returning to France and working for a chef of the same calibre. He and M. Meurin are lucky to have found each other.

I dined on the cheapest menu, *Le Menu Curiosité*, at 260f (at lunchtime there is a bargain 180f version). The meal started as it meant to go on - deliciously. When I tasted the preamble - three tiny *amuse-bouches* - I already knew I was in for an unforgettable experience.

A mousse of pumpkin with tomato jelly, a tender baby *langoustine* wrapped in a courgette shaving with a shellfish sauce, and a cauliflower soup, creamy beyond imagination, with chopped *cêpes* a surprise in the bottom, came in three little white porcelain dishes, one oblong, one square and one round, each holding a mere mouthful of ambrosia.

Marc is known not only for his imaginative use of unusual ingredients but also for his enthusiasm for local ones. Eel from the Somme came next - *anguille de la Somme au vert sur toast*. Three thin slices of fish, crisp on the outside, meltingly tender within. The *au vert* meant a creamy winey sauce, reduced to transparency and liberally sprinkled with herbs, served on a thin slice of unsweetened brioche.

More local produce next - the quails in his *suprême de caille fermière aux girolles, légumes étuvés à la fleur de sel* came from the little village of Licques, famous for its poultry. He used just the breasts (the extravagance totally justified by the result). They came in a sticky red wine sauce enlivened by punchy wild mushrooms. Perfect though they were, they were eclipsed by the vegetables. 'Étuvé' has no direct translation in English. 'stewed' certainly won't do. Here it meant cooked very gently in butter, covered, resulting in the most amazingly flavoursome potatoes ever, alongside melting baby onions, and juvenile carrots.

The dessert choice proved a real tug. True investigative spirit should have led me to *le flan de réglisse chocolate à l'infusion de thé vert*. Liquorice *(réglisse)*, rarely seen on English menus, is the flavour of the month in France for both savoury and sweet dishes and the infusion of green tea would have been a first. I chickened out, however, at the potential richness and settled for the alternative - *la galette crèmeuse à la pêche de vigne*. I knew that *pêches de vigne* were quite different from ordinary peaches, but this was my first sampling. Their flavour is much more intense and I shall certainly look out for them again. The Meurin treatment involved topping a mini-pancake, enriched with cream, with half a peach that had been poached in champagne. How could I regret missing the liquorice after that?

Petits fours were a chocoholic's fantasy - truffles to die for. And the two squares of glistening home-made toffee, one chocolate, one caramel, meant that a bag of the usual varieties will never be the same again.

Yes, I can tell the difference between one and two stars.

Remember you read it here first - hot from the press is the news that the Meurins have just completed six lavishly comfortable rooms above the restaurant. They show off the versatility of the red and white theme by being all different. The bathrooms stick with white - marble. Each room - more of a suite really, with sitting space - has a well-equipped kitchenette. Ingredients for breakfast - cereal, bread, fruit, eggs, etc - are supplied, then it's up to you to do the cooking. They cost either 500f or 600f, which is good value considering the luxury on offer, the fact that you can stock up the fridge with your own booze and thus avoid bar bills, and the delight of only having to stagger up the stairs after the Meurin feast.

Arrowed for the best cooking in the book.

BEUSSENT 62212 Pas-de-Calais.

31 km SE of Boulogne, 10 km N of Montreuil

The river Course flows wide and free here, past a picturesque and still functioning mill. On the D127 is an example of interesting local industry - Les Chocolats de Beussent. I had tasted the end result in various top restaurants in the vicinity, now I had the chance to find out how they were produced. I recommend the experience. The chocolate shop is open for purchases (preceded by complimentary tasting) from Mon. to Sat. from 9-12 and from 2-7 p.m. Group visits to the factory behind the shop are arranged by appointment in the afternoons and if you're lucky you can tag on and see the ingredients assembled and packed. The enterprise is run by two brothers, who have another shop in Paris, and one of them is likely to be your guide. Only the finest chocolate, rich in cacao, is used. If you want to be sure of seeing the workings of the factory on an English-speaking tour, telephone ahead to check on possible times (0)3.21.92.44.00. Les Chocolats de Beussent, 66 rte de Dèsvres.

Le Restaurant Lignier (R)S
4 pl. de la Mairie (0)3.21.86.50.55 Cl. Wed.; Sun. p.m.

I had been put off previously by Madame Lignier's indication that she specialised in groups, but repeated praise from readers persuaded me to put prejudice aside and I'm glad I did.

The building is in the heart of downtown Beussent - that is on a corner opposite the mill. True the big rear room is designed for groups but there is another more atmospheric one with just six tables, which I liked much better. The tables double up for use by bar customers. Lignier is very much the nerve-centre of the village.

During the week the 68f menu looks good value - *bouchées à la reine, omelette aux champignons*, dessert, wine or beer included - but look at the 97f version for something altogether fancier. *Terrine de légumes au Noilly Prat, Effiloché de saumon à la crème d'algue, millefeuille aux Maroilles, marinés à la bière*. Somewhere out there is a chef who enjoys cooking. Nothing amateurishly rustic about those dishes.

➤ **Josiane et Daniel Barsby** (Ch d'H)L

124 rte d'Hucqueliers, Hameau le Ménage (0)3.21.90.91.92; fax (0)3.21.86.38.24

The rule for including *chambres d'hôtes* in this book is that they must be special. The Barsbys' 19C home, part manor, part farmhouse, set deep in peaceful lanes, amply fulfils this requirement. To find it drive past the Restaurant Lignier and climb a narrow leafy hill, with picnic tables thoughtfully set out to make the most of the surprisingly good view. After 2 kms look for the house on the left - no sign, deliberately, but it's the only substantial property on the road.

They have hardly any need for signs - open just a year when I visited and already well-booked by word-of-mouth.

Daniel is a sculptor in wood, as will be very evident immediately inside the front door. Examples of his talent, bold and distinctive, some of them begging to be bought (but not for sale) are all over the house. His studio is a stunning room, rising up to lofty rafters, with a gallery from which to look down on him working either at his sculpture or at the lace patterns which he designs for *Calaisien* lace manufacturers. He will happily show you the delicate painstaking designs of which he is a master.

The five bedrooms are all generous, in size, fittings and views. Bathrooms are definitely in the luxury class, with power showers and deep tubs. Colours, in keeping with the scale of the house, are bold - lots of crimsons and forest greens, not pretty pretty pastels, No skimping of the extras - bowls of fruit are provided in the rooms, bon-bons too, and bathroom perks, along with thick new towels.

Their windows all look out onto unblemished countryside via extensive grounds. Two horses are available for accomplished riders. Outbuildings (more rooms in the future perhaps?) are as immaculately preserved as the house. The new owners have obviously invested untold time as well as money in the restoration.

Breakfast, included in the price of 350-400f, is special again. Not only the usual French standard bread and croissants but fresh farm eggs and of course freshly squeezed o.j. Or, I imagine, anything else that you fancied - Josiane is an extremely accommodating hostess.

An undoubted arrow for unusually comfortable rooms and a good breakfast at a very reasonable price, charming hosts and the guarantee of a peaceful night's sleep, far away from the crowds but only 20 minutes from Boulogne.

BÉZINGHEM 62650 Pas-de-Calais.
7 km of Dèsvres by D127 and D127E, 27 km SE of Boulogne

NEW La Ferme Auberge des Granges (R)S
(0)3.21.90.93.19

The unspoiled country either side of the valley of the Course cries out for unspoiled country eating, and this is just the spot to find it. The family Dacquin run this *ferme auberge* in a whitewashed farmhouse built round a cobbled courtyard, all as rustic as you could wish and unlike anything I know back home.

They do a 60f lunch of home-produced goodies, but for 80f, lunch or dinner, you are asked to tackle seven courses. Not much choice, just whatever is at its best that day and all the better for that.

You could settle for carrot soup, or *terrine*, or *quiche*, then guinea fowl, or a splendid roast farm chicken, then vegetables - the vanishing ingredient in many menus nowadays - then salad, then cheese, then fruit tart.

There are two other menus '*sur commande*', at 100f and 120f, for which you get home-made *foie gras*.

Reports welcome

BLENDECQUES 62575 Pas-de-Calais.
4 km S of St. Omer by D77

A surprisingly compact 'village' community feel, complete with church and market place, quite distinct from St. Omer's other amorphous suburbs.

Le Saint Sébastien (HR)S-M
2 Grand'Place (0)3.21.38.13.051; fax (0)3.21.39.77.85 Cl. Sat. lunch and Sun. p.m.

A real village pub. This is the kind of simple family-run hotel/restaurant that used to be so common in France and is now giving way to plastic and pop. There is a cosy wooden bar, a brasserie and a *restaurant gastronomic*, and each one is a star in its category.

The brasserie features salads, omelettes, as well as grills around 70f. In the more formal restaurant you need pay only 130f for melon and Parma ham, guinea fowl stuffed with mushrooms and apple tart with caramel sauce.

There is more choice on the 170f - oysters, *filet de boeuf* - and less on the 79.50f - *ficelle Picarde, poisson du jour* or the *plat du jour,* and then *dessert du jour.* Nothing wrong with that.

Double glazing takes care of possible traffic noise. AII except two rooms (which overlook the parking lot) look out onto the main road, so those who like to sleep with their windows open should maybe consider alternative accommodation. They cost 270f with bath or 250f with shower.

It's usually good news when the chef is a woman (my theory is that she has to try harder to get accepted, particularly in France) and that is the case here. Jeannette and Pierre Duhamel have reversed roles so that she cooks and he is front of house. And a friendly and helpful couple they are.

BOLLEZÉELLE 59470 Nord.
47 km SE of Calais, 22 km NE of St. Omer

One of the prettiest drives in this area is to take the D928 out of St. Omer, following the river Aa and then turn right at Watten on to the D226, which leads through some relatively (for this interminably flat territory) hilly countryside.

Bollezéelle itself is a village of neat little Flemish-style houses, a few shops, the church of St. Wandrille, built in 1606 with even earlier foundations, and a rash of new buildings spreading further every year.

➤ Hostellerie St. Louis (HR)M
(0)3.28.68.81.83; fax (0)3.28.68.01.17 Cl. Sun. Mon.

Built as a private house in 1760, it was bequeathed to the village at the end of the last century by its old, blind and unmarried owner for use as a home for the elderly. Now it has become a very popular middle-priced hotel, conveniently sited near both autoroute and ports.

As you approach the tall, narrow building, with grey slate roof and steeple topped by a flagpole, an encouraging sight is people sitting on wooden chairs on the terrace overlooking the extensive garden and watercourse, all socialising over their drinks. A hotel where no-one talks to anyone else is usually a sign of discontent.

Inside it's all very cheerful and very peachy. The cheerfulness extends to the ever-smiling *patronne* - "Just call me Bea" - who is bound to be at the reception. Flemish-born, multi-lingual, she soothes away any problems and helps with new ideas for local appreciation.

The bedrooms are named after regions of France - Artois, Flandres, Touraine. They cost 320f with shower, 360f with bath. Jura and Dauphiné are suites - 450f - and Brouilly is suitable for wheelchairs.

The food has been greatly enjoyed by most readers; there was one grumble about the cost but if you take the *menu du Marché*, three courses *selon le Marché*, it need cost no more than 140f, and that includes half a bottle of wine. Next one up is 180f.

Arrowed for safe convenience and a pleasant welcome.

BOUBERS-SUR-CANCHE 6270 Frévent. Pas-de-Calais.
4 km N of Frévent, 76 km SE of Boulogne

Another flowery little village in the pleasant valley of the Canche, dominated by the gates of a secretive château, next to the church; an agreeable place to stop for a picnic under the espaliered lime trees. There are lovely walks nearby.

Otherwise:
La Cremaillière (R)S
Place de l'Eglise (0)3.21.03.60.03 Cl. Tues. p.m.
 Just a village café, where an omelette and glass of wine, preferably taken at a table outside, would make a restful lunch break. During the week there is a different *menu du jour* every day, 70f, and two more at 95 and 120f.

BOULOGNE SUR MER 62200 Pas-de-Calais.
32 km S of Calais
M Sat., Wed.

A tale of two towns. To know Boulogne you must acquaint yourself with an industrialised, post-war, concrete-functional port and a 13th-century ramparted citadel. The former is noisy, traffic-beset, equipped with average shops, some better-than-average restaurants, and the buzz of a working fishing harbour; the latter is a community insulated by thick stone walls from the rest of the world. Footsteps echo in cobbled streets; on grey winter days ghosts outnumber tourists.

Shopping

The lower town, from which many quick-hoppers never venture, is not a thing of beauty in its post-bombing reincarnation. A grid of streets is lined with boutiques, a couple of chain stores and plenty of *charcuteries*, *pâtisseries* and *chocolatiers*. Here are the best:

Outstanding is **Philippe Olivier**, *maître fromager*, in the rue Thiers. Supplier of prime cheeses to most of the renowned restaurants in the North of France, not to mention a good few in England, he usually has around 300 varieties in stock. Beneath the narrow shop are his *caves*, kept at different temperatures to suit different varieties at different stages of their *affinage*. Show any interest in his great passion, and Philippe will no doubt escort you on a guided tour. Ask specialised advice on what to take home or consume on a picnic, the crucial question being: "When do you intend to eat your purchase?"

For *charcuterie* head for **Bourgeois**, 1 Grande Rue, the ideal pre-picnic stop. Choose from a confusingly extensive range of *saucissons*, *terrines*, *pâtés*, cooked meats and specialities like *petit salé aux lentilles* (salt pork with lentils). If you're self-catering consider the roast chicken sold in a bag in which it can be re-heated.

Irresistible *pâtisseries* come from **Fred**, on the Place Dalton, a decidedly upmarket but unintimidating establishment, where you can pick up a sandwich as well as a celebratory *gâteau*. But for the best bread in town Demarchez on the corner of the rues Faidherbe and Thiers has the edge. Two elegant pillars of gastronomy are the **Comtesse du Barry** in the Grande Rue and, even better if you want a truly impressive present, **Hediard's**, an outpost of Paris' famous foodies' paradise. This one is just outside the old town walls at 7 rue Porte Neuve. A one-off is **Idris** in the Grande Rue, whose window is ablaze with colour from dried and glacé fruits and nuts. **Nouvelles Galeries** sometimes comes up with interesting items a touch different from British chain store stock and is worth a look at Christmas time for toys and Christmas decorations.

In the Haute Ville there are several quirky specialist shops. I particularly like **Des Mystères de Fanny** (owned by Fanny Willemart), on a corner of the Place Godefroy de Bouillon, a needlework and crafts shop, which will sometimes sell you the stuffed toys expertly made up from kits. or decorative tapestries. Chantal and Pierre Vanheeckhoet's shop in the rue de Lille is crammed with present ideas.

Boulogne is not so hypermarketed as Calais. If you don't feel you've been to France unless you've pushed a trolley, there is Auchan, 6 km on the RN 42 at St. Martin-lès-Boulogne; or the Centre Commerciale de la Diane, with a PG supermarket. The latter is useful to know because of its 2 hour free parking, within easy walking distance from the town centre.

Wine shopping

Best hypermarkets we do not have. Best wine shop we do. The Grape Shop has always been my favourite booze stop and I was seriously upset when its town centre outlet closed. However it is now even less stressful to pick up a case or two from the Seacat depot. The building here is spacious and calm, the staff are knowledgeable, helpful and English speaking and the *dégustations* are generous. Over 300 wines are available and I particularly appreciate the absence of chauvinism in their country of origin. Wines from all over the world are here,

Boulogne

alongside an excellent French range. There are always special offers to look out for and if you don't have time to browse, just tell the salespersons exactly what you are looking for, at what price range, and you can trust them to make an expert choice for you. You can usually spot parents-of-the-bride sipping a range of fizz and asking hopefully if the Australian sparkling is really as good as the champagne. They certainly saved us a bob or two over two daughters' weddings, even if we did have to have a new car axle.

Best shopping of all is to be found in the Saturday morning market (smaller one on Wednesday). It's the biggest and best in the region, spilling out of the sloping cobbled Place Dalton into the adjoining streets. Farmers' wives come from miles around to set out their treasures - half a dozen creamy goats' cheeses, bunches of herbs, seasonal booty like wild mushrooms, and patently fresh eggs spattered with farmyard. One-stop shopping it is not but much more fun.

The Place Dalton, is the only part of the Basse Ville to have retained its pre-war character. It is presided over by the church of St. Nicolas, mostly 18C, transept vaulting a century earlier. This is the heart and belly of the town, the scene of ceremonies secular and religious. At Christmas-time the cobbled surrounds are charmingly decorated with white-painted birch trees sparkling with simulated frost and tiny lights, and the venerable patron saint, St. Nicolas himself, distributes sweets to the children. The stalls in the market sell cheap milk chocolate images of the saint; the smarter *chocolatiers* don't miss a commercial trick and offer dark and white chocolate versions.

There are plenty of bars around the *place* whose tables offer both sustenance and the opportunity to observe the action before climbing up the Grande Rue to the Haute Ville. You could take the car but somehow it will seem an anachronistic intrusion into the centuries-old calm. It's a ten-minute puff up to one of the four gates let into the massive ramparts. Built in the 13th century by the Count of Boulogne, on the site of a Gallo-Roman foundation, the ensemble is an impressive 400 metres square, decorated by 17 turrets. Try and find time for a pleasant stroll around the sentry walk, accessible from each gateway, for inspiring views of town and port.

From this fortress 3,000 Boulonnais put up a fierce resistance against 30,000 English troops ordered by Henry Vlll to capture the town. It was only after the betrayal by the Governor of Boulogne, Sire de Coucy de Vervins, that the English triumphed. The population fled from Boulogne to Étaples and Abbeville and the town remained an English possession until 1550 when Henri II paid a ransom for its return. In 1680 Louis XIV's ubiquitous architect, Vauban, advised the king that the outer walls of the citadel were in such bad repair that they would have to be demolished and re-built under his jurisdiction. These are the walls we see today.

The heart of the old town is named after Sir Godefroy de Bouillon, leader of the First Crusade and a member of the House of Boulogne. Here is the imposing 18th-century Hotel de Ville. From the interior you can scale the 12th-century belfry, the oldest monument in Boulogne, for more stupendous views over port and surrounding countryside. Adjacent is the place de la République, with 19th-century neo-classical law courts. Napoleon and Charlemagne are the occupants of the two niches.

Dominating the Boulonnais countryside for miles around is the dome of the basilica, and from the countryside is the best way to see it. Close up it somehow seems diminished and less impressive. It was built between 1827 and 1866 on the site of a previous cathedral destroyed during the Revolution, but retains the original Romanesque crypt. The cathedral was named after an apparition of the virgin in the 7th century. Her wooden statue, crowned with gems, stands in the central chapel, except on the last Sunday in August, when a procession in mediaeval costume, perpetuating the centuries-old pilgrimage in her honour, still takes place in the town.

It seems to me that fresh air is being pumped into the old town; it used to be a somewhat gloomy, lonely place, neglected by all but the most assiduous history-connoisseurs. Now there are new and interesting boutiques and restaurants lining the main street, the rue de Lille, and the tourists are outnumbering the locals. Well, you can't have it both ways. If only there were a recommendable hotel up here in the tranquillity.

Just Outside

Boulogne was heavily involved in Napoleon's project of invading England. The port, bristling with ships, was bombarded several times by Nelson's fleet. The first Légion d'Honneur was awarded by Napoleon himself in 1804 at Terlincthun, just outside the town. A small pyramid marks the spot where the Emperor's throne stood.

3 km north, by the N.l., is the Colonne de la Grande Armée. Napoleon assembled 132,000 men and 2,000 ships, ready to launch his attack on England, and the marble column was intended to commemorate his achievement. When the invasion fizzled out in 1805, because Napoleon had to concentrate his Grande Armée against the Austrians, he understandably lost interest. The column was completed eventually by Louis-Philippe. 263 steps lead to a platform, 623 feet above sea level. Here is the view on which Napoleon must have planned to train his telescope - the white cliffs of you-know-where.

The entire coastline was heavily fortified with gunsites and forts; one of them is Heurt Fort, 3 km to the south-west of Boulogne on the small island facing the resort of Le Portel. Here there is a sandy beach dotted with rocks and bordered by a promenade; in summer there are several good fish restaurants, but it is all very dead out of season.

Boulogne's history of fortification, bombardment and destruction continued; in the First World War it was a front line British base with a heavy flow of maritime traffic and surrounded by military camps, hospitals and munitions dumps - an obvious target for the heavy bombardment that followed from the Germans only sixty miles away. In WW2 the Germans invaded the town on the 25th May 1940 and occupied it for four years. It was transformed into a veritable fortress and an important submarine base, and this time the bombardment - 487 times - came from the Allies, with many civilian casualties. Liberation came on the 19th September 1944 by the Canadian army.

Nausicaa
Bvd Ste Beuve (0)3.21.30.99.99. Open weekdays 10am - 6pm. Weekends 10am - 7pm. Cl. Jan 5th - Feb 13th. Admission: Adults 53f. Children 36f. Children under 3 go free.

Not an aquarium. A Centre National de la Mer, aiming to educate as well as amuse, this gleaming glass edifice on the front is a must for any visitor, of whatever age, to the town. Graphically aided by state-of-the-art techniques it tells the ecological story of the submarine world. Fishing, farming, pollution, conservation are all dealt with imaginatively and forcefully.

Younger customers will find plenty to amuse and question. Like how does it feel to be caught up in a net with a shoal of tuna? What happens if I stroke the fish? Why does the starfish curl up in the palm of my hand? They will relish having a good shudder at the gruesome conger eels and toothy shark, and will probably suffer less from *mal de mer* than their elders when they stand on the bridge of the trawler simulation and are battered by noise and spray in a howling audio-visual gale.

For a more soothing experience make for the Caribbean. No need to travel, no need to learn to scuba, here is the sunshine dazzle, the humidity, and nose-to-nose contact with fish as vivid and bizarre as any diver ever witnessed.

The Centre includes a well-stocked library, gift shop, cinema, bar and smart restaurant. If possible avoid school holidays, when there are queues and chaos.

HOTELS

The dearth of interesting hotels in Boulogne continues to amaze me. Here are the two best of a very dull bunch but personally I would forget staying here and head for either Hesdin-le-Abbé (p.121), or Wimereux (p.180).

Le Métropole (H)M

51 rue Thiers (0)3.21.31.54.30; fax (0)3.21.30.45.72 Cl. 20/12-4/1

Central, well-run by the pleasant Lejeune family, with agreeable breakfast room and a small garden. There is now parking for 12 cars at 40f per night. Bedrooms are small but reasonably well-equipped with mod cons and adequate bathrooms. 25 rooms 400-440f.

Le Faidherbe (H)M

12 rue Faidherbe (0)3.21.31.60.93; fax (0)3.21.87.01.14

A modern hotel near the port, recently re-decorated in pleasant pastel tones and generally smartened up.

35 rooms: 180-350f.

RESTAURANTS
••

The Boulogne restaurant scene is deteriorating somewhat. The town's only Michelin star lost, Fats Domino closed and the decamping of La Liègoise to Wimereux have not been good news. The choice is narrowed, but there are at least two stars, so all is not completely lost.

La Matelote (R)L

80 bvd Ste Beuve (0)3.21.30.17.97; fax (0)3.21.83.29.24 Cl. Sun. p.m. o.o.s.; 34/10-10/1

Sometimes losing a *macaron* can be a much-needed kick in the pants. Tony Lestienne's cooking had been lack-lustre even when FE12 was being written, but now perhaps with everything to gain it will once again become innovative and exciting.

His dining room overlooking Nausicaa is just as pretty, the service still attentive, the covers elegant as ever, and the fish just as prime. Prices are high though - the cheapest menu is 175f; I look forward to seeing some changes here.

➤ **Chez Jules** (R)M

Place Dalton (0)3.21.31.54.12; fax (0)3.21.33.85.47

Several changes here in my favourite restaurant, and all for the better. Whenever I am asked where to eat in Boulogne I unhesitatingly indicate Chez Jules. There are lots of restaurants, bars and cafés taking advantage of their central position around the Place Dalton, but only one Jules. It is now bigger (not always a good thing) and better (if that were possible) in that with the option of eating upstairs in the first-floor light and pretty dining room, there is more likely to be a free table downstairs, where all the action is. Here is the huge wood-fired oven, where they cook the best pizzas in town, and all the pzazz of a busy popular brasserie that could only be French.

But Jules is not just a pretty pizzeria. You can eat as well here at a more sophisticated level as anywhere else in town. The fish is irreproachable, whether you choose a simple bowl of *moules*, a selection of oysters, a *brochette* of seafood or a classic *sole meunière*. There are three menus from 90-150f; on the cheapest is a touch I particularly applaud - the bowls of *rillettes* or *terrine* are left on the table for you to help yourself.

Wherever you eat in Boulogne it is inevitable that you will share the restaurant with fellow-Brits. At Chez Jules the ratio of locals to tourists is testimony to the value on offer.

An arrow for honest value.

➤ La Coquillette (R)S
10 rue de l'Enseignement-Mutuel (0)3.21.46.03.47.27; fax (0)3.21.46.04.55.70

I asked for endorsement for an arrow for La Coquillette in FE12, and in came the confirmations that this was indeed a find. It's tucked away in a residential area, off the Place Navarin, a brown-shuttered, colourfully window-boxed old house, where the specialities are Italian-based. Fresh pasta, like *tagliatelles au pistou et lardons*, or a more sophisticated version with fresh salmon, are the dishes to go for, but the *gratins* are excellent too and for those with healthy appetites, the menu at 67f is a sell.

With a modestly-priced wine list and friendly service from the *patronne*, this is the place to head for on a budget outing, secure in the knowledge that quality and quantity have not been sacrificed to keep the bill down.

"The best place has to be La Coquillette, which we would never have found without your guide. A delightful little restaurant, with simple, impeccably served food - we loved the andouillettes - and a very pleasant welcome." Jennifer Storey.

Arrowed for good value and the best Italian cooking in the area.

L'Huitrière (R)M
11 pl. de Lorraine (0)3.21.31.35.27

Gault-Millau describes l'Huitrière as *un restaurant de poche* and pocket-sized certainly seems appropriate for this miniature fish restaurant tucked away in a corner of the Place Lorraine, away from the less discriminating tourist's eye. Evidence that the fish is good and the price right is that at lunchtime the six tables are always occupied by local *hommes d'affaires* getting down to the serious part of their day.

Appropriately marine is the colour scheme - navy blue and white - fresh and functional. With time to spare, order the *plâteau de fruits de mer* (160f) served on a hollowed cork platter, or for the less intrepid the *assiette* (90f). *Moules* come three ways - *à la crème, marinière* or, *provençale* at 40-46f. Me, I'm happy with just a dozen oysters (75f). The simple *menu du jour* costs 95f, or an infinitely preferable one (oysters, skate, cheese and dessert) will set you back a mere 130f.

Sucré Salé (R)S
13 rue Monsigny (0)3.21.33.81.82
Look in the pedestrianised precinct by the theatre to find this pretty little *salon de thé*. Readers have agreed that it's a pleasant haven to sip an elegant cuppa and enjoy French *pâtisserie* at its best, or a home-made ice cream. It's popular at lunchtime too, for light dishes, salads and savoury tarts.

La Cave du Fromager (R)S
23 and 30 rue de Lille (0)3.21.80.49.69 Cl. Tues.
Only someone as passionate about cheese as Marie-Renée Frémont could possibly conceive devising a double-spread menu in which every item featured that heavenly cholesterol-laden ingredient - cheese. Her restaurant, unique in the region, is on one side of the main street of the Vieille Ville and the shop where you can buy take-homes is opposite.

'Le Welsh', for some reason I have yet to fathom, is almost a Boulogne speciality, with every brasserie in town serving a version, but none so good as here - just the thing for a chilly day warm-up. Cheese *feuilletés, fondues, raclettes, gratins, quiches,* salads, all around 30-50f, or just... cheese, *tout simple*. Or not, as the case may be. Some of the dishes are not simple at all, like *mousseline de bisque de homard au Brillat Savarin* which comes with any *entrée* and a *dégustation* of as many cheeses as you can tackle for 125f (makes even me feel queasy), or *noix de St. Jacques au Roquefort* (56f).

Three course menus are a good-value 79.50f.

Even the desserts veer cheesewards. *Fromage frais* with a blackcurrant syrup or tarts filled with fruit on a *mousse de fromage,* or even prunes stuffed with *Roquefort*. Hope the Channel's not too choppy on the way home.

NEW Estaminet du Château (R)S
2 rue du Château (0)3.21.49.66; fax (0)3.21.31.92.96 Cl. Wed. p.m. and Thurs.
I used to rack my brains to conjure up any eating suggestion, however doubtful, in the Haute Ville, but there are signs that restaurateurs are realising the potential up there, away from traffic fumes, where tables can be set with safety on the pavement and there is even room for a garden or two.

The **Estaminet** is the name that regularly crops up as the best of the bunch. Because it's prices are so reasonable - 65f for a good menu - and because there are still not many competitors, you will find the clientele is mostly Brits, but give it a try - the owners, M. and Mme Davenet, are trying hard.

NEW Brasserie Le Châtillon (R)S
6 rue Charles Tellier (0)3.21.31.43.95 Lunchtime only Cl. Sat. and Sun.

The opening times say it all - this is a restaurant for the workers. The workers in this case being the fishermen and those engaged in the fish canning business in the port. Perversely I am always more excited about finding a restaurant hidden in an unlikely setting, especially if it's away from the tourist track, than one obvious to all. When the Grape Shop personnel told me that the best place to eat fish in Boulogne was, surprise surprise, in the port, I couldn't rest until I had tracked down Le Châtillon.

I found it near the Bassin Napoleon. (Drive into the port and ask, or do as I did and buy wine first and profit by instructions in English). It is a large, totally unfussy brasserie, a bit smoky and still full of customers at 3 p.m. You eat fish and nothing but the fish, fried, baked, poached, or raw, and it couldn't be fresher. Prices vary according to the catch of the day, chalked up on the blackboard.

An experience. I look forward to the reports on this one.

Incidentally, the owner of Le Châtillon also runs a good fish shop, l'Ecailler in the rue de la Lampe.

Otherwise:

Recommended but not yet sampled by me: Gourmandière, 6 rue des Religieuses (off the rue Faidherbe). For interesting salads, quiches, omelettes, Philippe Olivier's cheeses and traditional dishes like *boeuf Bourguignon*.

And from a trusty local correspondent: "*The Cyrano almost opposite the France Telecom office at the end of the rue Victor Hugo (9 rue Cooquelin) is where my French chums eat when they're in town, with old fashioned chef and equally rotund wife.*

Across the river is La Braserade (Chez Bruno, 9, rue Alma). Managers from the fishing port eat here each lunchtime, enjoying the smart surroundings and a copious menu at 85f which includes the largest hors d'oeuvre board imaginable. It's difficult to find, being reached through an archway under the modern block of flats facing the Ibis on the far bank. Cl. Sun. Mon. p.m." Bob Smyth

---

BOURNONVILLE 62240 Pas-de-Calais.

6 km N of Dèsvres, 19 km E of Boulogne

Lovely countryside around here, due east of Boulogne, in the forests of Boulogne and Dèsvres, along the river Liane, past sleepy undiscovered villages. Bournonville is the hub of five mini-roads, so check the map carefully unless you want to get lost, which is a most agreeable prospect in these parts. Whatever you do make sure you work up an appetite for:

➤ **Auberge du Moulin** (R)S
(0)3.21.83.87.81

I have to admire the stamina of FE faithfuls. When I rashly offered many years ago to pay the bill if anyone could produce proof that they had waded through the full menu here, I never expected to be still receiving applications all these years later! Nothing much has changed in this unpretentious café/restaurant/bar, least of all the menu, which costs 85f. In these days of weight/cholesterol/calories consciousness it does you good just to read it:

1. Cream soup - tureen left on table for seconds and thirds (strictly inadvisable).
2. Smoked salmon - steaks of it. Or trout *meunière,* or fresh salmon or *terrine* of chicken.
3. Braised ham or tongue, with carrots and lots of gravy.
4. *Gigôt* of lamb - three steaks this time, with enough haricot beans and potato to feed a family for a week. Or guinea fowl, or quail.
5. Salad
6. Cheese
7. Apple tart, with cream naturally.

Arrowed for sheer political incorrectness and the amount of pleasure it has given happy guzzlers.

N.B. Don't think of going on a Sunday without a reservation.

"We spent three hours there, having struggled our way through their now famous six course lunch, aperitif, coffee and wine, for 110f. The place was teeming, both dining rooms in use, with a huge log fire in ours. We kept walking outside to cool off. I am attaching a couple of menus, signed on behalf of two of the couples who managed to finish every course, though we did leave some of the wine." Ian Skelton.

P.S. I now disclaim all responsibility.

```
┌─────────────────────────────────────────────────┐
│               BRAY DUNES Nord.                    │
│             11 km N of Dunkerque                  │
└─────────────────────────────────────────────────┘
```

Otherwise:
It's a strange coast road to Bray, the northernmost limit to this book, through housing estates where the omnipresent sand dunes make fine playgrounds for local kids, skirting hamlets with unpronounceable Flemish names, and past factory blocks and secretive high concrete walls. The railway line is one side and the autoroute on the other, but here in between is a kind of no-man's land. Access to the beach, which is the real *raison d'être* for development here in the first place, is amazingly difficult. When you do find a turning to the left in Bray it leads down to a windswept promenade and mile upon mile of beach up to and beyond the Belgian border. It's good for a breath of the briny, but not recommendable for much else. The restaurants and cafés are strictly for the tourists and snap shut out of season. I don't think many of those tourists can be Brits. Sheltering from the gale, we asked for tea in a café and were told they didn't have any. *"Les Anglais!"* they said with a despising gallic shrug.

```
┌─────────────────────────────────────────────────┐
│             BROUCKERQUE 59630 Nord.               │
│    4 km E of Bourbourg on the D2, 35 km E of Calais,│
│             with easy autoroute access            │
└─────────────────────────────────────────────────┘
```

A nothing-special village, mostly modern, set in the flat Flemish countryside.

Middle Houck (HR)S-M
pl. du Village (0)3.28.27. 13.46; fax (0)3.28.27.15.10 R Cl. Sun. p.m.; H and R cl. 24/12-31/12
This spic-and-span brick restaurant in the village centre, heavily be-geraniummed, has been thoroughly approved of by numerous readers. I say 'restaurant' rather than 'hotel' because it is in the dining room that its priorities lie. The four bedrooms are clean and adequate but no more (215f); nevertheless I am sure they are a very welcome retreat after a substantial dinner here, with absolutely no driving.
The mid-week menu is 90f, and this is the one that most of the businessmen, from Dunkerque I surmised, were tucking into when I re-visited. Lots of hearty Flemish dishes but salads too. Nice Madame Morez told me that at weekends the atmosphere is more *familiale* and the menu

price then is 188f. Recognised as being the best cooking for a long way around, so you should book.

"We had two pleasantly furnished and very comfortable neighbouring rooms. There was plenty of choice on the 90f menu. Two of us started with a kind of Welsh rarebit on salad and the other had chicken liver salad. We all chose tender pork medallions surrounded with nouvelle cuisine-fashion new potatoes, leeks and cauliflower. Sweets were a large plate of profiteroles for one, cherries and chocolate for no 2 and I chose a tarte aux pommes, beautifully flambéed at the table.

The village was just the right size for a short walk to the charcuterie where we shopped for our return journey and the boulangerie where sweets to take home were gift-wrapped by Madame while the locals waited for their bread quite cheerfully."

CALAIS 62100 Pas-de-Calais. 37 km N of Boulogne
M Sat., Wed.: Place d'Armes; Sat., Thurs., Sun.: Z.U.P. du Beau Marais

---

No wonder that English visitors feel at home in Calais. For more than two centuries, from 1347 to 1558, it was indeed an English town. After his victory at Crécy in 1346 King Edward III laid a vicious and determined siege to Calais, which its courageous citizens resisted for almost a year before, starving, they capitulated. In retaliation for their unwillingness to co-operate earlier, the king proposed to exact revenge on its burghers. The famous group depicted so vividly by Rodin volunteered their lives in exchange for a promise that the rest of the town should be spared. It took the compassionate pleading of his wife, Queen Phillippa, to persuade the king to pardon the brave hostages.

Rodin's statue, simple and dignified, stands outside the bizarre Town Hall, grey, sombre, and intensely moving amongst the strident begonias. Walk round the group and see that each man is a masterpiece of character-drawing, from the patriarchal St. Eustache to the agonised youthful Pierre de Wissant. Maquettes and studies for this masterpiece are in the Musée de Calais, well worth a visit. Don't miss the watercolours of the English artist Bonington, and look at the views of early Calais, like the 19th-century William Callows of the Place d'Armes, to realise the extent of our loss.

In the museum too are more examples of English influences - the lace for which Calais is famous, once an important industry, for which the machinery, designs and artists were brought over from Nottingham in the 19th century.

Under English rule, protected by great walls and moats, garrisoned by a force of 2,000, Calais flourished for two centuries under the royal flags of Plantagent, Lancaster, York and Tudor until it fell to the Duc de Guise in 1558. When the town was signed away to the French forever in the 1564 Treaty of Troyes, the English queen, Mary Tudor, was so shocked at its loss that she declared that on her heart after death would for ever be engraved the word Calais.

Yet the links continued. After Napoleon's defeat British entrepreneurs flocked into Calais eager for new commercial pickings, and when Dunkirk was being evacuated in 1940 it was the troops in Calais who stood firm to the bitter end. Churchill recognised their bravery by calling the town the little bit of grit that saved us.

The English invasion of Calais still happens every day when thousands of shoppers pour off the ferries - more passengers than in any other port in the world. A peaceful, mutually beneficial invasion nowadays. We get the cheap booze and a (diluted) taste of le Continent, and the shopkeepers get busy tills. Equally profitable has been the intrusion of British supermarkets, irritated at the profits drifting towards the wine trade in France and staking their claim to a share of this highly lucrative market while the duty-free going is good.

Calais

Booze-buying

No-one knows for sure how much longer before this wine bubble is burst, but pro tem it would be foolish not to take advantage of the savings to be made and Calais is well-equipped to help you do so. Here are some suggestions:

Calais Wine and Beer, rue de Judée, Zone d'Activités Marcel-Doret. Near exit 3 off the A26. Open daily from 6 a.m. to midnight. Wide range of international wines in cheaper bracket. British staffed.

Pérardel Wine Market, 365 ave. Antoine-de-St. Exupéry. Just beyond above. Turn left at bottom of rue de Judée. Open daily 9.30 a.m. - 7 p.m. 500 varieties, from plonk to exclusive vintages.

Champagne Charlies, 14 rue de Cronstadt (off rue de Moscou). Foot passengers should follow signs to Centre Ville. Wide selection of wines and beers.

Beer Lovers, ave. de Verdun. Take exit 14 before Chunnel on the road to Calais beach. Open daily. Wide range of wines and beers. Tastings.

Just outside Calais, at the entrance to the tunnel, is the **Cité Europe**. This is where most Brit booze-fanciers with cars will head for, playing safe with familiar names like Sainsbury and Tesco. Like it says, it's a cité. Vast. So allow plenty of time to find it (appallingly badly signed, and all in French) and navigate within it. You either love huge shopping centres or you hate em; I belong to the latter camp, but can just see how, if it's wet outside and you have hours to kill, this might be the answer. I wish it had the cheerful atmosphere of American malls, rather than that generated by cross, tired, bored customers. In true investigative spirit, I tackled the mammoth, in order to be able to report first-hand:

No signs to guide me to my target, Tescos. Which car park to head for? Toss a coin. Parking outside the sign which read Tescos seemed a good idea, but no. I had to walk the full length of the parade back to the main door. No sign of Tescos inside. Subsequently found it one floor down. Dying for a loo. Back to starting point. Four loos for how many cross-legged ladies? Headed purposefully to *dégustation* station. What you want? asked bored fat Frenchman. I didn't *know* what I wanted and had hoped he would tell me. Loaded two trolleys with cases of un-sampled wine at severe risk to back. Lad at check-out said would I take em all out again. I pointed at sign saying 'We are here to help you' and said, *"You* take 'em out." Apparently his brief to help didn't extend this far, so made nasty scene pretending not to speak French, exasperating queue behind me and eventually getting results. Not a load of fun.

I had got it all wrong. Some of the wine was good and some was terrible. So I shall have to buy the successes at my local Tesco (since I never intend to tackle la Cité again). It should have been the other way round - sample before you leave and arrive equipped with a list of goodies. It will be with great relief that I return to beloved Grapevine at Boulogne.

Other Shopping
The main shopping streets are: the rue Royale, best for chocolates, *pâtisserie, charcuterie,* fashions and presents; then past the Tourist Office, where it all gets a bit seedy around the railway station and becomes the bvd Jacquard. Here is the French Woolies - Monoprix - and the slightly more upmarket Le Printemps. At the busy Place Albert 1er (with its opulent baroque theatre, and a statue of Joseph-Marie Jacquard, who invented the loom for unskilled workers to produce lace) turn left into the bvd Lafayette. There's a much more gallic atmosphere than the streets nearer the port. This is where the Calaisiens do their daily shopping and the market is in one of the side streets in the pl. Crêvecoeur.

Natural Assets
If all this shopping has included picnic ingredients, where to consume them? There are two park possibilities: one is by the rue Richelieu, off the rue Royale, and the other, the parc St. Pierre, with plenty of shade and benches, is opposite the town hall. Here is the *Musée de la Guerre*, the war museum, housed in an old German bunker, used for telephone communications during WW2. Posters, tracts, memorabilia and letters are a poignant reminder of the Resistance, the occupation and the bombing. Open 20/2-20/12, daily from 10 a.m. to 5 p.m.

Calais has another asset that, surprisingly, is rarely mentioned - a magnificent beach. Infinitely superior to any across the water, with literally miles of fine sand when the tide is out. With time to spare before the ferry or on a day trip with the kids, head in this direction. If you are not picnic-equipped there are plenty of cafés that will fill the gap.

HOTELS
The hotel scene is not bright. The old Meurice used to have a certain faded grandeur, but nowadays there is more fade than grand and nowhere else that offers anything more enticing than a modicum of comfort and a useful first or last night bed. The Bellevue in the Place d'Armes was being torn apart last time I visited, so perhaps there might one day be good news here. At least I can suggest three options that won't break the bank and are good representatives of the two-star bracket:

NEW OWNERS Windsor (H)S
2 rue du Commandant Bonningues (0)3.21.34.59.40; fax (0)3.21.97.68.59
Patronne Madame Houston is French, married to an Englishman, so there will be no language problems. They took over a year ago and have made few changes. The 15 rooms are clean, cheerful and well equipped - 285f double

with bath, 265f with shower, 175f and 160f with neither.

Good value, and three minutes from the ferry or town centre, with pleasant owners, and the bonus of a lock-up garage.

Richelieu (H)S

17 rue Richelieu (0)3.21.34.61.60; fax (0)3.21.85.89.28 Cl. Christmas and New Year

In a quiet side street, overlooking the park, run by the same management for many years. All 15 rooms, whether with bath or shower, are 284f; they're all differently furnished, some with tiny balconies looking out onto greenery, so it's worth asking to see more than one if possible.

NEW OWNERS Pacific (H)S

40 rue du Duc-de-Guise (0)3.21.34.50.24; fax (0)3.21.97.58.02 Cl. Christmas and New Year

Madame Duhamel has taken over here and is re-decorating the 19 rooms one by one. They cost 250f with bath, 240f with shower and loo, or 185f just with shower. The garage is an extra 20f. There's a particularly spacious lounge and p.d. room, which used once to be the restaurant. Madame Duhamel is happy to offer special prices out of season, so try negotiating.

Otherwise:

For those who are happier with three-star accommodation (though in this case I think the more modest hotels offer better value), there is the **Metropol**, which looks more interesting, situated on the quayside, than proves to be the case. 40 rooms 250-400f. 43 quay du Rhin (0)3.21.97.54.00; fax (0)3.21.96.69.00. Or the **George V**, 36 rue Royale (0)3.21.97.68.00 fax (0)3.21.97.34.73. The 39 rooms are often engulfed by groups or seminars. 310-380f. The only option if you insist on dining in your hotel. See under Restaurants.

RESTAURANTS
....

➤ Le Channel (R)M

3 bvd de la Résistance (0)3.21.34.42.30; fax (0)3.21.97.42.43 Cl. Sun. p.m. and Tues. (except fêtes) 23/7-6/8

If I say there is nothing new to write about Le Channel, that is high praise indeed. As long as there have been French Entrées, and a good time before that, Le Channel has been no. 1 restaurant in Calais, and never once let that go to its head. It may be old hat to recommend a restaurant that everyone knows and is in every guidebook, but that is exactly what I do when asked

Where shall we eat in Calais? Playing safe was never my style, but here it would be folly not to do so. Reliability is Le Channel's middle name.

From time to time the decor changes - currently raspberry velvet high backed chairs, matching carpet, oil paintings on panelled walls - and a few new dishes join the menu. Perhaps we can expect more experiments now that the two Crespo sons have joined forces, one as *sommelier,* one after a *stage* at *Robuchon,* but I don't think that the *hommes d'affaires* that are the mainstay of the clientele (always a good sign) would like to see their favourite menus messed about too much.

Madame Crespo's welcome has not wavered. However busy the service, she miraculously contrives to be near the door when new customers arrive, to show them to their table and make them feel at ease. Likewise Joseph Crespo, installed behind the glass of the open plan kitchen, supervising his team of chefs and *commis,* manipulating his pans, still finds time to lean over the counter to shake hands with old friends. I stood there for a while, watching the dexterity and speed, and every single dish that emerged looked totally admirable.

The staff, in their formal black and white, seem to have assimilated their bosses' spirit - they know that the right orders have to appear on the right tables in double-quick time if the recipients are to catch their ferry (and in order to re-use the table) and manage to combine efficient briskness with a smile.

The 98f weekday menu is a snip - well worth crossing from one Channel to another expressly - and never skimps with expensive choices like Dover sole or *langoustines.* Fish is always good but so are the *terrines* and local dishes like *coq à la bière.* Tarts are home-made of course and so are the ice creams. You really can't go wrong.

The arrow is for consistently high standards, excellent ingredients, well-cooked, and delightful owners.

Le George V (R)M
36 rue Royale (0)3.21.97.68.00; fax (0)3.21.97.34.73 Cl. Sun. p.m.; 23/12-4/1

Long-established Calais restaurateur Bernard Beauvalot successfully combines two restaurants under the same roof: 'Le George' is the gastronomic leg and 'Le Petit George' the bistro. The former is surprisingly elegant, with a welcoming fire for inclement weather, and serves hefty portions of traditional food. Fish and pastry are its declared specialities, but I think of it more in terms of *choucroute* and casseroles.

The livelier bistro 'accepte les jeans' and feeds their owners on menus from 98f. *À la carte* too for express meals for those with a ferry to catch. In both establishments the standards are high.

NEW ➤ **Aquar Aile (R)M**
Plage de Calais. 255 rue Jean-Moulin (0)3.21.34.00.00; fax (0)3.21.34.15.00 Cl. Sun. p.m.

I had been put off by the situation - outside the town heading west, and the building, an ugly modern block of flats - but I'd been missing a treat. Take the lift up to the first floor for a view that merits the word fabulous. The décor is the sea. Vast curving windows enclose the prospect of waves, yachts, ferries, beach huts, sand, giving a whole new meaning to panoramic. Do not fail to book a window table to get your money's worth.

The marine theme continues with a blue/green/grey colour-scheme, glossy ceiling painted to match. For those who missed out on the view, the other seating is still pretty good news - comfortable tapestry banquettes, ideal for intimate dining. The tone is decidedly upmarket, with pristine starched napkins, expensive china and smooth service from professional black-and-white-garbed staff.

Smooth service does not always come with smiles; at Aquar Aile the waiters have forgotten they're French and actually seem to be pleased to see you, even when, as I did, you order just nine oysters and a glass of Muscadet for lunch. Husband redressed the balance somewhat by choosing his favourite turbot and it came cooked to perfection - still pearly, 90f worth of irreproachable freshness. For one franc less we could have spent the afternoon tackling a *palette de pecheur*, a generous assortment of fish, wet and shell. Complimentary appetisers of a fishy persuasion and *petits fours* even if you don't order coffee. It's all excellent value for the quality on offer.

Menus from 80f, including wine during weekdays, or 100f with wine;135 or 250f for the serious lobster-fanciers.

An arrow for Calais No.1 fish restaurant, with good value and pleasant service thrown in.

➤ **L'Histoire Ancienne (R)M**
20 rue Royale (0)3.21.34.11.20; fax (0)3.21.96.19.58 Cl. Sun., Mon. p.m.

Décor 1930ish, with art déco lamps, leather banquettes and Toulouse-Lautrec approximates decorating the bar walls; bistro-style, but with cooking that combines bistro simplicity with a touch of sophistication. The Comtes, Patrick, and Claire, used to run La Diligence, next door to the Meurice, which had less of the bistro, more of the plush about it. I like this version far better.

The bistro bit that pleases me is that there were no tut-tuts when I ordered only a starter at lunchtime and husband fancied just a good steak. The sophisticated part came with the quality and the presentation. My stuffed mushrooms came beautifully arranged on a classy black plate, sprinkled with chopped chives and scattered with designer leaves. The dressing was spot on, the stuffing generous with the garlic, the herbs and whatever the delicious toothsome filling was. An excellent 35f worth, especially as there was no quibbling about entitlement to their special offer - a takeaway bottle of wine for every table on production of a ferry or tunnel ticket - "We like our English friends." (Just as well, because there's a lot of 'em about.)

Husband's *entrecôte* proved large and juicy with lavish garnish of *chanterelles* and melting baked potatoes (not many French know about them) 65f. Next door ordered the 98f menu and oohed and ahed over the *soupe de poisson*, again presented with style and an array of white side dishes for the *rouille, croutons* and cheese. Their children ate well for 45f - egg mayo, escalope of chicken and ice cream, but you have to be under 12 to qualify. There is another excellent menu at 158f.

It is not difficult to guess that Patrick sometimes likes to cook special dishes, a touch more interesting than the menu basics - *Les Petits Plats de Patrick*. These involve some of his favourite sauces, like saffron cream sauce and a deep dark mushroom version. Fish is another speciality and, as it says on his brochure, "Good tasty roasts at a price you can afford."

Only one black mark to spoil this panegyric - in this country of rude waiters, ours was the rudest. If Claire hadn't taken over some of the serving I am afraid we should have left without ever discovering *l'Histoire Ancienne* delights. I'm very glad we stayed, and the arrow is totally justified (but don't stand any nonsense from the *personnel*).

NEW ➤ La Pléiade (R)M
32 rue Jean Quehen (0)3.21.34.03.70 Cl. Sat. lunch, Mon.

In one of the turnings west of the rue Royale at the sea end, a pleasant little restaurant, green façade, nondescript décor, paintings of boats indicating a fishy emphasis. Daily specialities written on the blackboard are always a good sign. In this case they include dishes like *'l'épaule d'agneau, confits de rognons, timbale de poissons à l'aneth, filet de cabillaud à geniève* - all interesting stuff. The 85f menu offered plenty of choice (other more sophisticated versions with an extra course at 125f and 165f).

My choice was a light flaky *feuillété de moules*, with flavoursome sauce featuring plenty of garlic, and mussels cooked *à point*, then crispy halibut filled with mustard seeds and white wine sauce, roast local cheeses and local ice cream. All excellent value, even if you can only manage half a dozen oysters at 48f.

Arrowed as the most promising newcomer to the Calais restaurant scene.

> **Grand Bleu** (R)M-S
5 rue J-P Avron (0)3.21.97.97.98 Cl. Sat. lunch; Sun.

A little nautically-themed restaurant just where it ought to be - on the quay. It's good to have a fishy meal where freshness of the produce takes precedence over flashy presentation and expensive décor, and the cost is kept proportionately low. That said, fresh fish nowadays costs plenty, wherever you buy or eat it, and if it doesn't it probably doesn't answer the job description.

Here the dining room is modern and unfussy, with navy blue cloths and napkins and grey chairs. M. Olivier's cooking can be unfussy too - nothing beats a perfect *sole meunière*, which here costs 85f - but he can knock you up a professional version of *aumonière aux deux saumons* or le *saint-pierre à la fleur de thym* if that is your wish.

Menus start at 98f weekday, 155f otherwise, but as in most fish restaurants, my view is that it is preferable to eat *à la carte*, from a bowl of mussels to a lobster, according to appetite and budget.

Arrowed for excellent fishy value.

Côte d'Argent (R)M
1 Digue Gaston-Berthe (0)3.21.96.42.10 Cl. Sun. p.m., Mon.

The third of the recommended fishy restaurants, and the longest established, here overlooking the beach. The owners have changed not so long ago, and the youthful Lefèvbres, Roland cooking, Sophie welcoming, have added considerably to its appeal. The décor has been spiced up, albeit in a predictably marine style, and the service and table settings are suave.

The 98f cheapest menu is simple but good - mussels in white wine, poached skate, cheeses and patisserie. If you invest 160f you get to sample *langoustines*, sole, cheeses from Wierre Effroy and dessert. You have to eat *à la carte* to savour Roland's declared specialities - a *fricassée* of lobster or *goujonettes* of sole - but personally I prefer my lobster unfricasséed and my sole looking much as it did when it came out of the sea, give or take a golden tint, some butter, a squeeze of lemon and a sprinkling of herbs.

Otherwise:
NEW Le St. Charles (R)S
47 Place d'Armes (0)3.21.96.02.96 Cl. Sun. p.m., Tues.

I disregarded the St. Charles because it was so obvious, here in the middle of the Place d'Armes, that I suspected it would be just a tourist easy option, cashing in on its convenience. Not a bit of it; there are actually French people eating here, and that's saying something in Calais. In fact it's very

French in ambience, small and cosy, lace-curtained, with plump waiters whose English is decidedly pidgin.

Menus suit all purses, from 59-185f, with some promising fish specialities. An example of the 75f menu would be *soupe de poisson* (with all the trimmings), wing of skate with raspberry butter, and home-made ice cream. More reports please to elevate this welcome newcomer into the main category.

CAMIERS 62176 Pas-de-Calais.
19 km S of Boulogne, 10 km N of Le Touquet
M Mon.

The sand dunes and pines around here remind me of the Mediterranean, but the windswept appearance of the Plage St. Gabriel gives the game away.

Turn off the main road just opposite the sign to the *plage* to find the by-passed village of Camiers.

Les Cèdres (HR)S
(0)3.21.84.94.54; fax (0)3.21.09.23.29 R cl. Sun. p.m. o.o.s.

Drive round the back of this seemingly typical French bourgeois villa to find the new guest wing built around a courtyard. There are 29 simple rooms at 160-315f, which I call good value in this popular holiday area, and so near Le Touquet. It would certainly make a good family base, with the sands so near. You can be assured of a peaceful night's sleep, away from the main road, and there is safe parking.

Menus from 80f-199f, of which I know nothing because no-one has passed on any experiences.

CAP BLANC NEZ 62179 Escalles.
10 km SW of Calais

This is the part of the Côte d'Opale that irrefutably confounds those still labouring under the misapprehension that the North of France is (a) flat and (b) dull. The coast road leaves behind the sand dunes and weekend chalets after Sangatte and sweeps up and up to reveal a stunning panorama of rolling farmland to the left and white cliffs dipping into the sea to the right. Do not fail to turn off at the sign to Cap Blanc Nez, park the car by the memorial to the WW1 victims and walk to the cliff edge to enjoy the spectacular view. Better still carry on walking down the well-maintained cliff path to Escalles, far below. This is just part of the network of cliff walks, all taking advantage of the truly glorious countryside around here.

NEW Le Thome de Gamond (R)M
Mont d'Hubert (0)3.21.82.32.03; fax (0)3.21.82.32.61 Open every lunchtime
On the opposite side of the road, signed to the *musée transmanche,* is an example of what the French do so well - a restaurant that takes advantage of an unusually attractive feature (in this case the view) and does not take advantage of the built-in custom.

The Frechou family have designed their sizeable modern restaurant to make the most of the view over the Boulonnais countryside, with huge windows to take in the panorama. Fresh from the ferry on a Sunday afternoon, we found the place still full of happy eaters demolishing *plâteaux de fruits de mer* (135f). There is a two-course menu at 76f for the fainthearted, and my yardstick for prices - *moules* and sole - cost 35f and 90f respectively.

CAP GRIS NEZ 62179 Pas-de-Calais.
30 km N of Boulogne, 32 km S of Calais

Not the best beach along this privileged stretch, but then the standards are high - there's sand enough to satisfy most. To the cross-channel swimmers it must look like heaven. Just across the water are those cliffs, and yes they are very white.

Les Mauves (HR)M-S
(0)3.21.32.96.06 Cl. 15/11-1/4

Can't understand why I get so little feedback to this pleasant old-fashioned hotel, quietly situated at the approach to the Cap, 500 metres from the sea. It has a peaceful flowery garden ideal for relaxing after a long day, a nice rustic dining room, with carved chairs, polished floor, copper whatnots, and there is that rare amenity for little French hotels - a bar in which guests can mingle when it's too cold to sit in the garden. Pristine bedrooms have all mod cons and *patronne* Madame Cugny is friendly and helpful. Perhaps it's a touch expensive? But then the season is so short.

Menus from 120f, 16 rooms 380-460f, breakfast 42f.

Otherwise:

There's the famous (the modest claim is 'renowned as far as Brussels, London and even beyond') La Sirene, perched on the cliff edge, with unbeatable views through its panoramic windows. Madame Bouloy continues to dispense her seafood specialities, with lobster from her *vivier* a speciality. Menus from 120f (0)3.21.32.95.97 lunch and Sat. dinner only from Sept. to Easter. Cl. Sun. p.m. and Mon. o.o.s.

CASSEL 59670 Nord.
50 km SE of Calais, 32 km NE of St. Omer

High on the list of must-sees in the whole region, Cassel is unique. The approach, slowed down because of the cobbles, past prosperous villas, through avenues of chestnut trees bent in combat with the habitual wind, gives little hint of what to expect until you drive through the 17C porte de Bergues, which makes a fine proscenium arch for centre stage - the Grand'Place. The scene is more stage setting than reality, with the huge Place - one of the largest in Flanders and steeply sloping - surrounded by aristocratic buildings. There are coats of arms of noble families over doorways that lead into secluded courtyards and weathered rooftops that might have existed since mediaeval times. Might have, but probably didn't, thanks to the fire that roared through the town in 1940, destroying everything in its course.

The slopes of Mont Cassel, 176m high, have been fortified since time immemorial - understandably so since they are the highest for many a league. Normans, Flemish, French, Spanish and English all fought here; Romans camped here and engineered seven roads from the town towards the coast or to connect with their other strongholds.

Marechal Foch, Commander-in-Chief of the Armies of the North, made this his headquarters and spent "the most distressing hours of his life" here, between 23rd October 1914 and 21st June 1915. With the English General Rumer, he directed the Battle of Flanders from the town. His statue is still in command, high above the town in the Place du Château (no château now) by the old windmill (or copy of the 16th original that was burnt down in 1911). From here, abetted by a *table d'orientation,* you can see five kingdoms, they say - those of France, Belgium, Holland, England, and heaven. So pick a clear day.

It is a town that inspires stories and legends. It was the local giants, Reuze Papa and Reuze Maman (still paraded through northern towns on feastdays) who dropped the huge mound of earth on which it stands.

There is a peaceful 'English garden' up here, with shady benches and walks marked out through the trees. Those disinclined to climb can drive all the way up and stop for refreshment at an establishment as unusual as Cassel itself:

NEW ➤ Estaminet T'Kasteel Hof

8 rue St. Nicolas (0)3.28.40.59.29 Cl. Tues., Wed. p.m. and Thurs. o.o.s. and Mon. throughout the year

Clinging to the side of the very steep hill, with fabulous views from its terraces, this little wooden restaurant has bags of character, totally uncontrived. The ground floor looks like a shop - perhaps it was once - with the counter still in position and an eclectic assortment of objects hanging from the ceiling, on mantelpiece, floor, niches, every available surface. Baskets are suspended from on high, with a rocking horse, a collection of hats, enamel pans, flat-irons, enamel jugs, dried flowers and hops. An antique stove takes care of the heating; floor is bare wood, tables ditto, chairs wicker. Upstairs is more of the same, with an amazing panorama from the veranda. Must be lovely in summer.

The flavour of the month is determinedly Flemish. No wine, because it does not come from this region. But beer... the menu lists pages of varieties, *blanches, blondes, ambres, brunes* and *fruitées.* You can even buy it by the kilo (30f). There are bottles of home-made fruit juice made from local produce - the friendly barman (owner?) encouraged me to taste. I sampled rhubarb, strawberry, blackcurrant, apple, raspberry and several more. All very fruity. With the addition of local gin, a range of tempting cocktails is on offer. I liked the sound of *'Gen'pom'* - gin with apple - and *'Cherche Mourette'* gin and blackcurrant.

Food follows suit: all farm produce is used to conjure up the *carbonades, flamiches* and of course the ubiquitous *Potje vleish.* You don't have to order a heavy main course though - there are *pâtés, saucissons* and *rillettes. Crêpes* and sweet tarts take care of the desserts. I had to try *paaptart* which I had not come across before - brown sugar and raisins. There are sorbets too, flavoured with *chicorée, bière,* and *genièvre.* Definitely different.

To the right of the entrance there is a little shop, selling some of the chef's produce, along with a great variety of beers. You could at least buy a postcard of the extraordinary décor.

Do go - great fun. Arrowed for delightful eccentricity.

Back in the town all round the square are eating/drinking possibilities cafés, restaurants, pizzerias, *crêperies* and a *cave à bieres.* Remember these are for the tourists and don't expect too much.

Otherwise:
La Taverne Flamande (R)M
34 Grand'Place (0)3.28.42.42.59 Cl. Tues. p.m. and Wed.

Every Flemish *place* has to have its Taverne Flamande and this is Cassel's. It's quite smart inside, with astonishing views of the Flanders plain far below from the *terrasse panoramique* at the rear.

Authentic Flanders cooking appears on the 98f *menu flamand.* This is the chance to try *waterzoi de volaille à la gantoise* - chicken in a kind of béchamel sauce - and *tarte flamande aux pommes et à la cassonade* - apple and blackcurrant tart - or even *crêpes flambées au Houlle* - pancakes doused with gin. Other menus at 89f and 138f.

Readers have approved, so don't let my impression, which was coloured by indifferent reception, put you off. The rival Hotel Foch across the square was even cooler, so perhaps they don't need to try too hard.

The course and its valley

Heading south from the ports you have several route choices. Stick to the *nationales* or the *autoroute* if you are in a hurry, consider the yellow and white roads on the Michelin map if leisurely delight is more important than speed. The D127, which follows the valley of the Course, is the pick of the bunch. Follow it from Dèsvres to Montreuil and any preconception that the Pas-de-Calais is all built up/boring/flat/same-as-home will vanish. Drive through the flowery unspoilt villages like Courset, Parenty, Recques, Beussent, Inxent, lining the rushing, sparkling little river that plays hide and seek, vanishing on one side to re-appear on the other; sometimes, as at Doudeauville, it disappears altogether, only to spout anew in the next village. Extend exploration to the lanes and valleys on either side of the river to find a succession of time-warped sleepy crossroads, cottage gardens, churches, ponds, bars, fruity-smelling farms and streams that run into the Course, with names more imposing than the reality - the Baillonne, the Bésinghem, the Brimoise are little more than trickles - but very attractive picnic-worthy trickles.

I cannot claim that the Course is a secret any more - there is even the *Circuit Boulonnais* marked out along it for first-time tourists to follow - and every time I drive down it I find more modern bungalows to regret, but the picturesque crumbling whitewashed barns still predominate and the way of life of the farming residents remains much as it has been for generations.

Accommodation and eating options are limited. The **Auberge d'Inxent** (page 127) is one possibility and there is now an excellent upmarket B&B at **Beussent** (page 73) as well as the long-established **Le Relais Equestre** at **Inxent** (buy the Chambres d'Hôtes book!). The **Restaurant Lignier** at **Beussent** has a loyal following (page 72) and for those who are looking for something definitely basic - perhaps an omelette or grilled chicken - there is **Grémont-Cocatrix** down by the trout farms in **Zérables** and the **Bon Accueil** at **Engoudsent**.

CRÉCY-EN-PONTHIEU 80150 Somme.
19 km N of Abbeville, 17 km E of Rue by D938

The scenery changes abruptly as you approach Crécy, from green valleys and hills to open plain. Good battle country.

At first glance there is nothing to distinguish this little town, wide market street, a timbered house or two, from any other. But stop the car and look at that war memorial. As in many another mourning Picard town, it takes pride of place in the centre of town. What is unique about this one is the date of the inscription: "*à la memoire des français morts en defendant leur patrie, 26 Aout, 1346*". The other side of the cross commemorates the bravery of Jean of Luxembourg, the blind King of Bohemia, brother of King Philippe, who opposed Edward III. Determined to 'strike a blow for France', he ordered his men to tie him to his horse during the battle, where he was slain along with 1,300 French knights, the cream of the French nobility, and 30,000 men-at-arms. In recognition of his gallantry, our Prince of Wales wears his badge of black shield and plumes to this day.

On the battle site itself, a lonely hilltop above the plains of wheat, there is little else to mark the battle, except the tattered flags of four countries - Bohemia, Luxembourg, France - and Britain.

It's a shame that there is no special restaurant or hotel in the town centre to revive pilgrims and to encourage more visitors to this historic site.

Otherwise:

There is the **Hotel La Maye** just outside, a modern building with nice garden and terrace. Rue de St. Ricquier (0)3.21.22.23.54.35 Cl. Sun. p.m. Mon. 11 rooms 255-320f; meals from 97f.

LE CROTOY 80550 Somme.
68 km S of Boulogne

There are encouraging signs that things in this little port on the north bank of the estuary of the Somme are looking up. Its history has been: fishing village/popular Sunday lunch treat/steady decay/new interest. Paint has been applied to shaky balconies, flowers embellish civic borders, new hotels emerge, old ones get spruced up, the customers return. All good news in fact.

I have always found it very agreeable to work up an appetite by promenading round the curve of the bay, photographing the fishing boats pulled up on the beach to be painted in vivid colours, past the nice old stone house built on the remains of the Château de Crotoy where Joan of Arc was imprisoned before crossing the bay on foot to St. Valéry, and on to Rouen. From here I continue the walk along the beach, which must be one of the finest of all the fine beaches of the North. Le Crotoy claims that it has the only south-facing beach along this coast. Well... true, for part of the way at least, but the bracing wind ensures that it never feels southern. More Skegness than St. Tropez.

Appetite assured, the next step is to scan the menus of the restaurants lined up by the port. There are plenty to choose from, and it is indeed very pleasant to commandeer a table on the pavement and order a plateful of steaming *moules* and a *demi* of Muscadet. But my advice is not to expect too much, These are strictly tourist restaurants and neither their prices nor their talents are geared for gourmets. If you spend 45f on *moules marinière* you will be well-satisfied; if you order a sole *meunière* you will not, even if the price (which says it all) appears to be a bargain at 75f. Fresh fish *never* comes cheap, even in a fishing port. For those looking for something different I have found a couple of alternatives, described below.

NEW Les Tourelles (HR)M
rue Pierre Guerlain 2-4 (0)3.22.27.16.33; fax (0)3.21.22.27.11.45 Cl. Jan.

The old home of the Guerlain perfume family has been transformed into a stylish new hotel. The red bricks have been restored, the witches' hats atop the towers and pinnacles painted blue, the balconies' paint newly whitened, the shutters renewed and, lo, we have an idea of how the mansion must have looked in its Edwardian heyday. Inside it's another story. The style here is more Scandinavian or New England seaside, with bare blond floorboards, unfussy white drapes, blue easy chairs, wicker, canvas, light filtering to every corner. Very Anouska Hempel, very chic, very nice indeed.

Outside is a well-furnished terrace overlooking that amazing estuary view, which must be the most attractive place in le Crotoy to have lunch or an aperitif, and at the rear a pleasant shady garden. A lounge bar with live piano music in the evenings takes care of the problem of where to gather in wet weather.

I loved it all and would have liked to see a room, some of which have magnificent views, which I am pretty confident would have earned an arrow, but of course they were all occupied, and the guests saw no reason to leave such an agreeable location so that I could have even a glimpse. So reports will be eagerly awaited.

Lunch I can report on. Another world from the town eating scene. The food was as light and modern as the hotel, well-cooked and presented. Unusually for France I was able to order a delicious starter (*terrine* of roast vegetables) and not feel inadequate. The dinner menu looked equally desirable, featuring a very un-Gallic range of dishes, abjuring anything ponderous. Menus from 95f.

17 double rooms, 2 singles, 175-450f.

NEW Aux Trois Jean (HR)M-S
Digue Jules-Noiret (0)3.22.26.16.17; fax (0)3.22.27.21.28 Cl. 25/8-10/10

Right opposite the best part of the beach, separated by a large terrace, where tables are set for refreshment throughout the day. Eating continues inside, with sensibly priced menus for families. The rooms are not particularly spacious but all are bright and light, with good bathrooms.

8 rooms at 330f.

NEW Mado (R)M

Hotel de la Baie (H)M-S (0)3.22.27.81.22; fax (0)3.22.27.85.43

This *used* to be the reason for coming to Le Crotoy - to eat at the legendary Mado's, presided over by the eponymous *patronne* and her parrot. Mado and parrot, alas, are no longer with us but the name and the restaurant continues. Everything has been smartened up, with fresh green and red paint and a dispersal of most of the atmospheric clutter of the glassed-in terrace (full of tourists) and the dark interior (full of French). The theme is still fishy, and the end product more reliable than those along the prom. Menus start at 75f. Be prepared to linger.

Upstairs are three rooms which have beaten me every time, both under the old regime and the new. They are always taken, often a year ahead. I believe that they must have superb views, but cannot speculate beyond that, except to confirm that readers, who have been cleverer than I, have been happy with their stay here.

Three rooms at 400f.

CUCQ 62780 Pas-de-Calais.
3 km S of Le Touquet

Virtually a suburb of Le Touquet, pleasant, well-groomed. Look out for a sharp bend in the D940 Berck road, and on the right is:

La Petite Auberge (R)M

933 ave. de la Libération (0)3.21.94.33.03 Cl. Sun. p.m. and Mon. o.o.s.

A ravishingly pretty, low, whitewashed old Picard farmhouse, with brown shutters and lace curtains, tables and chairs outside and loads of geraniums. Inside is pretty too in a beamy cottagey way. Menus are 89, 120, 155f, with my price guide ruler, the sole *meunière,* clocking in at an average 88f.

Popular, so be sure to book.

DÈSVRES 62440 Pas-de-Calais.
19 km SE of Boulogne
M Tue.

Dèsvres is devilishly difficult to drive out of. Getting in is easy - sometimes I've done it by mistake, finding myself in that huge sloping main square without even trying. But once trapped, they do not want to let you go, so they have contrived a hub of eight roads, with minor roads forking out of them, and obscure signs to ensure you end up back in the square. Last time, as we sat in the car poring over the map, determined not to be beaten, the kind driver parked alongside offered help. When we told him where we were heading, he tried to explain the route and then gave up - "just follow me" he said and set off corkscrewing round the town till he was satisfied that we could not go wrong.

It's worth taking this risk, however, because Dèsvres is a pleasant little town, with bags of character. It's best known for two assets, the Maison de la Faïence and the Café de l'Agriculture.

The town has been famous for its faïence since 1764, and celebrates the fact by establishing a museum showing in an audio-visual salon the history and in the *salle eau-terre-feu* the technique of the pottery. You can buy examples there or in one of several shops in the town. Open from 1/4-31/10 every day except Mon. from 10-13h and from 14-18.30h. In July and August it is open on Monday too. 25f admission fee.

That's dealt with a feast for the eye. Now how about the tastebuds?

Look no further than in the main square, the place Léon Blum, which is most animated on a Tuesday when the market takes over. Then you should certainly book your lunch table.

➤ Café de l'Agriculture (R)S
22 pl. Léon Blum Lunch only Cl. Sat.

As *rustique* as they come. Run by a team of jolly, beaming ladies. *Patronne* Madame Telliez does the welcoming, others are at the stove or peeling vast buckets of potatoes - you have to go past them to get to the lavs, which now have gained in hygiene what they have lost in character (no longer squatters).

The restaurant is surprisingly big, with cabbage roses flourishing on beige wallpaper, furnished with grandfather clocks, family *armoires,* a vintage gramophone, a corner fireplace and a photomontage of an autumn glade, but in early December it was hard to see the décor for the tinsel. It's a flexible dining room, at it's cosiest when confined by the first set of curtains to just eight tables. One set on and the size doubles, one set further and you're talking Sunday lunch and parties.

Main courses - rabbit, chicken, *fricassées,* stews - cost 50f and starters - *terrines,* crudités, soup - 25f. There is a three course menu, which changes daily, for 88f, a *plat du jour* for 49f and *pichet* wine at 22f.

Husband chose roast chicken - half a bird that had undoubtedly spent a gutsy life strutting round a courtyard, now charred and sizzling, rich brown juice accompanying and little *lardons* of bacon lending extra flavour.

Expecting fresh veg in an authentic French restaurant like this would be asking *trop*. Chips will have to do. But we did have the evidence of our own eyes en route loo-wise, that these were not out of the freezer.

I met my match in the *terrines de la maison*, served in hunks rather than slices. The rabbit was so good that it slipped down easily, the *fromage de tête* was only half consumed, the liver *pâté* less so, and as for the *rillettes* - a mere *dégustation* was all I could handle. All four perfect specimens, which, with a green salad, good bread, pickled samphire, gherkins and shallots, made a robust if not particularly elegant lunch for 25f.

I love the lack of affectation, the home cooking and the honest welcome of the good ladies and wish there were more of the same breed. Arrowed for good country value.

Otherwise:
Café Jules (R)S
11 pl. Léon Blum (0)3.21.91.69.72 Cl. Sat.

On the opposite side of the square and until recently a similar establishment to the Agriculture. Now there has been a change of management and it has gone all upmarket. The 89f menu lists dishes as esoteric as *gratin d'asperges* and *pavé de saumon frais à loseille*, but to be fair the *terrines* for which Café Jules was famous are still there and simple country dishes like pork chop with mustard sauce and jellied rabbit. On Sunday the price jumps to 139f and you get soup, then perhaps scallops in cream sauce, then a house speciality, *coq à la bière* or perhaps *civet de sanglier aux pruneaux*, and pud.

I liked Jules the way it was, but it is not fair to judge the new version by comparisons with the old. I'm pleased they've kept all that wonderful faience.

More reports please.

DUNKERQUE 59140 Nord.
46 km NE of Calais

The port that will forever be associated with the heroism and tragedy of the evacuation of May 1940, when 350,000 men were rescued, under heavy fire from the now fun-loving beaches of Mâlo and Bray-Dunes. Its growth since then has been phenomenal - it is now France's third largest port, divided into several basins. From the Bassin de Commerce you can take a boat tour around the waterways.

Dunkerque boasts two art museums, the *musée d'art contemporain*, surrounded by a sculpture park, and the *musée des beaux arts*, built in 1973, with collections of paintings from 16th-20th centuries.

I always get lost in Dunkerque. Can't even find the sea if I don't pay attention. Every time I dither between the conflicting directions - *port, plage, bassin, centre* - and end up totally confused and lost in the endless suburbs. I cannot claim that this is an easy-to-love town. It's just too big and sprawly and the flavour of the port does not spread far. There are no little fish restaurants to discover or hotels with character. I suppose it's not Dunkerque's fault that there is nothing antique to admire - 80% of the town was destroyed.

So, l would really counsel staying and eating outside the town. (See below for Tétéghem, Coudekerque and Cappelle la Grand.)

Otherwise:
Borel (H)S
6 rue l'Hermite (0)3.28.66.51.80; fax (0)3.28.59.33.32

If you have to stay in the town, at least you have a view of the port from this modern hotel between two bridges. 48 rooms cost from 360-420f.

Hirondelle (R)M-S
46 ave. Faidherbe (0)3.28.63.17.65; fax (0)3.28.6.15.43 R Cl. Sun. p.m.; Mon. lunch

Head eastwards down the main drag, the ave. Faidherbe, to Mâlo-les-Bains, which is Dunkerque's residential area, with a fine sandy beach, and look on the right for this ultra modern (and garish) hotel. 42 rooms cost 270-310f. 495f buys two people dinner, bed and breakfast.

Au Bon Coin (R)S-M
ave. Kleber, Malo les Bains (0)3.28.69.12.63

Decorated with yellowing photos of celebrities who have visited this long-established bistro in an insalubrious corner of the main road. Good for freshest fish and unpretentious atmosphere. 80f mid-week menu.

TÉTÉGHEM 59229 6 km SE of Dunkerque.
2 km from Calghouck by D4

A nondescript residential suburb, unremarkable except for:

➤ **La Meunerie** (HR)L
174 rue des Pierres (0)3.28.26.01.80; fax (0)3.28.26.17.32 R Cl. Sun. p.m.; Mon.
HR cl. 22/12-15/1

It's hard to imagine that this elegant complex was, as it name implies, a flour-mill. But indeed it was, transformed by Jean Pierre Delbé, whose widow carries on his good work.

In addition to the elegant restaurant there are now eight luxurious bedrooms, approached by a glass walkway. They are all different in size and style, but all come with a spacious marble bathroom, Louis XV decor and English telly, looking out onto an interesting interior garden. They vary from 550 to 850f, and there is also a highly luxurious suite with jacuzzi, which clocks in at 1,350f. Breakfast costs an additional 80f, but is one of the most desirable ever, on which you could certainly last out until dinnertime.

The restaurant is the big draw. The Michelin star stays firmly in place, for three menus, 280f (crab tart with oysters, flavoured with dill, noisette of salmon with hazelnut cream, roast chicken with seasonal veg and a magnificent pastry table, offering fresh fruit and home-made sorbets) all topped up with irresistible *petits fours*. Probably the best value, if you have the confidence to leave it to them who know best, is the *Laissez-nous Faire* menu at 330f. This one changes every day according to what is best in the market, and includes everything from kir to coffee, with carefully chosen wines accompanying four courses. An excellent deal, when you consider the high standards.

There are special *forfaits* available out of season which are worth enquiring about.

It is these high standards, obvious throughout every detail of Mme Delbé's operation, which earn La Meunerie an arrow for consistent excellence and star quality in this area.

COUDEKERQUE-BRANCHÉ 59210 Nord
4 km S by D916

Soubise (R)M
49bis rte de Berques (0)3.28.64.66.00 Cl. Sat. lunch, Sun. p.m. 11/4-22/4; 24/7-19/8; 18/12-6/1

This pleasant 18C building did escape the wartime destruction and is charmingly decorated with old Limoges porcelain. Chef Michel Hazebroucq has won one of Michelins red *'repas'* symbols for a menu whose price is not nearly as exalted as his reputation (95f). Go for it. The menu changes every day, as all good menus should, according to the whims of market and season, but there is always plenty of good fish. Other menus up to 198f. Traditional ingredients, traditionally cooked.

CAPELLE-LA-GRANDE 59180 Nord
5 km S by D916

Le Bois de Chêne (R)M
48 rte de Bergues (0)3.28.64.21.80 Cl. Sun. p.m.
  Mostly fish, well cooked by Flemish Christian Vandeneeckhoutte (phew) in this popular restaurant at the side of the road opposite the canal. Cooking is substantial northern fare. The cheapest menu at 110f includes three courses, three wines and coffee. The next one up at 198f had some more interesting offerings, like a *gratin de bouchots*, which I just can't imagine (*bouchots* are whelks - how do you tenderise them?).

ÉSCALLES 62179 Pas-de-Calais.
14 km SW of Calais

The best of the lovely coast road, the D940, between the two ports lies between the headlands, an area promoted as *Site de Deux Caps*. The views are spectacular, there is rarely much traffic and you can bowl along high above the Channel feeling that this is what a holiday is all about. The village of Éscalles lies below Cap Blanc Nez. Take the turning marked *Plage* for a pleasant stroll (or short drive) through fields of corn and beet down to the beach, with its variety of sand, stones and rocks. For lengthier walks, the coastal path is highly recommended.

Otherwise:
There are two family restaurants in the village, the **Restaurant du Cap** and **l'Escale**, which also has simple rooms from 235-315f. A good base for an unsophisticated family holiday.

> ÉTAPLES 62630 Pas-de-Calais.
> 27 km S of Boulogne
> **M** Tue., Fri.

If you need a contrast from Le Touquet's somewhat artificial atmosphere, cross the river Canche to the workaday port that WW1 troops knew as Eatapples. No gloss, no sophistication, no hotels to speak of here. The residents just get on with their everyday lives, often centred round the fishing boats that unload their catches on the quays. Tuesday and Fridays are the big days, when the central market takes over the main square.

There ought to be plenty of simple fish restaurants right alongside the boats and indeed there are, with predictable names like Au Marin Joyeux, La Marine, Les Trois Lanternes - but nothing special to recommend, and not one that inspires reader-enthusiasm. (I hope I'm wrong - let me know.)

Otherwise:
Les Pecheurs d'Étaples (R)M
quai de la Canche Open every day
> I had high hopes when the local fishermen set up a co-operative to market their fish and built a smart modern fish market topped by a restaurant with good river views. They have two other restaurants, one in Boulogne. All a bit so-so. The bill tends to be more than you'd expected and the fish less inspiring. But if you keep it simple, choosing perhaps the fish of the day, or just a bowl of moules you may not be disappointed. And the view is good.

> FAVIÈRES 80120 Somme.
> 5 km NE of Le Crotoy, 61 km S of Boulogne

Turn off the main coast road, the D940, on to the little D140, and drive through a maze of country lanes to find this village, amidst marshes, willows and not much else.

▶ Clé des Champs (R)M
(0)3.22.27.88.00 Cl. Sun. p.m.; Mon.; 31/8-11/9; 4/1-24/1; Feb. school holidays
> A pretty rustic low white building set alongside a patch of grass that serves as the village *place*. Surprising out here in the middle of nowhere to come across a bevy of cars, parked French-style, higgledy-piggledy, as near the

entrance as they can squeeze. That's because the French are prepared to drive some distance to the best value in the area. He who ventures thus far at the weekend without a reservation will not only be unable to park nearby - he won't find a free table.

The main dining room is as pretty as the exterior promises in a cosy, flowery *rustique* way. The overflow gets the much less attractive secondary room - another incentive to book early.

Four kinds of home-baked rolls are the kind of attention to detail that singles out le Clé as something special. Then, even on the cheapest menu, complimentary *amuse-bouches*, again indicating the generosity of the value here. The menus are sensibly short (another good sign), so even before we taste a morsel, we know the omens are good.

Seasonal ingredients, even to the extent of using blackberries picked nearby, are another plus point. Fish is particularly good, with not very far to travel, and vegetables are unusually lavish, but although the chef is wise enough to know when to treat perfect materials simply, that is not to say that he is not well able to produce more sophisticated fare, like a *terrine* of peppers topped with aspic flavoured with artichokes.

In order to qualify for the Michelin red *repas* rating, indicating good value, the price of the menu has to be kept below 100f. Le Clé qualifies - 95f. There are other menus up to 240f, but there is hardly any need to stray from the bargain cheapo.

The arrow remains for good value, unusually good cooking.

FRUGES 62310 Pas-de-Calais.
51 km from Boulogne, 19 km NE of Hesdin on the D928.
M Sat.

By local standards Fruges is a big town. All the action centres on the market square, around a couple of bars and restaurants.

Otherwise:
Café du Centre (R)S
2 rue du Marcehal Leclerc (0)3.21.41.46.50

A kind reader first alerted me to the joys of the Café du Centre, and on first glance I was not impressed - shabby dun-coloured façade on a busy street. Closer inspection then revealed that there was more to the café than originally met the eye and it went in the last book. This time again, I was on the brink of excluding it until I paid another visit and re-discovered the honest good value on offer here. Just like modest French restaurants used to be before the deep freeze and micro. Once past the vociferous bar and it all looks up. The back dining room has been redecorated in cheerfully bright colours and, as before, all is spotlessly clean and wholesome. There is even a small garden.

The clue to the worthiness of the restaurant is the fact that M. Logez-Mallet, the *patron*, is also a *traiteur*, so you can rely on the *terrines, saucissons* and made-up dishes being first-class. Midweek there are three choices from dishes like steak, lasagne, rabbit or couscous for 59f, including wine. On Sunday, for 80f you get *coquilles St. Jacques, ris de veau* and two other courses.

Go on - give it a try.

Le Fournil (R)S-M
2 rte de St. Omer (0)3.21.04.47.13 Cl. Mon. and every evening except Sat.

On the main road, the D928, between Fruges and Fauquembergues, Le Fournil used to be a lorry-drivers' caff. Fanny and David Caudron, ex Michelin-starred La Meunerie at Tétéghem, transformed it into a very pleasant little restaurant. David's cooking is way above average, thanks to stints in other prestigious restaurants, but his prices are rock bottom. I like the way the menus are kept limited to whatever was best in the market that day - 68f buys an *entrée du jour* then *plat du jour* or *poisson du jour* and a home-made dessert. The 98f version offers more choice.

GRAVELINES 59820 Nord.
20 km E of Calais

Gravelines owes its existence to the fact that six hundred years ago Philippe d'Alsace, Count of Flanders, deflected the course of the river Aa through the town. Today the town lies on the right bank of the Aa, still surrounded by the ramparts which have been necessary over the intervening centuries to defend the town from all manner of invaders. It was finally recaptured for the French monarchy, whose rights were confirmed by the Treaty of the Pyrenees in 1659. The ramparts you see today were built by the peripatetic Vauban, judiciously commissioned by Louis XIV. In 1706 Vauban became Governor of Gravelines, and from that post later rose to become Marshall of France. The very stones of the place are steeped in history. Spanish troops assembled here to invade England when the Armada arrived (the plan went awry); during the Napoleonic wars Bonaparte thought it would be a good idea to set up 'La Ville des

Smogglers', welcoming English smugglers to carry away brandy, in an attempt to evade the British blockade. The fortifications continued to serve their purpose well as recently as 1940 when they were an important factor in the defence of Dunkerque.

Nowadays the citadel, known as the arsenal, still intact, is set behind grassy banks and moat, and houses temporary exhibitions. Do take a walk inside the fortifications to discover a beautifully kept garden, with clipped yew pyramids and plenty of restful benches. Walk round above the moat - the view is a bit on the flat side but it's all remarkably peaceful nowadays.

The little town itself is agreeable, too, boasting a late flamboyant Gothic church with a Renaissance doorway carved in 1598. Superb 17C woodwork inside the church and some splendid tombs. The town's centre is a market square, and a fine belfry.

Hostellerie du Beffroi (HR)M
Place Charles Valentine (0)3.28.23.24.25; fax (0)3.28.65.59.71 R cl. Sat. lunch; Sun.

> An old building, tactfully restored ten years ago, in the main square. It boasts an Irish bar, which makes a good meeting place, a smart restaurant, La Tour, and a brasserie for casual foraging. Menus start at 99f in the restaurant and 55f in the brasserie, with good carafe wine. The 40 modern rooms are well-equipped, cheerful and bright. 360f with bath.

Otherwise:
I am told that the best fish restaurant hereabouts is Le Turbot in the rue de Dunkerque.

> **HALLINES** 62570 Pas-de-Calais.
> 6 km W of St. Omer

This is another of the three villages - Arques, Blendecques are the other two - which almost run into the south of St. Omer, but somehow manage to retain their individuality. To find it take the D928 and then the D211 to the prominent church and gaudy graveyard, with all the charm of the river Aa flowing through under a bridge in the village centre.

> **Hostellerie St. Hubert** (HR)M

1 rue au Moulin (0)3.21.39.77.77; fax (0)3.21.93.00.86 Cl. Sun. p.m.; Mon.

I predicted when I first found the Hostellerie for FE12 that it would be the next in the long line of château hotels near the Channel ports that have been swallowed up by the tour operators and subsequently over-run by our compatriots. Wrong. Don't ask me why but that just hasn't happened and even my file isn't overflowing with readers' comments. Don't understand it.

It is one of the many idiosyncratic 19C mansions that proliferate in the North of France. The interior is much more elegant than most, with many of the original decorative features retained and restored. An important white marble staircase leads to the truly lovely pine-panelled dining room. On a bleak winter's night, with a big fire crackling away in the marble fireplace, the crimson walls echoing the warmth and the chandelier glittering, it looks at its best. In summer though it must be very pleasant to look down through those tall windows to the lush grounds, with the river rushing through.

The place settings are Limoges and there is discreet piped classical music; the service is friendly but efficient and there is a pleasant family feel about the place, generated by Mme Delva, who welcomes and son Olivier, who is chef-*patron*. The young *maître d'* is helpful and knowledgeable. The cooking is sophisticated without being chichi - lots of good fish and perfect local cheeses. Menus start at a very reasonable 120f.

The nine rooms are all different, as the price range, from 350-800f, reveals. In summer I would certainly think it worth while to pay for one overlooking the lovely garden, but they are all spacious, with high ceilings and good mod cons. In winter we took the cheapest, with a fine view of the cemetery.

Arrowed for style, peacefulness, good cooking.

HARDELOT 62152 Pas-de-Calais.
20 km S of Boulogne

Possibly the best beach along this whole stretch of best beaches. Along with top-notch golfing, expensive villas set in extensive pine woods, well-manicured lawns and flowerbeds, this would seem to be the resort with everything going for it. Everything that is, except a heart. Hardelot tries hard to mirror Le Touquet, but it doesn't have Le Touquet's pedigree. In season it looks raw, out of season it's a shut-down ghost. But I don't suppose the kids will complain when they see the sands and the ice cream bars and the shops selling beach essentials, nor the golfers who often prefer the greens here to the busier Le Touquet scene. While I failed to find the ideal hotel for the former, the latter are well catered for at:

> **Hotel du Parc, Restaurant l'Orangerie** (HR)L
Probably the most agreeable combination of comfortable hotel and fine restaurant along the Côte. The hotel gets it just right - no glitz but rather an airy modernity, featuring white paint, cane furniture, big windows. The 81 bedrooms, mostly with a terrace overlooking the forest, follow the same style - lots of room, lots of light, bright and cheerful. Good bathrooms and all mod cons make the price of 525-720f a good deal in this luxurious setting.

A good place too for shoulder-season breaks, since the huge swimming pool surrounded by lavishly dotted recliners is well heated and, of the five tennis courts free to hotel guests, two are indoors. Golfers get special rates on the local course.

That's the good news, here's the extra good news: the restaurant, now known as l'Orangerie, is better than ever. Chef Bruno Andrieux uses not only local ingredients and recipes, like his *rable de lapin braisé à la bière* but other favourites from all over France like *tartare de canard fumé*, or cleverly combines the two, as in his *tian d'agneau de Montreuil au jus de tapenade*. The weekday menu costs a very reasonable 105f; others are 135 or 180f.

An arrow for casual luxury and excellent cooking.

HAZEBROUCK 59190 Nord.
62 km SE of Calais, 22 km E of St. Omer by N42

There is an air of bustle and purposefulness about Hazebrouck that I enjoy. The wide and wonderful main square is always full of cars (parking difficult but lots of animation), the restaurants and bars abuzz. If you are unlucky enough to hit a cold or wet day in the north, head here for a dose of cheerfulness.

The Germans launched one of the most damaging attacks (in terms of human life) on the town in WW1, aiming at its important railway network, and it suffered again in 1940 when the spire of one of the wonders of the north, the 15th-century church dedicated to St. Eloi, was bombed. The church is still worth a visit; walk behind it to discover a surprising peacefulness emanating from the *béguinage*. These little villages-within-a-town have been built in the Flemish region ever since the 12th century to shelter pious widows and to allow them to spend the rest of their lives in perfect harmony. There is a famous example in

Bruges, which is on all the tourist routes, but not many people discover this other example.

Back to the liveliness of the Grand'Place, dominated by the vast 19C Town Hall, with a most impressive façade. A row of chunky Doric pillars supports the arches of the colonnade, in which students socialise.

➤ Hotel Gambrinus (H)S

2 rue Nationale (0)3.28.41.98.79; fax (0)3.28.43.11.06

Look through the pillars and a large 19C building painted bright pink fits the frame. This is the Gambrinus, Hazebrouck's only hotel, conveniently situated between station and market square. The opportunity to cash in on this exclusivity has been firmly resisted by the exceptionally pleasant and friendly owners, Madame Delaere and her husband. They have decorated each floor in a different colour, peach for the first floor, green for the second, blue for the third. The 15 rooms are small but cheerful and spotless, with an en suite shower, and cost 290f. Breakfast is served in the raspberry red room downstairs.

Accueil is always important but never more so than in the simple hotels. There can be no doubt about it here, and Francis Delaere will do everything within her power to make your stay an enjoyable one. Ask her to advise about where to eat to suit your mood; there is no shortage of candidates.

Arrowed for good position, good value, good welcome.

➤ La Taverne Flamande (R)M-S

62 Grand'Place (0)3.21.41.63.09 Cl. Sun. p.m.; Mon.

In almost every market square in the north you will find a Taverne Flamande, but this is my favourite. It's an archetypal brasserie, with all the bustle of black-trousered, white-aproned waiters weaving through the tables, bearing aloft plates piled high. Piled particularly high in this case, especially with the indispensable northern *frites*, and very good they were. There are leather seats inside, occupied by well-fed perspiring local businessmen, and plastic ones outside occupied by hopeful tourists.

Maybe the latter, like me, had only wimpish appetites at lunchtime and settled for one of the famous quiches - Maroilles, Lorraine, *au poireaux, au saumon* and *aux oignons* (the best), served with green salad, but the *hommes d'affaires* obviously had no problem about getting stuck into the 90f *menu du jour* - *terrines, campagne* or *poisson,* then venison liver with onions, then cheese, then a *gratin de pommes.* The *plat de jour* was also going down well, a *sauté* of veal with mushrooms in a cream sauce for 49f.

I love the atmosphere, I love the warmth, I love the food, I love the prices,

I love the friendliness of the nice *patron*, Bernard, so an arrow of course.

Le Centre (R)S

48 Grand'Place (0)3.28.48.03.62 Cl. Tues. p.m.

If you get caught in Hazebrouck on a Sunday or Monday, or if the Taverne is full, do not despair. Le Centre, on the same side of the Place as its rival, is another praiseworthy *brasserie/creperie/pizzeria/saladerie/restaurant-traditionel*. Christian Van Inghelandt is *patron* here. Walk past the hectic flowered wallpaper of the bar to a long narrow room beyond (or sit outside or the terrace of course). Here 65f buys the local speciality the *tourte aux poireaux*, followed by a *rôti de boeuf* and dessert or coffee - good value. You can take the lighter option, the *formule fraicheur* for 69f, which entitles you to raid the *buffet froid* and top that up with dessert. The regional menu costs 110f and there is another at 175f.

Auberge St. Eloi (R)M

60 rue Eglise (0)3.28.40.70.23 Cl. Sun. p.m.; Mon.

As its name implies, near the church, on the main road. A little modern restaurant, unremarkable from the outside, comfortable within.

The 110f. menu (not Suns) offers good value, particularly as it includes wine. Home-made *rillettes* are of tunny fish and shrimp, followed by either the *poisson du jour* or the *viande du jour* - a formula of which I greatly approve - followed by desserts. There is a *menu affaire* at 140f which, together with the opening times, indicates who are the main customers, and another at 168f. More reports please.

HESDIN 62140 Pas-de-Calais.
61 km SE of Boulogne
M Thurs.

If only Hesdin had a hotel worthy of the delightful little town, I could wholeheartedly recommend it as the perfect choice for a short stay. Quite different from anywhere else in the region, with its cobbled streets, threaded by rivulets of the river Canche, crossed by hump-backed bridges, and spectacular market square.

Dominating the town from its vantage point in the square is the imposing Hotel de Ville, originally the home of Charles V of Austria's sister, Mary of Hungary. The sumptuously decorated balcony was added in 1629 and the belfry in 1875. Inside are some rare 17th-century Flemish tapestries. It's an incredibly rich and majestic building to find in what is now such an insignificant little town, as indeed is another treasure just off the square - the church of Notre Dame. Built in brick in the second half of the 16C, it was further embellished with a wonderful stone Renaissance doorway, an ensemble of Corinthian columns, swags, coats of arms, angels and towers. The interior is richly furnished - look for the 18C misericords in the choir stalls.

I like the size of the town too - big enough to support some interesting shops, small enough to wander round comfortably before settling down in the square preferably outside one of the several bars and brasseries. *The Globe* is the one I recommend but you'll have to be there early if you want to claim a table from the locals, especially on market days.

Thursday is the day when the square and surrounding streets fill up with the stalls of farmers and their wives from neighbouring villages. It's worthwhile arranging your tour around it.

Another bonus is the surrounding countryside. The most attractive approach is from the north via the D108, through the pretty villages of Embry, with a stream flowing by and a white folly church on a hill, and Lebiez on the river Crécquoise is just as charming. Wamin, centred round its château, is another pleasing hamlet if you're in detouring mood. This will lead through the deep forest of Hesdin, amongst whose oak and beech trees wild boar are still hunted. A good place to consume the goodies bought in the market, on picnic tables set out in the glades.

Absolutely no joy with hotel accommodation in the town itself.

Otherwise:
Just outside is the **Trois Fontaines** at 16 rte Abbeville à Marconne (0)3.21.86.81.65, which has 10 quiet rooms at 280-320f and serves meals from 95f.

RESTAURANTS

A brighter picture here, with three good reasons for visiting Hesdin:

NEW L'Ecurie (R)M
17 rue Jacquemont (0)3.21.86.86.86 Cl. Mon. o.o.s.

An enchanted setting, through a courtyard, in an old stable. It was always an attractive building but now that it has been completely renovated it is understandably the most popular restaurant in town, involving a booking if you want to be sure of a table. When they are full, as on Thursday mid-day, service tends to get a bit fraught and the reception is not all one could wish for. Even at other times, it is distinctly on the languid side, so don't go in a hurry.

The décor does not rely entirely on the historic building for character, nor does it tend to the dark and gloomy norm of antiquity; the owners have boldly decided to go for fresh pastels and a contemporary feel, with lots of light. Similarly, chef Jean Luc Lecoutre combines traditional dishes with modern interpretation. Fresh produce, everything home-made. During the week his *'menu affaire'* appeals as much to the shoppers as to the businessmen, including as it does three courses and a drink. Other menus are 95f and 145f, the latter chosen entirely from the *carte*.

This would undoubtedly rank as an arrow if only they would get the service sorted out. Let me know of any recent experiences.

NEW ➤ La Brêteche (R)M

19 rue du General Daulle (0)3.21.86.80.87 Cl. Wed. o.o.s.

Very good news to see this old restaurant revitalised in new hands. Young and friendly Christine and Fabien Oudart have been installed here for just a year and have already made many improvements and innovations. There are three dining rooms: upstairs, with big windows overlooking the town and a big fireplace, is the pink version; the two alternatives are yellow and blue or red and white, all three now fresh and cheerful.

Fabien is gratifyingly obsessed with using only fresh ingredients and it shows. His specialities include home-smoked salmon, rabbit used in a *carbonade* and local farm chicken, cooked until it becomes *fondant*. Menus are 90f or 175f, with a special *terroir* version at 130f.

Arrowed for good value, good cooking, good welcome.

Flandres (H)S (R)M

rue Arras (0)3.21.86.87.21 fax (0)3.21.86.28.01 Cl. 27/6-8/7 and 20/12-10/1

Sadly the hotel Flandres does not live up to the restaurant. I have a list of grumbles about several aspects of the former, but only plaudits for the latter.

"The welcome was as dire as usual and our room just as drab but nevertheless it is good value if it is simply used as an overnight stop. There certainly should not be an arrow as far as the hotel is concerned but the food was up to its usual high standard with excellent fresh crudités on the hors d'oeuvre table and superb rare spit-roast beef". Jonathan Paul Diamond.

"Extremely good value for money. The first course was a mountain of white fish and boiled potatoes with delicious home-made mayonnaise - simple, yet so effective. Next came a salmon steak in light sorrel sauce and some really toothsome chips and finally a good selection of sorbets. As you say, the dining room was full of local businessmen - as well as all the local gendarmerie who were clearly

enjoying themselves."

All of which doesn't leave me much to add, except to say that a slight falling off of standards detected since these letters were written means the arrow has to go. I would probably choose either of the other recommendations in the town nowadays because the atmosphere there is less serious. That said, if you are looking for straightforward French cooking, approved of by local businessmen (sure sign of reliable high standards), in substantial quantities, you could do far worse than try the Flandres.

Menus start at 92f with good carafe wine. The 14 rooms cost from 250-340f.

HESDIN L'ABBE 62360 Pas-de-Calais.
8 km SE of Boulogne on the N1

The hotel is between the *nationale* and the village (which is only a church and a *boulangerie*), and well signed.

➤ **Hotel Cléry** (HR)M
(0)3.21.83.19.83; fax (0)3.21.87.52.59. H Cl. 11/12-29/1. R (residents only) Cl. Sat. and Sun.

The hotel takes its name from Baron de Cléry who built this architectural gem in the late 18th century. It's not grand or large enough to be termed a château, - just an elegant gentleman's country home. It's a very thin building, which means that light pours in from the floor-to-ceiling windows from both sides. Straight ahead from the front door is a small salon, and there are two more to the right, perfect for aperitifs and teatime cuppas, smart but not intimidating, cosy fire in winter.

To the left are two pleasant dining rooms. Given the rooms' perfect proportions and the amount of light, it would be almost impossible to furnish them badly. The present young owners have opted for contemporary patterned curtains on pine poles, primrose walls, defining the panels in the ceiling by painting them golden yellow and white.

Elsewhere in the main building the decoration is more traditional. Up the elegant Louis XV staircase are the best rooms, spacious, furnished with antiques, some with stunning views over the extensive grounds.

In the rooms contrived from the old stable block Laura Ashley reigns supreme. Variations of her familiar flowery fabrics and paper are in every room, and very attractive too. The French think so - L.A. is the height of decorator-chic. I certainly felt very much at home in ours - the same sweet-peas. The bed was king-sized, there was a good bathroom and, unusually, plenty of putting-down space for sponge bags and paraphernalia.

The 5 hectares of gardens are now a major attraction. Quite extensive walks have been marked out in the woodland, and it is all very peaceful and

HOTEL CLÉRY HÉSDIN - L'ABBÉ

pleasant to stretch car-weary legs in the shady tracks. There is a tennis court too, but the idea of a swimming pool was scotched as being too noisy. The whole concept of the hotel is rest and relaxation (Relais de Silence). Certainly the occupants of the numerous recliners on the lawns looked peaceful enough.

Breakfast costs an additional 55f but is worth it. Apart from the usual croissants and bread there are cereals, fresh fruit, yoghurt, three kinds of jam in pots not foil, and ultimate test - freshly squeezed o.j. Service both at breakfast and at dinner is suave, the china is fine, and the ambience refined. Unfortunately the cooking did not live up to the rest of the experience (135f and 175f).

The rates vary according to season. The six cheapest rooms, with shower, cost from 330-395f, and the most expensive range from 620-795f.

The hotel is arrowed for charm, comfort and pleasant owners, but I counsel eating elsewhere until the cooking is sorted out.

HESDRES 62720 Wierre Effroy. Pas-de-Calais.
3 km SW of Wierre Effroy, 20 km SE of Boulogne

Just a hamlet perched up a hill. Road numbers are not a lot of help in this maze of white minor roads and it will be a case of 'I wouldn't start from here' on whichever direction I suggest. So look for it in the pretty unspoiled countryside due east of Wimereux, threaded by the river of the same name.

La Rencontre (R)S
(0)3.21.33.20.72 Cl. Mon. p.m. and Tues. Last orders by 8.30 p.m.

A tiny cottage on the corner of two very minor roads; Madame Roland is the cook and Madame Courand serves. Inside is everyone's idea of a cottage interior, charmingly rustic, simply furnished.

The food is totally in keeping, prepared from fresh local ingredients and organically grown vegetables. I learned a new term - *'légumes bio'*. Menus are 80, 90 and 130f, four courses apiece.

This one is a unique country treat. Let me know if it deserves an arrow. Many wily locals think it does, so make sure you book.

In the rear garden are some attractive gites, if anyone should be interested.

HOULLE 62910 Pas-de-Calais.
6 km NW of St. Omer

It really is a surprising area to be found east of the N43. Water is the dominant theme and canals, streams and rivulets criss-cross the flat Flemish farmlands and dictate the setting of villages. Houlle is particularly watery, with shimmering lakes providing homes for waterfowl. There are several alternative eating possibilities in or near the village and all you have to do is to back your fancy, hopefully follow the signs from the main road and get lost in the watery wilderness a couple of times.

L'Auberge de l'Étang

11 Impasse des Étangs (0)3.21.93.05.26 Cl. evenings from Mon. to Thurs., all day Mon. 15/10-15/3

This ridiculously pretty little whitewashed old farmhouse used to be called after its previous owner, Mère Poupart, and then it was really rustic, both in food and character. The new owner, Jérome Delplace, has realised the potential of the place - all low beams, gleaming copper, flagged floor - and worked out his own formula for capitalising on his property and packing most of his trade into lunchtime. Here is one reader's view:

"Set menu at lunch is amazing value at 110f for four courses of really good well-presented food. Total bill for three including aperitif, bottle wine and coffee 448f. Still can't believe what good value it was for such an excellent meal." Mr. and Mrs. M. Shaw.

The Shaws are quite right - it is good food, it is good value and the auberge is strikingly attractive. That's the good news.

The bad is that M. Delplace is totally inflexible. The Shaws had his set menu and it suited them fine. If there had been one item on it that did not suit them - say an allergy to fish or offal - there would have been absolutely no alternative. Nor can you request a slighter meal. We took two friends there for lunch and none of us wanted all three courses. We ended up paying the 110f per person for *terrine* for one (request for green salad to go with it refused), and chicken for the other two. At no stage when we booked the table or arrived at the auberge had we been warned of the house rules and they certainly are not mentioned in the brochure.

The other caveat is that there are two rooms and the larger of the two is usually occupied by groups. This was the case for us - one large table taken over by vociferous Germans, which left us very much in the minority, alone next door. The large coach outside would normally have warned us off but we had arranged to meet our friends at the table and anyway I wanted first hand experience. M. Delplace, quite unabashed, told me that it was groups he was trying to attract.

So the answer is certainly try the auberge if you can manage a full lunch and are prepared to risk an obdurate no-choice menu. If these conditions apply you will enjoy the excursion.

HUBY-ST-LEU 62140 Hesdin. Pas-de-Calais.
1 km NE of Hesdin

The local forest is nicknamed The Cathedral of Old Oaks, because its lofty oak trees are so dense that you can hardly see the sky above, and the result is awe-inspiring. This is the valley of the Ternoise, a good base for exploring that river and the other six that thread through the green countryside.

Take the St. Omer road and on the steep hill climbing out of the town look on the right for:

➤ La Garenne (R)M

(0)3.21.86.95.09 Cl. Tues.; Wed. lunch; one week in Feb.

An ancient posting inn, dating back to the 16th century, where Didier, front of house, and Bernard, chef, hold court. If the atmosphere strikes you as theatrical it is hardly surprising - Didier was well known on the Paris stage, and has brought with him to Huby his love of colour and originality, so that a meal here is going to be a performance in more ways than one.

Depending on the number of customers, there are two optional dining rooms, each with a huge eye-level log fire. Even in chilly July there was a cheerful blaze. The smaller room has cherry painted walls stencilled with green ivy leaves, flimsy white muslin is draped artistically if confusingly over ancient beams, a cartwheel hangs from the ceiling, and on every available surface is an assortment of objets, not necessarily d'art, but certainly eclectic - saddles, mirrors, fossils, paintings... Tablecloths are pink, flowers, not necessarily in their first flush of youth, are lavishly scattered in anything that will hold water, tablecloths are rosy pink, and the general effect is of warmth and generosity.

At weekends the larger room next door is used too, also with a log fire, also cosily unconventional. On my last summer visit, Didier was lamenting that the weather had been so gloomy that they had not been able to eat in the garden as he had planned. It's a pleasing prospect - not all like the rabbit warren that the house name suggests, but well-tended and organised, with tables and chairs shaded beneath white parasols, good lighting, gravel paths, lots of shade - all one could wish for in fact for summer carousing, if only the sun would co-operate.

The menu changes each week. The 145f version offered, for example, *ficelle de Picardie, jambon grillé,* cheese or fruit tart. You get an extra course on the 177f menu, which has some interesting translations like 'scallop marine

LA GARENNE, HUDY-ST-LÉO.

mollusc'. *Delice de sainte Feriole* does not appeal when it becomes 'duck fatted liver rolled in ham' and I never did get to work out what a *medaillon du grand large* approximates, but my scallops were perfectly cooked and the tunny steak with white wine shallots and 'slip of bacon sauce' was irreproachable.

La Garenne's hospitality never stops. The place is open all day for crêpes, drinks, tea and coffee. A comfortable lounge and bar is a rare asset.

I had wondered if the eccentricity would be to readers' taste as much as it is to mine. You bet it would - thumbs up all the way. So, for the third time, the arrow stays firmly in place.

HUCQUELIERS Pas-de-Calais.
29 km SE of Boulogne by D341 and D343

Hucqueliers is easy to navigate just two main roads, crossing neatly in the middle, which is the heart of all the action, centring on a couple of bars and restaurants.

Otherwise:
NEW Auberge d'Hucqueliers (R)S
GrandPlace Cl. Mon.

As we were peering doubtfully at the hectic décor of the auberge - bright green and brighter green - one of those battered old Peugeots that spell instant France pulled up and a rubicund face leaned out of the window to inform us, with many an illustrative gesture, that "*On mange très très bien ici*".

Well we couldn't ignore a tip like that; unfortunately the infuriating *journée de fermeture* beat us once again; it was Monday, and we never got the chance even to peer inside. All I could do was to check out the menus. An omelette and chips costing 30f would have done us fine. Other menus, starting at 45f, looked just what one would wish for in a simple country inn - *poulet aux fines herbes,* or *plat du jour.*

Rooms, uninspected, cost 200f.

> INXENT 62170 Montreuil. Pas-de-Calais. 3
> 2 km S of Boulogne

Probably the best-known village along the D 127, following the river Course. Take the path beside the church to walk along the river without a road intervening. It flows fast and wide here - hang over the bridge and you may see one of the trout for which the region is famous. The main reason for the village's popularity is that it is the site for a restaurant well-loved by several generations:

Auberge d'Inxent. (HR)M
218 rue de la Vallée (0)3.21.90.71.19; fax (0)3.21.86.31.67 Cl. Tues. p.m. and Wed. o.o.s.

Having been in the same family for many years, the auberge then had several new owners in the past few years and there have been changes. The great and the good Elizabeth David, who wrote about the simple inn serving simple country food - trout and chicken were about the limit of the menu - would not recognise the place now, nor its menu. Mercifully the exterior remains the same - wisteria tumbling from the wall of the old Picard farmhouse - nor has the entrance hall, with its flagged stone floor and wonderful old white tiled stove. Walls have been knocked down, however, to enlarge the dining room, and a certain intimacy lost in the process. We were the only diners, which made the musak even more obtrusive.

Fate took a hand in deciding that Jean-Marc Six should be the owner of the Auberge. Working in a restaurant in the north, he bought a ticket in a raffle and won first prize - around £150,000. He heard that the Auberge was for sale and the chance to be his own boss was too good to miss.

He is passionately devoted to the ingredients and recipes of his home territory, buying locally and in the valley itself if possible. Trout come from the ponds at Zérables, flour from the mill at Beussent, bread from the excellent baker at Montcavrel, jams and honey from farmers' wives, strawberries from Montechort, and of course chocolates from the famous chocolate factory down the road (see Beussent).

His 79f menu is fairly limited - *terrine,* fillet of pork or fish of the day - but on the four-course 135f version, you get the chance to sample *ficelle de l'auberge,* and *potje vleisch,* both Flanders specialities, or the famous *truite au bleu. Crème brulée* comes *à la chicorée,* using the roots as subtle flavouring. The house speciality is a dish from a village near Lille, *tarte au Wambrechies.* Just right for a light lunch, I thought. Potatoes are piled into the flan, topped with *crème fraiche* and flavoured with juniper and a touch of gin.

Jean-Marc and his wife Laurence have actually reduced the price of their rooms. "I want people to come back," he says. And anyway, his love is in the restaurant not the hotel, so naturally he wants the bargain rooms to encourage people to eat there. They are unchanged since the tenancy of the former owner, are quite small but pleasant and well equipped. Two with shower cost 295f and four with bath 350f. P.d. is 35f.

LAVENTIE 62840 Pas-de-Calais.
33 km E of Lille

A rather grim little northern town in which to find such a treasure:

NEW ➤ Le Cerisier (R)M and S
3 rue de la Gare (0)3.21.27.60.59; fax (0)3.21.65.35.85 Cl. Sun. p.m. Mon. and Sat. lunch

Eric Delerue learned his trade with Marc Meurin at Béthune - see p.69 and it shows. He has been cooking in his own delightful little restaurant for twelve years now and has readily adopted the Meurin trademarks of impeccably fresh ingredients, local where possible, and imaginative flavour combinations. The noticeable difference is in the price. To be able to sample cooking like this for peanuts (lunch Tues.-Fri.) would alone merit a cross-Channel venture. Go on - it's just off the autoroute. Or at very least turn off on your way south in order to get the holiday off to a good start. Here's what to expect:

There are two formulae, gastronomic and simple. The latter is served in a pretty little room painted appropriately cerise and known as La Griotte. Take the *plat du jour* and you will pay a mere 39f. For us it was a *filet mignon* and *gratin dauphinois*, both perfect. Alternatively there are, sensibly, just four *entrées* and four *plats* on the *à la carte* menu, costing 29f and 55f respectively. Try the local dish *tourte au fromage* and top it up with a *mignon de porc à la moutarde*, or, if you're saving your appetite, order just one dish, even a starter, and there will be no raised eyebrows. A platter of good cheeses or a home-made dessert costs 20f and coffee the least I have paid in France recently - 8f.

The gastronomic restaurant, Le Cerisier, has a yellow theme and is as pretty and comfortable as its neighbour. This is where Eric can show off his talents without too much price restriction. Nevertheless the 150f menu is astonishing value. A *ragout* of baby asparagus is served with orange hollandaise sauce, seabass is topped with grated truffle and served on a base of potato *purée* whipped with olive oil and garlic. Roast pigeon is twinned with breasts of smoked duck and *carré d'agneau* is basted with honey. Exquisite desserts show off his skill as a *pâtissier*.

Don't go in a hurry because everything is cooked to order. Charming young Madame Delerue will help to make the waiting time fly.

Arrowed for excellent food of one-star-Michelin quality, with non-Michelin-star prices. Go soon.

LUMBRES 62380 Pas-de-Calais.
42 km SE of Calais, 10 km SW of St. Omer.

Moulin de Mombreux (HR)L

rte de Bayenghem (0)3.21.39.62.44 and (0)3.21.39.13.13, fax (0)3.1.93.61.34

There have been many changes in the road system around Lumbres and it is approaching spaghetti junction proportions. For the first time we approached the village from the south and discovered to our surprise quite a substantial small town. I had always imagined that it was just a factory complex.

The setting - grey dusty papermills belching grey dusty effluvia into the grey dusty Pas-de-Calais - makes arrival at the Moulin all the more sensational.

No trace of industry here except a few ducks working hard to combat the force of the fast-flowing river Bléquin. Even the ancient wooden mill-wheel is at rest. The building's venerable exterior is striped with honey brick and cream stone, its green lawn and wide terrace scattered with white recliners. All is very peaceful, very colourful - the antithesis of the activity down the valley and the busy network of roads above it.

The 24 bedrooms are in an annexe, pleasantly flowery, well equipped, french windows looking across to a photo-opportunity of the old mill. 500-750f. In the annexe is a comfy lounge, bar and breakfast room.

Moulin de Mombreux.

Back in the main building the reception area centres on another bar, huge, semicircular, stone, beyond which is an open log-burning fire just by the mammoth mill-wheel. Everything twinkles - glass, brass and polished flagstones. A corkscrew staircase leads up to the restaurant, a dignified room whose rough white walls are hung with Flemish tapestries.

The cheapest menu, at 215f, includes wine, and offers three choices in each course - e.g. a *terrine* of guinea fowl stuffed with pistachios and served with a *confiture* of red onions, then a breast of chicken from Licques (just down the road), and then any item on the dessert menu. The next one up is 345f, with more sophisticated fare, like home-made *foie gras* and seabass *en croûte*.

I have always eaten well at Le Moulin, but there have been one or two dissenters - chiefly about the price - so the arrow has to go for the time being.

LA MADELAINE-SOUS-MONTREUIL 62170
5 km W of Montreuil.

A pleasant hamlet sheltering in a valley beneath the towering ramparts of Montreuil. The Canche flows wide and free here and there is usually a fisherman or two spending a patient hour on the banks.

➤ **La Grenouillère** (H)M (R)L
(0)3.21.06.07.22; fax (0)3.21.86.36.36 Cl. Tues.; Wed. o.o.s.; Jan.

At every available opportunity I find an excuse to visit The Froggery and its amiable chef-patron Roland Gauthier. I must stop describing him as youthful, since I see that he is now *quadragenaire,* but his welcoming smile is still decidedly boyish, as is his untiring enthusiasm for cooking and interesting ingredients.

For the first time I recently managed a July visit and I had been looking forward to dining on the terrace of his utterly charming whitewashed Picard erstwhile farmhouse. On previous out-of-season occasions it had understandably been impracticable but surely in July... Well we all know what kind of summer '98 proved to be and although the flowers bloomed bravely and the white tables and chairs were waiting for customers, the terrace was just as windswept as it had been in November.

So inside it had to be. No hardship whatsoever. Cosiness and warmth instead of chill. Even the frogs were smiling (for those unfortunates who have never visited La Grenouillère, the restaurant takes its name from the caricatures on the dark varnished walls of La Fontaine's fable of the frog who wished he were a bull and ate so much that he exploded, to the dismay of his lady frog companion - a recommendation for *nouvelle cuisine* if ever there was one).

Fresh flowers casually arranged as though they had just been picked, gleaming copper, uneven flagged floors, all add to the rustic ambience. There is nothing casual or rustic, however, about the place settings and the service - both highly polished, as is befitting a Michelin-starred establishment.

There are three menus: *Mer & Terre* for 290f, *Dégustation* for 400f and *du Terroir* for 190f, which is such good value we rarely look elsewhere. I learned a new word - *Crème Froide à l'Ortie du Marais* is a chilled cream soup flavoured with nettles. Trust Roland to make good use of every conceivable ingredient that his beloved region can produce. The photograph on the front of his brochure depicts him hoeing his *potager,* and herbs and infantile vegetables are always prominent in his cooking.

Then the star course of the meal - a *Risotto aux Crustaces et Brunoise de Légumes de Saison,* a risotto perfumed with shellfish and served with tiny broad beans and carrots. Course three was sucking pig, skin caramelised, aromatic spices cutting the richness. Then, after a refreshing *sorbet,* a *millefeuille* of strawberries, which are a speciality of the region, cream scented with thyme.

This four-course menu - six if you count the *amuses bouches* and the *sorbet,* is obviously good value, but be prepared for a costly wine list, on which there is no opportunity to economise.

The value continues with the lodging. All four rooms were predictably occupied in July so I could not see the redecoration that Roland assured me had improved them still further. I hardly think it matters - they were all so attractive and comfortable last time I stayed there. There are two doubles at 380f, one with twins at 450f and a flat which sleeps two adults with three children for 550f. All have luxurious bathrooms, so it's not surprising that you have to be quick off the mark to book one. It's an ideal combination with a memorable meal and breakfast, with any luck, on the terrace, to the sound of birds and rushing water. During the winter (not Saturday) you get a room thrown in if you tackle the 400f menu.

Arrowed for some of the best cooking in the region.

Auberge du Vieux Logis (R)S-M
pl. de la Mairie (0)3.21.06.10.92 Cl. Mon.; 8 days in Feb., 8 days in Oct.
This is where the locals go if they want an unpretentious evening out. It's an extremely pretty cottagey building dating from 1859, on the corner of a bend of the D139. Outside are plenty of tables, well-patronised in fine weather for drinks as well as meals. All very peaceful and countrified. Inside the tiny rustic dining room it's as archetypally French as you could wish for, with red-and-white checked table-cloths and low beams.

Véronique and Étienne Boutin have been owners here for nearly eight years; Etienne likes to cook classical French dishes like his *cassoulet maison,* prepared every day. Menus from 80 to 170f feature veal kidneys, grills, and just a nod to more recent favourites like a *carpaccio* of raw fish. Nice atmosphere, nice people, all contribute to happy eaters.

> MAINTENAY 62870 Pas-de-Calais
>
> 2 km S of Montreuil, 40 km SE of Boulogne

To get in the right rustic mood, turn off the main road south from Montreuil and take the D139E through Écuires, Boisjean and Roussent past whitewashed farmhouses, through fields of corn and poppies, into dark woods, then turn left onto the D119, where lines of willow follow the river Authie.

Turn right to the Moulin, beyond the church, into an avenue of poplars festooned with mistletoe, past lakes on both sides and elegant Charolais cattle munching the rich pastures.

▶ **Le Moulin de Maintenay** (R)S
open 12-9 p.m. (0)3.21.90.43.74

The moulin has come up in the world since I first wrote about the enchanting scene of creaky waterwheel churning, lilies floating, and café serving lunchtime crêpes. Now it merits a mention in Gault-Millau and is altogether more sophisticated, in an artfully simple way. Pretty though the interior is, with all kinds of home-made goodies on sale in the shop, the terrace is the place to be. Here white tables, parasol shaded, directly overlook the water and nothing but that word idyllic will do for the scene.

Try one of Maître Paul's specialities, *Rhubarbois,* at 16f a glass and snack elegantly on not only *crêpes* and *galettes* but quiches and *salades composées.* Just the thing for lunch on a hot day, but very agreeable too, early on a fine summer's evening.

Arrowed for unique charm.

There are organised tours of the 12C mill, describing its history from the time it belonged to the abbey at Valloires and its function. You can visit from 10-12 and from 2-9 p.m. for 24f but phone first to check that there is not a group at the same time.

> MARQUENTERRE. Somme.
>
> 60km S of Boulogne, East of Rue, south of Fort-Mahon Plage

Marquenterre the sea (*mar*) that (*que*) enters (*ent*) the land (*terre*). Well-named indeed. Here the opalescent light that gives the Côte d'Opale its name does indeed have the effect of merging sea, land and sky. Sand dunes stretch to the horizon with no clear boundaries. Mud flats provide the perfect habitat for all manner of birds.

Parc Ornithologique du Marquenterre
St. Quentin-en-Tourmont (0)3.22 25.03.06

I strongly recommend an outing here for both bird-fanciers and beginners alike, especially for kids who might well become addicts after spotting spoonbills and cranes, using the hides that are dotted about the 5,000 acre reserve, and counting some of the 300 species that are known to drop in on their way to warmer/colder climes. Binoculars are provided and the whole enterprise is admirably well organised. Help-yourself restaurant on site.

Open daily March 20th to November 14th, 9.30-7. Admission 42f; concessions 32f.

MARQUISE 62250 Pas-de-Calais.
13 km NE of Boulogne
M Thurs.

For years I imagined that Marquise began and ended along the *nationale*. I now know that behind the Grand Cerf is a quieter Marquise, centred around a market square.

Le Grand Cerf (R)M-L
(0)3.21.87.55.05; fax (0)3.21.33.61.09 Cl. Sun. p.m. Mon.

For serious eating by serious eaters. You do not drop in here for a snack. Echoes of le Grand Cerf's glorious past, when it justified a Michelin star, still remain. Generations of Englishmen have taken nourishment here before toiling down the old main route to the capital, ever since doors first opened as a *relais de diligence* - a posting stop for carriages. The place is very conscious of it's illustrious past; the stone bench where Victor Hugo rested in 1837 is proudly *in situ* at the entrance.

Stéphane Pruvot too has an impressive past. His previous cooking experience was at the Côte St. Jacques in Joigny, of three-star fame.

Not surprising that his style is strongly traditional, but he insists on adding regional touches, like stuffed pancakes served with a beer-flavoured sauce, ox cheek again with beer, and chicory as a spice. This is what his customers ask for, but he is not afraid to experiment occasionally, with more exotic combinations, like his cauliflower mousse served with giant prawns gently curried. Fish, local of course, is predictably big - turbot is served with *petits gris*.

Menus start at 95f. This is high quality at reasonable prices, and if I do not award an arrow, perhaps it is because the establishment seems to lack a woman's touch - a touch of *tristesse* maybe. No feed-back from readers hasn't helped. However, if you bring your own atmosphere and rate the cooking as of paramount importance, you will relish Le Grand Cerf.

MOLINGHEM 62330 Pas-de-Calais.
9km SE of Aire-sur-la-Lys by D188

All very confusing - Molinghem runs into Isbergues which runs into Berguettes. It is the station of Molinghem that you are aiming for.

➤ Le Buffet (H)S (R)M

22 rue de la Gare (0)3.21.25.82.40 Cl. Sun. p.m.; Mon. 1/8-22/8

Well, who would have thought it. This indeed was once the station buffet but that would be hard to guess in its reincarnation as one of the most attractive restaurants in the district. It has swapped dinginess for pastels - peach and almond green - white painted beams, and bleached wood, resulting in pleasing lightness and brightness.

With the aperitif white-jacketed waiters brought little stuffed cherry tomatoes and, during menu-perusal, a mouthful of delicate cauliflower soup sprinkled with crab in a tiny white porcelain pot.

There's a commendable 80f menu mid-day but for dinner I had to go mad and fork out 100f for three courses on the *Le Terroir* menu and husband staked even more on the *Le Gourmand* version at 158f. I've noticed before that the youthful Thierry Wident has a penchant for *petits gris* (small snails); perhaps he knows where to find a good supply in his garden. Sure enough, here they were again, this time in a risotto. And very good too, with shreds of leeks and deep fried chervil as a garnish. The parmesan was the expensive fresh shaven kind not the dried stuff out of a plastic shaker. Husband's menu yielded very tender Licques chicken, braised with mushrooms and an unusually good selection of *petits farcis de l'été*, in other words seasonal vegetables stuffed with breadcrumbs and lots of garlic.

Christine Wident is a welcoming efficient hostess; she makes no bones about the fact that the restaurant is their first love and that the bedrooms are mere accessories. They are clean but very small and cost a modest 180f.

Readers have unanimously enthused about the set-up here, so the arrow stays.

MONTREUIL SUR MER 62170 Pas-de-Calais.
38 km S of Boulogne
M Sat.

Hard to credit nowadays, when Montreuil, perched on an escarpment, looks down on miles of fertile countryside, that indeed it was once 'sur mer'. In fact, in the days when the kings of France controlled very few provinces, it was France's only royal port. Now the estuary of the Canche has silted up and there are ten miles or so between sea and town.

A glimpse of the sea can still be snatched if you look hard enough in the right direction from the ramparts that surround the town, and a walk around them is a very good idea in any case. It takes 40 minutes to complete the circuit, high above the weathered roofs and cobbled streets, but there are numerous narrow alleys along the way, down which to escape if it's all a bit breezy up there. The view is over rolling farmlands, the valley of the Canche, the lighthouse marking the estuary, Le Touquet and Étaples and the old monastery of Notre Dame des Prés. Consider the cobwebs blown away.

With the advent of the autoroute there is now a choice of four roughly parallel roads approaching the town from the north. The coast road, the D940, runs through the sand dunes and forest of Hardelot and crosses the river at the old fishing village of Étaples; next comes the A16 which whisks you into Boulogne in no time, then the N1, which used to be lorry-loaded but might be relieved now, and then, for those who have time on their hands and enjoy the journey as much as the destination, the D127, following the valley of the Course (see p.101).

As you cross the river, wind up the steep hill to the town, and drive under the bridge, the oldest part of the town presents itself; the cavée St. Firmin, picturesquely cobbled with 17th-century cottages clinging precariously to its slopes, will be familiar from many a postcard.

First comes the little place Darnétal, flower-bedecked, fountain-spraying, tree-lined, and behind it the former church of St. Saulve, part 12th century, with flamboyant Gothic nave. Montreuil takes its name from the original monastery (monasteriolum) founded here in the 7C by St. Saulve, Bishop of Amiens.

Follow the Grande Rue to park in the Grande Place, where Douglas Haig, who had his WW1 headquarters here, is commemorated by a statue. And Grande the Place certainly is, spacious enough to accommodate the colourful Saturday market, which is just one more reason why Montreuil is a good weekend-break idea. Around the square are plenty of coffee/beer opportunities, and an excellent picnic-supplier, M. Vasseur. *"Outstanding range of delicious dishes are made on the premises every day. We tried two of M. Vasseur's pâtés, some mini-quiches and a local speciality, potje vleisch, a cold dish made from veal, chicken, pork and rabbit. The bread came from the Boulangerie Coulon in the Place Darnétal and delicious that was too"*. Roger Davies.

The charm of this peaceful old town has always appealed to artists and writers, and anyone who has seen *Les Miserables* will know that Jean Valjean, having attained respectability, became mayor of Montreuil. Victor Hugo had visited the town in 1837 and it obviously impressed him so much that he decided to use it as the setting for one of the main episodes in his book. Laurence Sterne, author of *A Sentimental Journey through France and Italy,* lodged at the old coaching inn, the Hotel de France in the 18th century (see below).

Of recent years there have been many changes in Montreuil and nowadays it has become somewhat of a gastro-centre, with more than its share of hotels and restaurants to choose from. So near the beaches, so easily approached from the ports, on the way to Paris, in lovely countryside, it would be my No. 1 choice for a short break in the area.

Château de Montreuil (HR)L
4 Chausée Capucins (0)3.21.81.53.04. fax.(0)3.21.81.36.43 R cl., Mon from Sept to May; Thurs lunch throughout the year. H and R cl. 15/12-6/2.

How lucky we Brits are to have a luxurious bolthole like the Château de Montreuil waiting to pamper us just across the Channel. How lucky too that Lindsey and Christian Germain never rest on their considerable laurels but just go on making this little bit of paradise more and more heavenly. And in case you think this eulogy is totally o.t.t. (or that I'm being paid to write it!) I shall now get over and done with the single criticism that crops up is occasionally in the pile of praise - i.e. that the château is full of Brits. Just tell me how one could avoid that, when it has been an Anglo-haven for so many years, even before the Germain regime, and word of mouth continues to do a better job than any advertising. It is, after all, far and away the most comfortable hotel in the region, with superb cooking thrown in, so what do you expect? Lindsay is very conscious of the problem and tries hard to get a continental mix, but with contented customers reserving a year ahead, she has her work cut out.

At least half the credit for the Chateau's popularity must be attributed to Lindsay, who looks after the hotel bit while Christian cooks. 'The English Rose' as the French guidebooks tend to describe her, provides not only the perfect reception - smiles, warm welcome for her new customers, remembering the names of old ones - but is also an extremely efficient housekeeper. No detail, however small, escapes her scrutiny, and, just as Christian runs cooking seminars, she could handle one on how to run the perfect hotel.

Château de Montreuil.

As usual, most of the rooms were occupied (book well ahead if you have a favourite), but she showed me round some of the newer (and cheaper) ones in the annexe, all of which were perfectly delightful. Good sized, furnished with Laura Ashley fabrics and pleasant furniture and with luxurious marble bathrooms. Then of course I had to peek at some of the old favourites - the one with the four poster and the copper-ceilinged bathroom is understandably the American's favourite. They are all different, but each one would stand up to the test - if you want to make sure your guests are comfortable try sleeping in the guestroom. I wouldn't put it past Lindsay to have done that.

Back at reception, an elderly couple, regular visitors, were departing. While his wife settled in the car, her husband nipped back for a farewell kiss from Lindsey.

The Château is a rare example of food perfectly complementing bed. Usually either the restaurant or the hotel dominates; here they are perfectly in harmony. Christian Germain, Roux protégé, continues to be in fine fettle. It must be hard to stay as passionate about one's metier for as long as he has but the cuisine shows no sign of fade. Insisting on the finest, freshest ingredients, as many as possible from local sources, he and his second, Laurent Collin, experiment with new combinations and techniques, never resorting to clichés, as do so many traditional French chefs. I have never had a bad meal at the château and neither, according to my postbag, have any readers. You can rest assured that his cheapest menu, 300f in the evening, 200f or 270f inclusive of wine for lunch, will be a treat, but if you really want to see what he can do, go for the *dégustation* menu, where you trust the team to tease and delight your taste buds for 400f.

Some of my favourites: *tartare de concombre et huitres de pleine mer, pressé de légumes de saison, vinaigrette de tapenade,* then for a main course *tronçons de lotte en croûte d'herbes sur palette de poivrons,* or *filet de canette de barbarie en croûte de sésamé, jus aux navets et gingembre.* For dessert: *Minestrone de fruits glacés à la feuille déstragon, sorbet au yaourt de brébis,* or *larme de chocolat blanc, abricot rôti à la vanille Bourbon, sauce amande amère.* All these feature on the 300f Menu Carte.

The dining room, freshly decorated in blue and yellow, with swags of dried flowers, looks out on to the new swimming pool, surrounded by expensive recliners, and the terrace, where summer sipping is the perfect preface to the meal. The gardens are leafy and extensive, and like the building itself, in the *style Anglaise.* You could be in Weybridge, but I bet you're glad you're not.

13 rooms cost from 760-1,010f, demi-pension from 825-875f per person, but there are all kinds of special deals, from two nights *gastronomique* break to a special mid-week out of season offer, which is particularly good value. Check with Lindsey Germain. Cookery breaks are for three days for groups of six people, out of season, three mornings in the kitchen, three dinners, B&B, one wine tasting, around 3,000-4,000f per person.

"We again stayed at the château, where we tend to go every six months, and it was absolutely fabulous. The service was absolutely wonderful. I had the wonderful boulognaise scallops as one of the courses on the menu gastronomique and they were the best scallops I have ever tasted. Also the foie gras was wonderful, the first night served with cabbage and red cherry beer and the second night with baby rhubarb. My wife has many allergies and she was looked after very well; this included croissants being made without any egg, no eggwash on the bread and on the menu gastronomique there were certain dishes prepared just for her, as she cannot eat any fish. There was no extra charge for this." Jonathan Paul Diamond.

> **Hotel de France** (H)M
rue Coquempot (0)3.21.06.05.36
Patronne Janie Hall has achieved the near-impossible. She has integrated herself into Montreuil society, from dustman to *duc,* and endeared herself to them so thoroughly that they are able to forget and forgive the fact that she

Montreuil.

is not French, and taken her to their hearts. Her cosy bar is the favoured rendezvous for *le tout monde*, and if there are Montreuil politics to be discussed (there usually are) she is there in the heart of the action.

It's not hard to see why Janie is so popular. She is warm and friendly and always has time for a chat. She tells me that her clients nowadays are 80% repeats. On my last visit there were a boisterous party of golfers, who stay with her at least twice a year, and a foursome who had got into the habit of dropping in whenever they flew their private plane from Birmingham to Le Touquet.

But here is a hazard warning. Do not even think of staying in the Hotel de France if your ideal is conventional mod cons, sanitised, sterilised and safe. This is a very idiosyncratic establishment, with Janie's somewhat bohemian personality stamped on every inch.

Take the décor for example. Not everyone warms to such an abundance of plastic flowers, red, orange and yellow, playing such a large part in the decoration, nor the daze of blue and gold painted walls embellished with pineapple stencils. In the huge breakfast room, appropriately equipped with a stage and piano, erratically paint-spattered canvas flaps, as though someone had lost inspiration halfway through. There are baubles, gold ivy leaves, stars on ceilings, posters, antlers, African drums, tambourines, and a hat-stand overflowing with assorted garments (whose? abandoned?) our friends described their loo as psychedelic and very pink with it (but were delightedly bemused with the whole set-up). Our shower curtain first resisted all attempts to draw and then came away in our hands, and the towels were off-white scratchy.

But consider the positive touches - fresh flowers in all the bedrooms, mineral water and bon-bons, deep comfortable chintzy armchairs in the bar/lounge and above all Janie dispensing welcomes, smiles and alcohol.

A mural in the courtyard commemorates Laurence Sterne's stay in the old coaching inn. In summer, this is the place to sit with a glass or three, on the cobbles, among the miscellaneous pots and tubs full of colour. (Admittedly it wasn't looking quite so attractive during our April visit, when Janie hadn't quite got around to sorting out all the winter debris.) Sadly the useful connection with the restaurant across the courtyard has foundered and further association is doubtful, but there is no shortage of alternatives in the town.

This is a love-it-or-hate-it entry. Readers have been divided 80/20 in favour, but they did have my cautionary description to weed out the doubters in advance. I would advise choosing your room carefully, because some are on the bend of a noisy road and have only mediocre showers, while the best are quieter, lighter, and have bathrooms. You may have to book well in advance.

Rooms from 350-500f

Arrowed for personality.

Les Hauts de Montreuil (RH)M
21 rue Pierre Ledent (0)3.21.81.95.93; fax (0)3.21.86.28.83 Cl. 2/1-6/2

The oldest building in Montreuil, dating from 1537. Ridiculously picturesque in traditional black and white, with plentiful beams and flowers. Behind the façade is a modern hotel, the antithesis of the quirky Hotel de France. The rooms have been cleverly contrived round a courtyard, complete with fountain. We drew the short straw and got the one on the ground floor next to the tradesmen's entrance. Not much hope of sleep after dustmen, deliveries and laundry services started work at dawn. Tip! - avoid room no.1.

Parking is in the two narrow wings of the courtyard, involving some tricky manoeuvring if your car is parked first. It all worked out very smoothly during our visit, but it does assume a lot of goodwill from guests being asked to move their vehicles to allow access.

The rooms are excellent - surprisingly spacious and well-equipped with big double beds and a good bathroom. Breakfast is served in a converted stable, and a superb breakfast - or rather brunch; tuck into smoked salmon, pâté, ham, eggs, melon, strawberries, pineapple, compôtes of berries, cheeseboard, yoghurt, twenty different home-made jams and the usual pâtisserie and French bread and there should be little need for lunch expenditure. Only the mindless pop spoiled the perfect harmony. As every breakfaster was at least middle-aged (and British) I would have thought Ole Blue Eyes would have been more appropriate than youth-appeasing wail and thump.

The hirsute M. Gantiez is a hands-on *patron*, running his establishment with total efficiency and marketing it diligently. In the 16C caves beneath the hotel he offers wine-tasting (preferably followed by wine-buying) and a range of well-cared-for cheeses for sale, as are other *produits regionaux*, which guests can select as classy take-home presents. Fifteen wines are available by the glass (rare in France) so anyone like me, who thinks the perfect lunch is a platter of cheeses and a glass of red, will score here. The bar makes a cosy meeting place to partake of such a snack if the tables outside in the courtyard do not appeal.

The cheapest menu, termed *'Terroir'* is 150f, featuring *flamiche montreuilloise* - a pie filled with cheese, smoked breast of duck and leeks, or there is *l'assiette du saurisseur, tartare de brébis desgrange aux salicornes*, which should cause a few puzzled brows. Let me translate - a plate of smoked fish, with marinated kid and seaweed. An appealing third course option is a trilogy of regional farm cheeses served with a walnut salad. Other menus at 185 and 245f.

27 rooms cost 430f (shower) or 500f (bath). Breakfast is an additional 65f per person, making this a pricey stop, but it is very popular and booked well ahead.

➤ Le Darnétal (HR)M
pl. Darnétal (0)3.21.06.04.87; fax (0)3.21.86.64.67 Cl. Mon.p.m; Tues. 1st week in July

Everybody loves the Darnétal, established on the corner of a pretty, be-limed, be-fountained, be-geraniummed square for over a century. It's all very neat, very freshly painted, very French, with brown shutters and overflowing windowboxes and tables outside for summer imbibing. Indoors not a lot has changed, thank goodness. There's still a lovely warm cosy atmosphere, generated by bright red tablecloths, lots of flowers and polished old furniture.

Chef-*patron* Jean-Paul Verney sticks with trad. French. Expect to find fresh local fish, plenty of oysters, hot and cold, ragouts, and good pastry on his menus, which start at 95f (go for it), (not weekends). Others at 140 and 190f.

The Darnétal cooking is generally acclaimed as among the best in the town, with special mention made of his oysters in champagne sauce. "*Simply the best dish I have eaten in France. This should be double or even triple arrowed*".

A relatively new innovation are the four bedrooms, each one different, furnished in vaguely *Belle Epoque* style. No telephone, no telly, just a lot of comfort, plenty of space and a good night's sleep after an intensely satisfying meal. 220-300f.

Numerous testimonials to the credit of le Darnétal and utter reliability earn it an arrow.

NEW ➤ Le Clos des Capucins (HR)M
46 place du Général-de-Gaulle (0)3.21.06.08.65; fax (0)3.21.81.20.45 Cl. Sun. p.m.; Mon.

Jean-Luc Bigot installed his *sous-chef* in his former premier restaurant, Le Relais du Roy (which subsequently closed down) and transferred his main operation to the main square. Here he and his wife have smartened up the hotel part of the old Les Remparts, and now the bedrooms are attractively furnished with cane beds and pastel floral prints and equipped with modern bathrooms. At the rear of the hotel is an unexpected sheltered terrace, a very pleasant spot for summer breakfasts.

Jean-Luc's skill in the kitchen is well-documented and now the combination of his culinary talents with comfortable bedrooms in the town centre merits an arrow.

Rooms at 340f. Menus at 90f, 140f (recommended) and 180f.

NEW Hotel Bellevue (HR)S

6 Ave du 11 Novembre. (0)3.21.06.04.19; fax (0)3.21.81.01.94

The Bellevue was always prominent, situated as it is on the hill winding up to the town, but now it is impossible to miss, since the new owners, a young English-speaking couple who have lived in America and Madagascar, have adopted the colours of Montreuil - blue and yellow - and painted the whole hotel, inside and out, in various combinations of those two hues. It's good to see the old hotel brought back to life from former shabbiness.

All the bedrooms have been re-decorated, some more blue and some more yellow, and new bathrooms installed. Further rooms were being contrived from the sheer rock behind the hotel last time I visited. The obvious question for a hotel in this site is "Are they noisy?" and the obvious answer from the *patron* is, "Not now they are double-glazed and in any case the heavy lorries do not toil up the hill after dark."

The bar is usually busy with locals and there is a welcoming fire in the adjoining dining room whenever appropriate, so the atmosphere is altogether cheerful. The enthusiastic *patron* is very proud of his food, and certainly the value is there, especially if you take advantage of the special weekend break prices (enquire within).

Rooms from 290-380f, menus from 85f-149f.

➤ Le Coquempot (R)M

2 pl. de la Poissonnerie (0)3.21.81.05.61; fax (0)3.21.86.46.73 Cl. Mon.; Sun. p.m. o.o.s.

The responsibility was dreadful. Being asked to select the perfect venue for a friend's important birthday dinner is bad enough for anyone, but for those of us who claim to know a thing or two about French restaurants, it was asking for trouble. I need not have worried. Le Coquempot rose to the occasion admirably, as it rises to any occasion, from a romantic table for two amongst the flowers in the enchanting new terrace garden, to a boisterous party of twelve like ourselves.

I was delighted to find this delightful restaurant, with equally delightful young owners, just in time for FE12, and staked my reputation on guessing it would be a winner without any more back-up than my own instinct on good vibes. Since then the plaudits have amply supported the gamble. There have been a few changes, but all of them good ones, like the terrace. The young Poussets have gained in confidence; she is just as modest and retiring but even more quietly efficient at welcoming and taking orders, and he is not afraid to extend his repertoire.

The exterior of the tall 19th-century, typically French, house in the square is now softened by abundant geraniums trailing from nine window boxes. Inside the two dining rooms windows are high, oak floors are polished, napery, wallpaper and curtains are peachy. It remains a dignified gentleman's house, and perhaps first impressions are a touch stuffy, but Madame Pousset soon dispels any inhibitions.

We ate off the set 155f menu and every one of our party was incredulous at the modesty of the eventual bill. Each item on the menu was sampled - mussels and clams stuffed with sauerkraut and garnished with smoked salmon; marinated salmon flavoured with dill and Guérande salt; livers of chicken, duck and goose. Main courses were '*coq du cocquempot*' (Coquempot is a corruption of *coq au pot*), garlicky lamb *noisettes,* or cod cooked *en papillote*. Third course was cheeses, before a selection of desserts. Thumbs up all round.

A great pleasure to re-award this arrow, for fine cooking, pleasant surroundings, delightful owners, and good value.

LA MOTTE-AU-BOIS
59190 Hazebrouck Nord. 5 km S of Hazebrouck on the D946

The countryside around here is deep and green, with the Forest of Nieppe and the banks of the river Lys providing good picnicking/walking possibilities.

Auberge de la Forêt (HR)M
(0)3.28.48.08.78; fax (0)3.28.40.77.76 Cl. Sun. p.m.; Mon.; 26/12-16/1

There is an air of opulency about this large chalet-type building nowadays. The restaurant is very grand, with tapestry chairs, draped curtains, big stone fireplace and smart waiters. M. and Mme Bécu have been here for many years and have been steadily improving their property. The 12 bedrooms have all been agreeably renovated and cost a reasonable 320f. As they are nearly always fully booked, you should not arrive on chance.

Prices have increased substantially. The cheapest menu, now 135f (not Sunday) offered *rillettes maison, contrefilet rôtie aux oignons* and dessert. There is also a midweek *suggestion du jour* for 70f. Other menus are from 165-275f.

Until recently there was nothing but praise for the set-up - comfortable rooms and excellent cooking. Unfortunately the praise for the latter had dried up of late and I hear the odd grumble about short cuts. This is very bad news for the l'Auberge because it is essentially a restaurant with rooms rather than the other way round and its reputation hinges on the cuisine. Let's hope that this is only a temporary hiccup and that the arrow that would have been assured a year ago can be restored soon.

Auberge de la Foret   La Motte-au-Bois

NOEUX-LES-MINES 62990 Pas-de-Calais.
5 km S of Béthune

As its name indicates, a mining town, with plenty of evidence, in the shape of surrounding slag tips, of the local industry. The main streets, however, seem prosperous and clean, with an astonishing preponderance of furniture and home decorating shops. Why should this be, I wonder?

Les Tourterelles (HR)M
374 Route Nationale (0)3.21.66.90.75; fax (0)3.21.26.98.98 R cl. Sat. lunch, Sun. p.m. and fêtes

More astonishment to find an establishment called The Doves perched on the main road of a mining town, and more astonishment again to find it peaceful and altogether charming.

The nice old white building is set well back from the traffic hazard in a sizeable, well-maintained garden. Inside are high ceilings and a sense of the elegance of the time it was built - a century or so ago I would guess. The dining room is welcoming and warm - panelled walls, pink cloths, and a white grand piano (but I forgot to ask when it got played). Chef Noel Verbrugge likes to introduce regional recipes and ingredients from Flanders and Artois on his menus at 135 and 165f but on the former we stuck to the more familiar avocado and shrimps and then salmon escalope and '*sorbet du jour*'. The menus don't excite on first reading, but the quality is high and the portions generous. Good carafe wine.

There are 21 well-furnished and comfortable bedrooms, with a bathroom apiece, at 250-350f. Management is helpful and friendly and there is private parking. Altogether a good deal in an unexpected quarter.

Les Tourterelles.

PETIT FORT-PHILIPPE 59820 Pas-de-Calais.
20 km E of Calais

On the eastern side of the estuary of the Aa. On the other side is Grand Fort - Philippe, with gravelly beach, benches for picnics, marshes, fish market and bizarre gabled lifeboat station. They were both named after King Philippe II of Spain. In 1557 his army had beaten the French troops at St. Quentin and in the following year they repeated their success at Gravelines and Henri II was forced to admit defeat. Philippe constructed the splendid lock in Petit Fort-Philippe and the twin towns took on his name.

On both sides of the estuary the walks are superb - miles of fabulous sand and endless skies. In P.T.P. walk out on the beach, along the prom, or out towards the often invisible sea on the breakwater - the best leg-stretch and ozone gulp imaginable. The sands are so firm that the local footballers have their pitch and goalposts thereon. There's another pleasant short walk along the river bank, good for watching the colourful boats. Plenty of benches for picnicking.

There's an important lighthouse here and I love the lighthouse-keeper's cottage, all spic and span and painted blue and white. The keeper was digging his spruce little garden and planting out his vegetables. Not many lighthouse keepers can do that.

Appropriately along the river frontage is a series of fish restaurants, all very popular for a fine weekend outing, with tables outside to catch the sun. You can hardly go wrong with a plateful of *moules* or a fine sole, but the two special recommendations are:

NEW L'Arlequin (R)M-S
Bvd de l'Est (0)3.28.65.56.04 Cl. Mon. o.o.s.

A tiny narrow restaurant, looking very fresh with its green-and-white banquettes. There are 80 and 98f menus but I preferred the 120f *menu du poisson*, which produced an interesting *gratin de moules* with leeks, an immaculately fresh cod fillet in *beurre blanc*, a hot goat's cheese and salad and a good home-made apple tart.

NEW La Matelote (R)M
Bvd de l'Est (0)3.28.65.47.94

Almost next door, larger, more tables outside. Their 98f menu offered, for example, six oysters, an *entrecôte* steak, cheese and dessert. Had it not been Sunday it would have been 76f, for *soupe de poisson*, a *moussaka de poisson* and dessert. Meat featured too - for 135f you could desert the prevailing fishiness after a first course of *gratin* of crab and feast on a baron of lamb.

Or of course settle just for a dozen oysters for a mere 70f. With a glass of Chablis and some good bread, what better lunch?

"A plâteau de fruits de mer was followed by dorade in a nouvelle-ish cuisine sauce, with toasted cheese and baked fruits for afters. A Muscadet accompanied the meal, with the patron adding local gin with the coffee." Bob Smyth.

PONCHES-ESTRUVAL 80150 Somme.
14 km SW of Hesdin

Take the D136 out of Hesdin to a particularly pretty unspoiled region. If tourists bother to explore the river Authie at all they usually stop short at Argoules or Saulchoy. If they went a few km further they would arrive in the hamlet of Ponches which seems to run into Estruval, the combined names being a very grand title for a very small village.

NEW La Table de Ferme (R)S

(0)3.22.23.54.02 Cl. 15/11-1/3 Cl. Sun. p.m.; Mon.; weekdays from 10/9-15/11 (i.e. open Fri. p.m. Sat. lunch and evening and Sun. lunch)

We turned off the road and drove into the kind of rusticity that has not changed for centuries. This is a *real* farm that does a bit of tourist business on the side, not the other way round. Nothing cosmetic about the muddy courtyard nor the crumbling, whitewashed (but not recently) barns surrounding it. Low and picturesque, with photogenic dove lofts, they would make a property dealer's eyes glisten for their development potential.

No-one around to answer my banging on the ancient door of the main farmhouse, so I pushed it open and peeked inside. It looked like a stage setting, with scrubbed pine tables, a big log fire with smoke hood, copper pans and a clock stopped at 2.15. No artifice, just the way farm folk live.

Still no-one around, so a case for more exploring. I investigated the next door barn and found an attractive young woman mucking out. No less than Odile Testu, who runs the place, both farm and cooking. She told me that she uses only her own produce. That means you get whatever is ready that day. There could be no better formula. For example, the set meal, after a complimentary aperitif, might include a duck *terrine,* an omelette made with orange-yoked farm eggs and flavoured with sorrel, then farm chicken, duck or guinea fowl, salad, a range of cheeses from different local farmers served with home-made bread and farm butter, a fruit tart, cider or beer for 91f. You should telephone ahead to reserve.

I love the feel of the place and would be delighted to award an arrow if someone will confirm my impressions.

PONT-DE-BRIQUES 62360 Pas-de-Calais.
5 km S of Boulogne by D940

Boulogne sprawls all the way to Pont-de-Briques, which must once have been an independent village but is now virtually a suburb.

Hostellerie de la Rivière (R)L
rue Gare (0)3.21.32.22.81; fax (0)3.21.87.45.48 Cl. Mon. p.m. Sun.; 16/8-6/9

An unlikely spot to find a Michelin-starred restaurant, but it must work because the Martin family has been cooking here for two generations, and the accolades keep on coming. The recipe has been refined and improved over the years, with re-decoration of the restaurant and rooms; in the kitchen there has been acknowledgement of lighter culinary textures and even recognition of foreign influences and ingredients. The accent is on fish, fresh from the boats, with some sophisticated accents, like a celeriac *confit* with haddock, bass with bacon, but meat does get a look in - witness one of the star turns - braised hare. Menus start at 160f.

The rooms are small but perfectly formed, and very comfortable, each one differently decorated, all with bath or shower. As this is emphatically a restaurant-with-rooms I would not advise trying to book a room without taking dinner but, that accepted, it would be very agreeable to have only the stairs to negotiate having done justice to M. Martin's cooking and wine list (not cheap).

Eight rooms cost from 305-380f.

QUEND 80120 Pas-de-Calais.
26 km S of Le Touquet, 29 km S of Boulogne

The setting is flat windswept dunes and vast skies, with most traffic turning off the main road towards the beaches and tourist facilities of Fort Mahon Plage. (Don't bother say I.)

➤ Auberge le Fiacre (HR)M

Route de Fort Mahon, Routhiaville (0)3.21.22.23.47.30 fax (0)3.22.27.19.80

This old farmhouse, picturesquely timbered in black and white, has been converted into a luxurious hotel and upmarket restaurant. The new rooms are built round a well-kept garden, focussing on a white awning shading the many recliners tidily arranged to make the most of the sun. Lovely for al fresco breakfasts and evening drinks. Loads of charm here and in the raftered dining room, where high-backed rush-seated chairs accent the studied rusticity and expensive flowers add colour.

The bedrooms are lovely. All recently re-decorated in glazed chintzes, all with luxurious bathrooms, excellent value at 380f. In July, when most other hotels were heaving, there were still rooms available here, probably because it is so remote or perhaps because its recent upgrading has not been noticed yet.

The Fiacre would make a soothing oasis of calm after a busy day, or an excellent base for exploring the Marquenterre Ornithological Park, the abbeys of Valloires and St. Riquier, Crécy, and the often overlooked town of Rue. Arrowed for inexpensive luxury.

RUE 80120 Somme,
24 km NW of Abbeville, 54 km S of Boulogne

I never cease to wonder at the contrasts in the region covered in this book. There are some amazing one-offs - Cassel, Le Touquet, Bergues, Montreuil and Rue, all as different as chalk from cheese from one another and anything else. Rue is surprising simply because it is a typical French market town and there aren't many of them in this tourist/seaside/British-dominated area.

It is the capital of the Marquenterre. No big deal you might say. But once, before 5 km of silt intervened between it and the coast, Rue was an important seaport and if I try hard enough I like to think I can still detect a salty flavour in the air. Stronghold of the Counts of Ponthieu, it also prospered as the site of a pilgrimage centred on the tomb of St. Vulphy and of a crucifix borne by an unmanned boat and said to have been discovered under the house of Nicodemus in Jerusalem. Rue's church is named after its benefactor-saint and the chapel of the St. Esprit on the north side remains a magnificent flamboyant Gothic gem, decorated with impressive statues of the evangelists, as well as more secular figures like Charlemagne and Charles VIII. Its double porch, whose doors were carved in the 15th century, is sculpted with scenes from the Passion and the Seven Sorrows of Mary. The cloister, equally rich, has statues of Louis XI and Isabeau of Portugal and carvings telling the story of the miraculous crucifix. In the interior, festooned with hanging bosses, are four nails - all that remains from the crucifix.

Whit Monday still sees a pilgrimage to the chapel. The pilgrims' hospice stands in the Grande Rue, dating from the 16C; the imposing Gothic Hotel de Ville's belfry has four round towers wearing witches' hats.

All this a few miles from the beaches! Not many people know that.

It's a surprisingly big town in this wild wind-swept corner, with wide main streets, and very important on Saturday morning when the market takes over, especially in the hunting season. Every man and boy in Picardy loves *la chasse* and shops to supply their needs are plentiful. Guns, nets, waterproofed clothing, bags and windowfuls of grey and green paraphernalia - can there really be enough huntsmen/poachers/fishermen/shooters to buy all that gear? Obviously yes. Local restaurants naturally follow the trend, especially:

Lion d'Or (HR)M
rue Barrière (0)3.22.25.74.18; fax (0)3.22.25.66.63 Cl. Sun. p.m. o.o.s.; 20/12-10/1
> Very popular with the locals, and understandably so. Inside the black-and-white façade, past the bar, is to be found a surprisingly smart restaurant, raftered and furnished with light furniture and table settings. Good solid reliable cooking on menus from 85f, with quaffable carafe wine available. In season of course there is a *menu de chasse*, which is not to be missed, especially if you haven't eaten for days.

ST AUBIN 62170. Pas-de-Calais.
8 km SE of Le Touquet by D143 and D144E, 27 km SE of Boulogne

---

The new autoroute has sliced its concrete way through this triangle of unspoiled countryside between Montreuil, Le Touquet and Berck. I feared the worst, but once one has got used to the raw gash the aspect is still peaceful, flowery and surprisingly rural. St. Aubin is one of several pretty hamlets therein.

Otherwise:
Auberge du Cronquelet (HR)S
3 rue de Montreuil (0)3.21.94.60.76 open 7 days a week.

Once the village forge, whose fireplace is still visible in the 'banquet room'. Now run by Véronique and Laurent Pérard, the latter a nephew of the more famous Pérard in Le Touquet.

There are 8 rooms, pretty basic, 200f, and a restaurant serving menus from 58-180f based on *cuisine du terroir*.

ST. JOSSE 62170 Pas-de-Calais.
8 km SE of Le Touquet, 9 km W of Montreuil

One of the cluster of interesting dining possibilities in the pretty flowery villages in the rustic triangle south of the Canche. The D144 off the D143 is the easiest way to find it.

NEW ➤ Auberge du Moulinel (R)M-S
116 Chaussée Avant Pays (0)3.21.94.79.03 Cl. Mon. and Tues. o.o.s. Otherwise open every day, with no annual holidays

An old village inn, purchased by Alain and Annique Lévy four years ago. Inside the wooden beams and open fireplace make for a warm and cosy atmosphere. Alain, who has cooked at three- and two-star Michelin establishments, insists on only fresh produce, makes his own bread and comes highly recommended by the head chef of the Westminster in Le Touquet, who should know what he's talking about.

The 135f menu featured, for example, ravioli stuffed with *maroilles* cheese and served with cumin sauce, then the *queue de boeuf* for which Alain is rightly famous, then cheese or *crème brulée*. For 185f you get an extra course thrown in - a judicious mixture of traditional and innovative.

"It was wonderful décor, food and service. There were 7 of us with one small child who ordered the usual hamburger and chips and was served a very tender steak and sliced potatoes gently fried in butter, which impressed me no end. It's so nice to come across a restaurant which takes the same care catering for children and adults. I had the famous Parmentier of ox tail, which melted in the mouth. My 135f menu more than fulfilled expectations." D. H.

That's just the kind of recommendation from a well-informed local resident that I like to confirm my arrow. Go catch it while you can.

Le Relais de St. Josse (R)M-S
17 Grand'Place (0)3.21.94.61.75 Cl. Mon.; Sun. p.m and every evening o.o.s.; no
annual holidays

Fabienne and Etienne Delmer have been in this pretty little auberge in the
village centre for seven years now and have built up a reputation for good
traditional cuisine. Tables outside in the sunshine ensure a combination of
good food and good gossip. Inside there are low beams, pink tablecloths and
fresh flowers on the tables.

Weekday menus start at 75f, the 98f version is entitled *Le Petit Royal*, the
150f is *Regal du Palais* and 195f *Gourmand de Relais*, but I don't think I could
ever live up to that one.

ST OMER 62500 Pas-de-Calais,
40km SE of Calais
M Sat.

An interesting, multi-facetted town, which does not reveal its charms easily; it
took me several visits to appreciate it fully. Set at the junction of the Neufossé
canal and the river Aa (whose name I'm told is the French crossword-deviser's
delight), it is the heart of a complicated network of waterways, known by the
Flemish word *watergangs*.

A pleasant interlude in a timetable of driving and sightseeing is to take a ride
on one of the large flat-bottomed black boats typical of the region or on a more
modern version like the 'Emeraude'. Information about the numerous options
is best attained by ringing (0)3.21.98.66.74, since the service is not regular.
Among the possibilities are three trips starting from the canal on the D209: one
goes to Arques as far as the unique hydraulic boat-lift at Fontinettes, one cruises
the St. Omer *marais* and another explores the Aa to Houlle. Given a fine day,
with a glitter to the ubiquitous wateriness, it's all very peaceful and miles away
from the traffic tangle.

The banks of the *watergangs* are inhabited by sturdy market gardeners, who
glide from their rich dark plot, intensively cultivated to yield several crops a
year, to the market depots in time-warped flat-bottom punts laden down with
fat cauliflowers, leeks, chicory and cabbages. At weekends the roadside to
Clairmarais is lined with stalls selling their produce and people drive over from
Lille to pick up the freshest vegetables in the region. The bungalows along the
banks of the main waterways have mini-canals marking their borders, where
small boys sit for hours, bemused, watching their fish floats drift on the water.

On Saturdays all this *marais* produce is displayed on stalls in the most

Cathédrale Notre Dame

important market in the area which takes place in a great splash of colour in the Grand'Place, the centre of the town. The dignified Town Hall is the focus; the tourist information is there currently, but not for long - it is destined to be housed in the new complex at the entrance to the town that was causing such muddy confusion at the time of my last visit. On the other side of the square is a disreputable collection of cafés leaning drunkenly one on another. This disparity of styles and moods is a feature of the whole town, with the ruins of the 15C St. Bertin, the ponderous Gothic cathedral of Notre Dame, the chapel of the Jesuits, and the elegant 18C Hotel Sandelin, in the rue Carnot, now a museum, full of treasures, including 2,000 pipes made in St. Omer (open from Wed. to Sun. 10-14 and 14-18 p.m.).

Hard to believe now that St. Omer was once a prosperous maritime town, Its rich merchants invested their profits in the substantial classical houses lining the wide streets. Those in quiet backwaters, like the rue Gambetta, have been sympathetically restored, revealing their honey-coloured stone and intricate ironwork. The town is a series of quiet and not so quiet squares, opening one out of the other, with one street off the square, the rue de Dunkerque, for everyday shopping and a more upmarket section in the pedestrianised area.

The best place to stock up for a picnic is the rue des Clouteries. Le Terroir, at no. 31, has an excellent range of cheeses, *foie gras* and *terrines*. They will even make up a picnic basket for you. You have a choice of the formal or informal in which to enjoy your purchases al fresco. St. Omer is rightly proud of its public gardens, built on the ancient ramparts of the town, where the neat beds and bedding make a colourful background for benches on which to consume a sandwich and a glass of whatever. For those who prefer to set up tables and chairs as the French do for a serious picnic, the nearby forest of Clairmarais is deep and green and silent. St. Thomas à Becket took refuge here in a Cistercian abbey, of which only the farm now remains. The lake of Harcelles is the haunt of modern fishermen just as keen to land a trout for supper as were the monks who first stocked the water.

A favourite visit from St. Omer is to the crystal factory at Arques, 2 km outside the town on the RN43. There is an audio visual presentation of the various stages of manufacture and a visit to the factory floor to see the molten glass transformed into the finished article. A Christmas booze cruise can profitably be combined with a visit to the factory shop, which offers a 20% discount on their wares and periodical special offers. Opening times are from Mon. to Sat. from 9.30-11.30 and 1400 to 16.30 by appointment. Entrance 30f. The shop is open to all from 9.30-18.30 from 2/1-31/3 and from 10 to 19 from 1/4-31/12 except Sundays and public holidays. Ring (0)3.21.12.74.74 for further details.

Unfortunately all the hotels in St. Omer have to be in the 'Otherwise' category at present because of changes in management and lack of a strong contender.

Otherwise:

St Louis (HR)S-M

25 rue Arras. (0)3.21.38.35.21 R cl. Sat. and Sun. lunch

The manager of my old standby has moved on to the Ibis and I know nothing of his successor. In a quiet street, five minutes walk from the town centre. 30 rooms from 195-305f. Menus from 75f.

Le Bretagne (HR)M
2 pl. Vainquai (0)3.21.38.25.78 Cl. R cl. Sat. lunch, Sun. p.m; 10-23/8; 2/1-11/1
On the other side of town, a solid modern building, with two eating possibilities, a restaurant and the Maeva grill. 75 functional rooms 290-400f. Meals from 79f.

RESTAURANTS

Plenty to choose from, but reports vary wildly from exceptionally good to exceptionally bad. Only one that is consistent:

Le Cygne (R)M
8 rue Caventou (0)3.21.98.20.52 Cl. Sun. p.m.; Mon.
The name is taken from the lovely stone swan that is the centrepiece of the fountain outside. It's an 18C house in a quiet square, with a smart ground-floor restaurant all blue and yellow, and another pink version downstairs in the ancient cellars.

I suspect that Le Cygne might be suffering from the rush of new cheap restaurants in the town centre. Certainly its prices, which used to be a cause for complaint, seem to have come down and now compare favourably, considering that this is a quality restaurant of long-standing and high repute. There is a 72f lunch menu, which offers a sensible choice of *Entrée du jour* or *quiche* or salad, then *plat du jour* or *poulet sauté chasseur*, followed by dessert. Otherwise the 95f menu offers excellent value - for example a game *terrine et ses légumes oubliés* (must try that one to find out what exactly are forgotten vegetables), then seabass with a horseradish sauce, and a trolley of either cheeses or desserts. Other menus at 145, 185 and even 260f. If this sounds a lot, you might like to know that it includes *foie gras*, lobster, beef fillet, cheeses and an *assiette gourmande de desserts*.

N.B. There is a particularly good charcutier, Mignot, just opposite the restaurant.

La place Pierre Bonhomme, leading off the main square, is the restaurant drag of St. Omer. You can eat there in a variety of establishments at whatever level your budget demands. My choice proved a disaster. **Les Trois Caves** had been highly recommended, but one glance at the empty dining room when the other restaurants were all busy told me most of what I needed to know. The chef is said to have worked for Onassis, but in what capacity I cannot imagine. Our meal was pretentious and expensive and I could have hit the waiter who insisted on translating every word on the menu as though for an idiot. Pity, because the room, in the ancient cellars, is absolutely charming and there is a pleasant garden behind for summer dining. Please someone tell me they've changed both chef and *maître d'*.

Otherwise:
Au Vieux Marché (R)S
(0)3.21.98.29.39 Cl. Sun.

If I had trusted my inclination I would have headed straight for this lively restaurant on the opposite side of the street, simply because it was so full. It's a large restaurant divided by a straw-canopied central bar and decorated with engravings of St. Omer's old market *halles*. Cane chairs and a bistro atmosphere.

The value looks amazing - 65f includes a drink. Can't answer for the cooking because I have yet to try it, but a sample of what was on offer would be chicken liver pâté, fish of the day (or guinea fowl or pork), and dessert. At that price it's not surprising that the place was heaving. They also do pizzas and a good range of grills and the pastry-based desserts looked good. Certainly this is where I shall head next time but in the meanwhile all reports would be valuable for a main entry.

Le P'tit Montmartre (R)M
11 Place Pierre Bonhomme (0)3.21.98.33.33 Cl. Mon.

I really didn't have much luck in St. Omer one way and another. This was one restaurant I really wanted to try, after several readers' recommendations and no, it wasn't Monday, but a *fermeture exceptionelle* barred the way. All I can tell you therefore is that menus start at 90f and that the 120f one looked most interesting. Others at 150 and 230f.

Au Vivier (HR)M
22 rue Louis Martel (0)3.21.95.76.00; fax (0)3.21.95.42.20 Cl. Sun. p.m.

It says a lot for my beautiful nature that I even mention Au Vivier, the scene of the worst crisis of my last round-up. We had prudently reserved a room there, knowing that St. Omer tends to be full year-round, and after a long day trailing round in torrential rain, decided that the late afternoon would be better spent putting our feet up than getting them even more sodden. The road is pedestrianised, so we got saturated scuttling with suitcases to the door. Which was firmly locked. Banging and shouting got us nowhere and the lady in Le Terroir told us that the hotel was never opened until the evening staff for the restaurant came on duty at 6.30 p.m. Two hours to go. We tried every hotel in town and the only room available was overlooking the main road at Les Frangins. Sleepless night guaranteed. I am still waiting for a letter of apology from Au Vivier.

I couldn't bring myself to eat there after that experience, but I have to admit it looks good. On that dismal dank evening the rain did not prevent the terrace restaurant, covered with green-and-white awning, from being full. Fish is the speciality and no doubt when the memory fades a bit I shall be able to report further. Menus start at 85f and if you don't mind not having access to your room before aperitif time, the seven rooms cost 275f.

L'Entrecôte (R)S
1 rue Henri Dupuis (0)3.21.98.14.38 Cl. Sun. Tues p.m.

Mainly for carnivores but fish too is grilled over a charcoal fire. Meat grills cost from 59-89f and fish grills from 109 to 149f.

Chlorophylle (R)S
3 Place Foch (0)3.21.98.02.46 Cl. Mon.

An antidote to all that meat is this little vegetarian restaurant/*salon de thé* serving tarts, savoury and sweet.

LA COUPOLE
5 km from St. Omer, access from the autoroute by exits 3 or 4, well-signed. (0)3.21.93.07.07

The publicity describes this new 'attraction' as "From the war to the moon", and indeed this sums up the two aspects. It is a contemporary exhibition of aspects of WW2, when this was the most important subterranean base for the V2 rockets, constructed in a giant bunker built by Russian and Polish prisoners. The conquest of space is the other theme, re-living the first steps on the moon by Neil Armstrong. There are two cinemas, 18 audio-visual films and more than three hours of projection. That should keep 'em quiet on a wet day.

Information and Reservation on (0)3.21.93.07.07 Cl. the second week in January. Otherwise open every day from 9 a.m. to 7 p.m. from 1/4-31/10, and from 10 a.m. to 6 p.m. from 1/11-31/3.

Admission 55f for adults and 40f for children.

> ## ST. VALÉRY-SUR-SOMME 80230 Somme.
> ### 49 km S of Boulogne

A tablet on the quayside by the canal commemorates the fact that William the Conqueror set off from St. Valéry in 1066 for the conquest of England, taking with him some bare essentials: a sword to fight with, wine to fortify him and a bishop to give him absolution. Joan of Arc stopped here on her way to Rouen. Layers of history, illuminative details of past encounters, add richness to what is in any case an utterly delightful town, probably the most interesting along the whole littoral.

St. Valéry's position at the mouth of the Somme, the natural guardian against invasion, led to its being pillaged by the Vikings, occupied by the English during the Hundred Years' War, sacked by the Spanish under Charles of Austria, and passed to and fro between the Catholics and the Huguenots. A walk up the cobbled streets to the Vieille Ville, around the ramparts, is the best way to soak up the old-time atmosphere. This second, fortified town, secluded behind massive wooden gates, with flowery beamed houses and a freedom from traffic, comes as a pleasant shock after the bustle of the port and shopping street down below (pleasant though these are). Take the camera to record the astonishing views across the estuary to Le Crotoy.

Saint Valery sur Somme

The approach to the town is from the Abbeville road, across the flat marshes; then as you cross the bridge, the prospect becomes more enticing, with the photogenic masts of yachts lined up in the canal. In the port fishing boats unloading their catch accentuate the salty flavour. Essential to walk along the tree-shaded walks by the water's edge, where the expanse of river, marsh and sky ahead, stretching for ever towards the Somme's mouth, can best be appreciated. Great picnicking opportunities - benches, shade, views, calm.

Or not so calm - after a while it strikes you that it is in fact rather noisy. The volume comes not from engines and people but from the millions of birds in colonies across the water, their chatter vying with the bleating of the picturesque sheep dotted about the marshes. The salty vegetation they are so innocently cropping will ultimately prove their undoing. *Pré-salé gigôts*, naturally flavoured, are greatly prized by French gourmets.

Bathing depends on the tide; there is a little beach at the end of the quays, but when the tide recedes literally for miles, swimming is cancelled. This is the opportunity to walk over the sea lavender or along the path towards Le Hourdel, admiring the opalescence of the light and understanding why this is a favourite artists' haunt.

Among the manifold attractions of St. Valéry, there are few modern manifestations. Fitting therefore that the preferred method of transport should be 70 years old; the best way to appreciate the bay scenery and to visit Le Crotoy, Noyelles and Cayeux is to take the *Chemin de Fer de la Baie de Somme*, proudly twinned with the Kent and East Sussex Railway. The engine driver leans out of his cabin to check the single track is clear, pulls his whistle and with an impressive hiss, off puffs No. 3714, across fields, past leafy lanes and willow-lined streams.

The train runs every day from 15/3-15/11. Reservation office (0)3.22.26.95.66. In April there is a steam gala, with other trains joining in, and a model railway exhibition and just before Christmas there is a departure from the Christmas market stalls in St. Valéry as far as Noyelles, with a special night-time journey on the Saturday night. Fares are from 42f-63f depending on how far you travel.

Le Relais Guillaume de Normandy (HR)M-S

Quai de Romerol (0)3.22.60.82.36; fax: (0)3.22.60.81.82 Cl. Tues. o.o.s.; 22/11-26/12
Rising six storeys high from its own valley between port and the old town, Le Relais could have been a Disney fantasy. Half-château, half villa, with towers and turrets and balconies and curlicues, brown peeling paint, quintessentially French. It was actually built a century or so ago by an eccentric English milord as a romantic lovenest-by-the-sea for his mistress.

The view that he chose for her can now be enjoyed by diners in the first-floor restaurant. The food prepared by chef-*patron* Thierry Dupré is copious and good and greatly appreciated by the French on Sunday lunchtimes. He makes full use of local fish and the saltmarsh lamb. Menus from 80f, with carafe wine available.

The rooms vary greatly. If you get a dud one you might just as well not bother about a sea view - some are dark and overcast by the trees outside. On the other hand if you are lucky enough to book no.1, with its own charming little terrace, or no. 7 with its Picard furniture, you're on to a winner. 14 rooms at 220-340f. Good value.

Otherwise:

The old **Hotel de Port** and **des Bains** might look shabby, but readers have continued to report favourably on the value on offer here:

Excursion: Take a drive to the tip of the promontory that marks the extremity of the estuary; in the little harbour of **Le Hourdel** is a good bistro, **La pointe du Hourdel**, serving 120 beers from all over the world. Nice terrace, good place to eat a simple fish lunch.

STE-MARIE-CAPPEL 59670 Nord
3.5 km S of Cassel

Just a name on a sign on the *nationale* the D916.

Le Petit Bruxelles (R)M

rte Nationale (0)3.28.42.44.64 Cl. Sun. p.m.; Mon.; Tues. p.m. and Wed. p.m. o.o.s.; Feb. hols

There was a special menu on offer when I last visited, celebrating fifteen years of M. and Mme Desnave's tenure. They are kindly hosts who have made a lot of friends, including several FE readers. Their restaurant is typical comfortable bourgeois, serving copious helpings of well-cooked food guaranteed to keep out the northern chill.

The dishes under the heading *petites entrées pour petits faims* would suit me just fine, but forget the weight losing - one of them is home-made *foie gras* (49f) and the other a rich smoked salmon salad (46f). Fish features strongly and here the guilt can be assuaged, because all the fish and vegetables are *cuits à la vapeur* which sounds much more agreeable than 'steamed'. Mind you the accompanying sauces are not so virtuous. Fish are around 95f and meat dishes not far off - lots of duck, roast lamb and *fricassées* - all traditional stuff. There are special menus de la mer and, it being autumn when I visited, '*gibier*'; the *menu du marché* sounds expensive at 260f but it does include aperitifs, wine and coffee with the four courses, which makes it good value in the end.

"*We lunched at Le Petit Bruxelles. Not the cheapest, but for a special occasion the delicious food, attractive surroundings and the delightful Mme Desnave in attendance make this worth every centime.*" Red and Ann Harvey.

M. Desnave also sells attractive take-home presents in the shape of jams and conserves. 14 different varieties of *pâtés* cost around 45f a pot, enough for three to four persons. Jams are around 25f. For a special present a basket "*terroir*" would be a good idea, containing one duck *pâté*, one chicken *fricassée*, one local beer and the decorated basket for 202f.

SAULCHOY 62870
16km SE of Montiér. 17kms SW Hesdin.

On the north bank of the Authie, probably the largest village along the river valley, with a central grassy square lined with plane trees, on one side of which is to be found:

➤ **Val d'Authie** (R)S-M
(0)3.21.90.30.20 Cl. Thurs. o.o.s.; 31/8-12/9

Madame Pottier undoubtedly works hard. Just look at the closing hours to establish that. During the rest of the week she is keeping her pretty little restaurant spotless, welcoming her guests and doing all the cooking. She proudly showed me a rhubarb tart that had just come out of the oven, and very tempting it looked too, even soon after breakfast.

Her dining room (always full on Sunday and often on other days too, so book) is now hung with black flowered curtains in a pink and burgundy colour scheme. The dresser is polished like a mirror, the fireplace is wide and often in use and the grandfather clock has stopped at 3 o'clock.

The cheapest menu at 80f is a snip, bearing in mind that every course is not just thrown-together but the result of great care and attention. Choose, for example, the generous *hors d'oeuvres*, featuring items that originated in Madame Pottier's kitchen not in the local delicatessen, an excellent lasagne with local vegetables, and a slice of her signature fruity tarts. The price includes a carafe of house wine (good stuff) or beer.

For 125f you could sample Madame's version of the Picardy dish, *ficelle* (like a pancake), go on to *coquilles St. Jacques, gigôt d'agneau*, cheese and dessert, and for 150f you get yet another extra course.

Splendid value and arrowed of course.

An added asset is that you can bed down just up the road in the Pottiers' *chambres d'hôtes*, 575 rue de Haut (0)3.21.81.57.21.

It is a comfortable modern villa set in a well-tended garden. One room has bathroom and loo and the other just washbasin and loo; both have T.V. Use of a salon with log fire, and garage, all add up to a good deal for 200f.

STEENBECQUE 59189 Nord.
7 km S of Hazebrouck by D916

A nothing-special village, bisected by the main road.

Auberge de la Belle Siska (R)M
rte de Béthune (0)3.28.43.61.77 Cl. Sun. p.m.; Mon.; Tues. p.m.; 15/2-1/3

A chalet-like building beside a canal, with the deep forest opposite. The 120f *menu du marché* is good value, including as it does the wine, but it is served at lunch mid-week only. After that it's going to be 155f for the *gourmande* or 198 for the *douceur*. Fish is a speciality, particularly lobster, which weighs in at 160f, or sole with baby *langoustines*.

I always wanted to know who the Belle Siska was and had intended to ask on my next visit, but I picked the wrong day, the restaurant was shuttered and I still don't know. Enlightenment please?

TILQUES 62500 Pas-de-Calais
6 km NW of St. Omer, 30 km SE of Calais, signposted off the N43

Château Tilques (HR)M
(0)3.21.93.18.99; fax (0)3.21.3.23 open all year

"Why don't you include Château Tilques?" I get asked. The answer has been because it's so well-known, in the brochure of every tour operator, including the ferries, in every other guidebook, almost exclusively patronised by fellow-countrymen, I thought there was hardly any point.

But then I wondered if there was a degree of pique in all this (I found it first, sucks boo, when it was being converted from Le Vert Mesnil) and never let it be said.... So I went to have another look and have to confess that it is a lovely building (well, inside anyway), with high ceilings, light and cheerful, helpful reception staff, wide terrace, pleasant bedrooms overlooking the grounds, charming restaurant in the old stable block.

Not a lot has changed here, but there is now new management - French taking over from British - so the food might be improving and the atmosphere becoming a touch more gallic. It is always full, with either conferences or individuals, so make sure you book if you are not on a package deal, which is often better value here. If not, rooms cost a hefty 690-880f and dinner 200-230f.

For the first time I wandered past the château into the watery world beyond. I discovered that you could hire rowing boats on which to explore the inlets and canals on whose banks weekend gardeners grow giant vegetables on the fertile soil. Or you can opt for a ride on one of the traditional flat-bottomed black boats of the *marais,* the *bacoves.* Apply to Mme Lalart, Pont de la Guillotine (0)3.21.95.10.19. There are a couple of little cafés too, but even in September they were firmly shut for the season.

TORCY Pas-de-Calais.
43 km SE of Boulogne

Take the D341 to Dèsvres, D343 to Maninghem, D108 to Lebiez and finally the D130. Some of the prettiest countryside in the whole area; the valley of the Creqoise is particularly picturesque, with quiet villages like Embry, where a white shrine to Our Lady looks out over a surprisingly hilly terrain. Royan, where the river flows alongside the road is another village to plan a picnic around.

Otherwise:
NEW
Le Baladin, in the centre of the village, is a name that cropped up repeatedly from local advisers on where to go, what to see, what to do, where to eat and drink. I have tried repeatedly to work it into my schedule but it just never happens, so here is the hearsay. A fun place to be on Friday or Saturday evenings or Sunday lunchtimes (those are the only times it's open!) for lovers of jazz and

crêpes. The food is basic, simple and cheap. It's the atmosphere you go for. Everyone does a double take when they enter for the first time, since the furniture is on the ceiling! A piano, tables, chairs, you name it, are all upside down, suspended in space. Definitely different. Reports please.

LE TOUQUET 62520 Pas-de-Calais 32 km S of Boulogne
M Sat., Thurs.: Marché Couvert year-round; from 19th May to Sept. Mon., Thurs., Sat.

The oddball in the Côte d'Opale. Quite different from any of the other resorts and in many ways quite different from anywhere else in France. It has echoes of some of the spa towns, Biarritz perhaps, hints of past elegance, but proximity to England exerts a strong influence on its character. After all it was an English businessman who, at the end of the 19th century, fell in love with the perfect site of dunes, forest and sea and founded the Touquet Syndicate to develop the area attractively, build hotels and initiate tourism from across the Channel. Drive around today some of the quiet leafy side streets where expensive burglar-proofed villas are set back in gardener-intensive grounds and boards proclaim names like Byways, Wood End and Low Wood Manor, where the late lamented P. G. Wodehouse lived until he was snatched away to a German jail, and Weybridge or Sevenoaks spring to mind.

Between the wars the development accelerated rapidly but the town's heyday was in the Twenties and Thirties, when Le Touquet-Paris-Plage was about as chic as you could get for both Parisiens and Brits. The first casino was actually built as early as 1913, just in time to shut down for WW1; it reopened in 1919 and soon established itself as one of the major casinos in France, attracting the British aristocracy, including the Prince of Wales, and stars of stage and screen. A full orchestra played every day at "Le teatime". Le Touquet became known as "Part of England on French soil". To gain entry to the casino dinner jackets or tails were required for the gentlemen and for their shingled flapper companions here was the chance to air the most dashing frocks, furs, and fol-de-rols. Until quite recently the balls held here were strictly dress-to-kill affairs and James Bond would have been quite at home. Today the thrill of roulette takes second place to the largest slot machine room, the widest choice of games and Le Jumbo, the biggest "Slot" in France. Dress code somewhere between trainers and jeans and d.j.s and diamonds.

The Casino is open every evening. Take your passport. (0)3.21.05.01.05. You don't have to play, but it's worth while checking out this intrinsic part of the Le Touquet atmosphere. A White Lady cocktail on the summer terrace sets the scene perfectly.

Our grandparents, as children, sat on the beach with their nannies, and when they grew up came back to build eccentric villas on the sea front. A few of them remain, pinnacled, balconied, mock-beamed and large (the villas, not the grandparents). Too large for modern holiday homes, alas. Bulldozers attack them, one by one, and yesterday's hole in the ground becomes today's undistinguished and indistinguishable apartment block, so that in order to catch even a sniff of past character it is necessary to retreat further and further away from the beach.

And what a beach! Miles of firm golden sands, stretching into infinity left, right and, when the tide recedes, centre. Such an abundance of sand in fact that a large slice of it was covered with concrete and turned into a car park, and still left more than most resorts could dream of. A stroll along the prom still gives a taste of briny but it's better to gaze out to sea these days than be bored with the seafront architecture. There is every amusement a child could wish - beach clubs, sand yachting and the Aqualud complex, a very present help in times of inclement weather, especially for those who like their water heated and no sand between their toes. Here, under a glass pyramid the temperature all year round is a comfortable 29 degrees. Giant toboggan, rivers, wave pool, jacuzzi, cost 52f for three hours, up to 70f for a full day. Sauna and café extra.

The main street, the rue St. Jean, runs for half a mile or so from the floriferous, wooded, upmarket Westminster/Casino end of town, past the most expensive shops, designer labels, antiques and wickedly beguiling children's clothes, to the more popular, more crowded, T-shirted, seafront conclusion. In between, because, praise be, this is France after all, there is still space and customers for praiseworthy *chocolateries, pâtisseries*, cafés and restaurants. **Le Chat Bleu** is famous for its hand-made chocs; across the road is **Le Lido**, where I defy you to order a cappucino or Earl Grey and not be seduced by an accompanying calorific pastry.

However as the everyday food shops are being squeezed out of the main drag, the side streets, like the rue de Metz, take over, becoming more animated in the process, Here are good fruit and veg shops, butchers, and *charcutiers*, and that not-to-be-missed Touquetois institution, **Pérards**, part restaurant, part fish shop, where the inevitable take-home buy is a jar or two of their fish or crab soup and accompanying *rouille* and *croûtons*. Many a hostess has lied about the provenance of her, home-made, first course, bought thus.

The rue de Londres, another up-and-coming cross street, leads to the wide circus of the distinctive Art Deco covered market, built in 1927. Be there early for the best fish, on sale every day.

Le Touquet prides itself on being a year-round resort. It may not look its best when the sky lowers and the sea pounds in winter storms against the prom, but there are indoor attractions to compensate somewhat. Gambling aside, the casino is the scene for winter concerts, an international music festival and entertainments - and of course golfers are used to defying the weather. Golf is BIG, Le Touquet Golf Club is one of the largest golf set-ups in France and organises many prestigious competitions. 45 holes cover more than 250 hectares. Apart from the two famous courses, **La Mer**, established in 1931 and **La Forêt** in 1904, there is now **Le Manoir**, a nine holer, where beginners are welcome.

Le Manoir hotel, overlooking the fairways, is still dedicated to the sport that used to be played stylishly here in tweed plus-fours and brogues. It offers special golfers' rates, including green fees, from 335 to 395f for B&B per person (0)3.21.06.28.28; fax (0)3.21.06.28.29.

In summer the town regularly wins prizes for its flowers, and they are the first thing that strikes you as you turn the corner after the forest and approach the casino, spilling over from tubs, baskets, boxes and beds in Technicolor profusion. It's a very well-groomed, well-organised town altogether, and hard to beat in the area for the combination of sea air, shopping and walking.

The eating/lodging scene in Le Touquet has changed recently. Whereas the town was strong on restaurants and weak on hotels, the reverse is now true. It is particularly gratifying at last to have found a couple of budget hotels I can recommend.

Le Manoir
Le Touquet.

107

HOTELS
••••••••••••••••••••••••••••••••••••

➤ **Le Westminster** (HR)L
ave. Verger (0)3.21.05.48.48; fax (0)3.21.05.45.45 R cl. lunch Tues.; 2/1-15/3

Le Touquet's Grande Dame, Le West, has seen its share of celebrities since the palmy thirties when it was built and good casino customers were billeted gratis here, where they had just the road to cross before getting on with the serious business of losing money. Its transition into contemporary comfort and requirements has been skilful, and unashamedly luxurious. The spacious bedrooms have not been chopped into two, but have had en suite bathrooms attached, with marble basins, deep deep baths and fleecy bathrobes to wear en route to the indoor swimming pool. Good news, as is the retention of the original birdcage lifts that come clanking to your command.

The fortunes of the gastro restaurant, **Le Pavilion** decline or ascend with the incumbent chef. At present the cooking is in the capable hands of William Elliot, who combines imagination and insistence on prime ingredients. Menus start at 210f, including drinks and coffee; the wine list is reasonable considering the high standards. A more modest alternative is the **Coffee Shop,** where menus start at 115f, and expertise is just as high.

The Westminster has some particularly interesting *forfaits,* i.e. special offers, available throughout the year. The *Forfait 3 nuits* for example suggests three night's B&B, cocktails, one dinner in the Pavillon, one dinner in another posh Touquet restaurant, two hour's tennis, and - here is the unusual bit - two days instruction in *char-à-voile* (sand yacht racing) from the World Champion, all for 617f. per person per day.

"We stayed six nights in a very good room and the whole ambience was one of high-class professionalism. Everything required was provided without fuss. I enjoyed several swims in the pool, which was scrupulously clean. We ate once at the Pavillon and enjoyed some inventive dishes. We also ate once in the busier Le Coffee and found the standard of preparation as good, with the simpler fare and the prices very acceptable." Pat and John Corbett.

No doubt that if you feel like a pampering weekend in Le Touquet, Le West will fill the (considerable) bill. Arrowed accordingly.

113 rooms from 680 to 1150f, 2 apartments from 1700-1900f.

An arrow for unabashed luxury.

Red Fox (H)M
rue Metz (0)3.21.05.27.58; fax (0)3.21.05.27.56

A good middle-of-the-road choice, with the slightly high charge justified by this being popular Le Touquet, with an accommodation shortage in this bracket. On the corner of the main street, with the entrance in the rue Metz and parking available. The owner, who seems to be permanently behind the reception desk, night and day, is helpful and efficient. Rooms are nondescript - good sized, quite pleasantly decorated, but lacking in any memorable character. Bathroom ditto. Breakfast an averagely good buffet. It was not the Red Fox's fault that we elected to stay there on the night that France won their semi-final of the World Cup and the partying went on all night under our window, but I imagine that in any circumstances it would be a good idea to ask for a room at the side, rather than over the rue St. Jean.

48 rooms 410-510f.

Les Embruns (H)S
89 rue Paris (0)3.21.05.87.61; fax (0)3.21.05.85.89 Cl. Christmas week
A great find - a young couple have been working hard for two years now to restore this old hotel and now the atmosphere is light, bright and cheerful. They had seven newly decorated rooms out of a total of 19 when I visited and are working their way systematically redecorating the rest to the same high standards.

Prices are 290f for two, or 330f for three, with two rooms specially adapted for the handicapped.

Artois (H)S
123 rue Paris (0)3.21.05.17.09; fax (0)3.21.05.33.61 Cl. Whitsun holidays
A similar story. M. and Madame Barlet are the proprietors in this case, and have finished decorating 15 rooms. A terrace roof garden is the next project, but meanwhile breakfast is taken in a cheerful ground-floor dining room. 320-380f.

➤ Flavio's (R)L
1 Ave de Verger (0)3.21.05.10.22; fax (0)3.21.05.91.55 Cl. Mon. o.o.s.; 10/1-10/2
Flavio is dead. Long live Flavio's. The influence of the late lamented Flavio was felt right up to his death in 1995, when at 85 he was still in the habit of chatting to his guests. The influence is still felt, especially by his daughter Daniele Delmotte, who has capably taken on her father's colourful mantle. It helped that she married the chef. Guy Delmotte has been cooking here since 1968, but has somehow managed to retain enthusiasm and passion for his craft, as well as marrying the boss's daughter.

The restaurant, next to the Westminster, opposite the casino, has always attracted the rich and famous. It is almost an annexe to Le West, with the hotels clients booking up at Flavio's, where they know they can rely on consistently high standards. It has an air of well-manicured prosperity, with expensive chairs outside on the lawn, coloured awnings, lavish fresh flowers, well-upholstered seats, pristine napery, sparkling glass, and perfect service from waiters who know how to smile as well as bow, and an unfaultable *maître d'*, Laurent. They even managed not to make us feel unwanted when we booked for the night when France was playing in the World Cup and the rest of the restaurant and town were deserted. (We did the decent thing, ate up, declined a brandy, and allowed them to catch the last half hour.)

FLAVIO's.

Daniele is an efficient hostess, who really cares about her customers, and as her son Xavier helps out too, it is still very much a family concern.

If all this sounds expensive, well it can be, but not necessarily. Imagine a lunch in an English restaurant of equivalent standing for £15 including wine and service! The evening menus start at 240f; *Le Privé* depends on *la retour du marché*, three superb courses, topped up by *amuse-bouches* and including wines and service. Call that expensive?

The specialities appear on *La Découverte* at 380f: *Langoustines rôties aux épices et soupe de truffes, Meunière de volaille de Licques aux baies de genièvre fraîches, caramel de bière et petits ragoût de légumes*, but as this menu does not include wine, you can expect a considerable additional outlay, since the wine-list is famous for its prices as well as its range. Guy combines new ideas with traditional dishes and local ingredients, like the very local potatoes originating in Le Touquet, regrettably called *rattes*. And very delicious they are too. Order them whenever an opportunity arises.

Superb value if you stick to the menu, and arrowed accordingly.

"The restaurant is very comfortable and the tables are well spaced. I liked the extremely civilised atmosphere and the friendly but polished service of the efficient waiters. The cheapest menu is certainly the one to go for as it includes a bottle of red wine (Anjou and very acceptable). The wine list is outrageously expensive - even half a bottle of Sancerre was 190f. We ate a delicious little crab soufflé in a ramekin and smoked salmon, served with wonderfully fresh rolls, followed by fillets of sole, lightly sautéed in court bouillon. Breast of duck came next, served with a good selection of fresh vegetables including some unusually delicious cabbage. The dessert was a sort of superior apple turnover with beautifully light pastry, nicely garnished with fresh orange slices and raspberry coulis. I thought the package represented good value."

NEW Fierval (C d'H)L
6. Ave Leon Garet (0)3.21.05.10.22

The Delmotte hospitality has recently been extended. Daniele has put her father's old villa in a quiet residential area near the restaurant to excellent use as a B&B. It is luxuriously furnished in 1930s comfort, with the guests invited to use the deep deep armchairs and other solid furniture in the salon and dining room. At present there are four bedrooms, three with bathrooms attached, but Daniele is planning to open up another floor shortly, which will enable all her rooms to have their own baths/showers. The 450f includes a lavish breakfast, with bacon and eggs, since this is an English enclave (Daniele speaks the language fluently), and a 10% discount on meals at Flavio's. Daniele is an exceptionally kind hostess, who will ensure her guests enjoy their stay.

La Dune Aux Loups (R)M

ave. de la Dune aux Loups (0)3.21.05.42.54; fax (0)3.21.05.51.68 Cl. Tues. p.m.
o.o.s.; Wed. 12/11-4/12

Where other Touquetois restaurants seem to be on a downward slope, reports from La Dune are the reverse. Down in the forest something is stirring. Delve deeply through the trees into a quiet residential area to find this rustic hideaway. It's all very Hansel and Gretel, exposed beams and bricks outside, but indoors it gets more sophisticated with smart covers and efficient waiters. There's a leafy garden bordering an equestrian centre.

Arnaud Pannier, chef, dispenses mostly traditional dishes, like *blanquette de veau* and *meringue glacé* on his menus that start at 98f. Inexpensive wines result in an affordable bill.

Café des Arts (R)M

80 rue de Paris (0)3.21.05.21.55; fax (0)3.21.84.64.20 Cl. Wed. and Tues.

Local reports are disappointing on my erstwhile favourite. The décor was the only thing I disliked about the little restaurant and that has been changed. It's now very bright red and very bright yellow in and out. Eye-catching anyway. You can eat outside on the terrace, given fair weather. Jerome Pannis' cooking continues to be imaginative - witness his lobster with artichokes and green apples, or sole with grapefruit.

We stuck to the cheapo 100f menu (not Saturday evenings. Next menu 150f) and enjoyed our *moules à la biere, confit de porc à la Flamande* and *crème brulée à la Cassonata,* so I need some more reports to see who is right, but meanwhile the arrow will have to go.

Pérard (R)M

67 rue de Metz (0)3.21.05.13.33 Cl. never. No cards, no cheques

It's strange that there are not more good fish restaurants in Le Touquet, but perhaps they know that they could never compete with the famous Pérard, whose reputation gives him a headstart. Serge Pérard's fish soup sells all over the world; you can buy it here in the fish shop entrance to the bustling brasserie style restaurant.

There are reasonable menus but my advice is to keep it simple and go for one good piece of fish, like the sole for 75f, or the 169f *plâteau de fruits de mer*, and always bear in mind that the main reason for coming here is perpetuating a tradition.

Café des Sports (R)S

22 rue St. Jean (0)3.21.05.05.22. Cl. 6/1-3/1. Open non-stop, and that means 24 hours in the season

Everyone loves 'les Sports'. It fills the niche when you want a lively evening, or to eat early or late, some hungry, some less so, with a modest bill. A brasserie so well-known could take short cuts and serve fast foot, but no, Marcel Desseaux does it the hard way, serving huge helpings of real food. Sole *meunière* is sensibly priced at 97f (hard to find a really fresh, good-sized specimen for less). Offal is a speciality, from pigs trotters to sweetbreads, with home-made *andouillettes*. Or you can go for something simple, like a Welsh rarebit at 43f or an omelette at 45f. Something for everybody in other words, served by cheerful young waiters and waitresses in the best Parisian brasserie tradition.

Le Diamant Rose (R)S

110 rue de Paris (0)3.21.05.38.10

If there is one restaurant that is constantly recommended by locals and readers alike it is Le Diamant Rose. I have never seen it written up in any guidebook, it is not glitzy, nor dirt-cheap, but continues to offer excellent value with friendly service. Here is a view that sums it all up:

"No faltering of standards here and as popular as ever. Menus at 99f and 140f both very good. Moules marinières were ten times better than at Pérard. Well prepared, fresh ingredients and excellent friendly service. Passes the acid test - very popular with French extended families coming for their end of holiday blow-out." Jim Taylor.

Otherwise:

NEW L'Arléquin (R)S-M

91 rue de Paris (0)3.21.05.39.11 Cl. Wed. Thurs.

I know nothing about this little restaurant in a side street, except a gut feeling that it is worthwhile investigating, culled from peering in through the curtain chinks and inspecting the menu, on a Wednesday.

The 85f menu looked both good value and interesting. *Gougère de fromage maroillés, poulet de Licques, pot de crème à la chicorée* - all local dishes - promised well. There is a more extensive 132f version.

Reports please.

La Petite Charlotte (R)S
36 rue St. Jean (0)3.21.05.32.11 Cl. Wed. Thurs.
A pretty little bistro in the main street, good for light lunches and snacks but also serving evening meals. It used to be listed in FE, but was dropped after a couple of grumbles. Now a reader has better news:
   "*We took the 125f menu on which there was plenty of choice, which offered three courses with a supplement of 16f for cheese. First came a feuilleté of crab with salmon sauce, then skate in a delicious mustard sauce, followed by a plate of assorted pastries à la maison. Pouilly Fumé was 99f a bottle. Good, simple no-nonsense food at reasonable prices.*"

l'Escale (R)M
Aeroport (0)3.21.05.23.22 Cl. Thurs. o.o.s.
The French have a different attitude to restaurants in railway stations and airports from ours. There is no 'captive audience so let's milk them dry' attitude there, rather the idea that the 'facility' should be so good that it will attract not only the travellers but customers from outside as well. Certainly the *Touquettois,* and especially the *hommes d'affaires* use l'Escale for more than a hasty snack.
   It's all rather plush, and only the aeronautical activity outside and the elephantine old Dakota, still painted with wartime markings, parked directly outside remind you that this is not a city centre restaurant.
   There are two options, brasserie and restaurant. To say that the most expensive menu in the latter majors in lobster is grave understatement. Pay 350f and you get lobster salad, lobster *feuillété,* a whole grilled lobster, a sorbet and half a bottle of champagne! Very popular I'm told. Other less self-indulgent menus available. In the brasserie menus at 85, 120 and 150f feature regional dishes, like *ficelle Picarde, Waterzooi, genièvre sorbet* and local cheeses.

LE WAAST 62142 Pas-de-Calais.
19 km E of Boulogne

Well marked from the N42. Turn north on the D127 through an attractive rural area, the Parc Regional squeezed between the *autoroute* and the *nationale.*

Château des Tourelles (RH)M
(0)3.21.33.34.78; fax (0)3.21.87.59.57

The 'château' is hardly recognisable nowadays as the rather run-down manor house that Serge and Michelle Feutry took on as a base for Serge's excellent cooking abilities. Extensions have sprouted all over the place, tacked on to the old grey stone. Breakfast is served in a glassed-in extension into the garden at the rear. There is a new dining room, seating 70, one extension has rooms at 280f, with bath or shower room, and yet another add-on - the most radical yet - was still being completed last time I visited. This one is approached by a grandiose sweeping iron-railed staircase in an imposing new hall. There's a lot of mock walnut about. The new bedrooms here cost 390f and demi-pension runs between 260 and 310f depending whether you choose old or new section.

Hostellerie du Château des Tourelles

The new dining room sports an open kitchen, where Serge has a team of sous-chefs and commis working for him. His 85f menu changes every day, according to season and markets. For example: pan-fried cod with a coulis of leeks, roast beef and dessert. Other menus are from 130-190f.

'Improvements' and extensions are still going on. A family suite in the rafters of the latest add-on was being constructed, and will cost 550f.

The Feutrys have worked hard to achieve this considerable success and it is great to see their daughter carrying on the good work behind the reception desk.

WIERRE EFFROY 67200 Rinxent.
Pas-de-Calais. 5 km S of Marquise by D238. 21 km NE of Boulogne

---

The hamlet of Wierre Effroy is well marked from the main roads that encircle it. Just as well, because, in the middle of nowhere, it is not easy to locate on the map. Michelin lines the lanes that approach it in green (signifying particularly attractive countryside), and rightly so. Oddly enough, in the heart of this gently rolling, unspoiled farming land, there are two establishments, at opposite ends of the hamlet, that merit an inclusion here:

Ferme du Vert (HR)S
(0)3.21.87.67.00; fax (0)3.21.83.22.62 R cl. Sun. (check other dates)

No longer an undiscovered farmhouse with a few beds but a Logis-de-France that publicises its existence prominently with numerous signs. The same family, the friendly Bernards, still run the business, now with valuable input from their grown-up son. The farm complex centres on a large cobbled yard. Beside the front door is a shop selling home-produced cheeses, *terrines*, *quiches* and other farm produce. The dining room takes up another wing and the bedrooms the rest.

A reader chastised me for describing the rooms as monastic, so I went to look again. I stick by my view. They are small, whitewashed and furnished extremely simply. True, the en suite cons are immaculately mod, but the whole feeling of the ensemble is of peace and removal from daily cares.

The cooking is strictly based on local produce, usually their own, and the recipes are regional. Fillet of pork is cooked with juniper berries and the duck legs are braised in beer. There are the farm's own cheeses of course and a choice of five home-made desserts. The 130f menu has three courses and the 150 and 220f versions merit one extra. *Plâteaux de fruits de mer* are available too if you remember to order ahead.

Six rooms cost 220f.

Ferme Auberge de la Raterie (HR)S

(0)3.21.92.80.90 Cl. Sun. p.m.; Mon.

Draw in your mind's eye a picture of a typical picture-postcard-pretty unspoiled farm and the reality will not disappoint. The *auberge,* though nowadays more concerned with people than animals, still looks like a farm - low and rambling, rough stone walls, wooden shutters, courtyard, set among pastures - but with far more geraniums in pots, baskets and troughs, fresh white paint and white benches around from which to admire the view than the average farmer would have time for. At the rear is a surprisingly large flowery garden, with very un-farmer-like recliners scattered about for exhausted tourists.

Inside the farmhouse there is no evidence of the usual farm clutter, but all the best bits of the atmosphere remain. Low low beams, flagged floors, log fires, pine panelling, swinging lamps, and an old grandfather clock gleaming with polish.

The Coquerelle family team has been depleted by the departure of their daughters but Christophe's commitment to the *auberge* has been affirmed. He pointed out to me that they are now officially registered as '*Les Coquerelles, et leur fils'*. He injects a new generation's enthusiasm for sharing their adorable home. I am sure that it was the women in the family, though, who were responsible for choosing the furnishings of the prettiest bedrooms imaginable. They are all decorated in fresh and simple country style fabrics and wallpapers, with white frilly curtains and lace bedspreads. The older ones, up a steep polished wooden staircase, have hand-painted porcelain washbasins but have to share a bathroom with three other rooms. In two years' time they will all have their en suite bathrooms and will no doubt cost more but at present the bill is 230f. In the new block running along the garden, the bathrooms are in situ and the cost is 310f.

The dining room is as charming as the rest of the house. Farmhouse ingredients are used in menus from 100f. The next one up, at 145f, offered five courses, vegetable soup, *terrine,* roast chicken or ham, cheese, pudding.

Now, I have a problem. I thought on this last visit that the whole charming countryside set-up should have an arrow. On consulting my files however, I find a dichotomy. On the one hand: "*The cheapest evening meal was soup, roast chicken and burnt rhubarb tart. A total of 670f for a night stop for two makes La Raterie expensive and not deserving of an arrow,* and

"*The rooms were spotless and nicely decorated, but very cold with no heating on when we arrived. The dinner was extremely dull and the wine list impossible. Madame appeared to be away and we only ever saw one daughter who was not very welcoming. The Labrador was the only friendly being there."* And on the other hand:

"Sensational! The rooms at 300f were certainly pricey for that sort of thing but excellently furnished and beautifully set out. But it was the meal that persuaded us that Mme Coquerelle should receive an arrow. Glorious gammon, falling of the bone, preceded by a huge tureen of home made cream of vegetable soup and a quite superb Delice de Licques. This local delicacy, of onions, cream and chicken in a delightful little lidded pot was sensational and all on a menu costing just 139f. The hardworking family Coquerelle deserve all the praise we can give them". Mike Souter.

And:

"Excellent meal. A very thick potato soup followed by roast pork. The pork was large slices (no portion control) that had been roasted with garlic. Tarte aux pommes was also good. Their house wine was not very good but we felt the final bill was good value. Hearty French farmhouse cooking". Mark Girling.

Ah... put all these valuable opinions together and a clearer picture emerges. The simple farmhouse fare is always going to include thick vegetable soup for starters, then chicken or ham and a fruit tart. The two correspondents on the more expensive menu felt they had better value than those on the lowest-priced. But as all four had roughly the same menu, what happens if you stay for several nights? All agree that the wine is dicey - either not very good house, or expensive. I have to admit that 300f is plenty for a *ferme auberge* room, but personally I thought it justified because it was so exceptionally atmospheric. However, if they cannot be bothered to switch on the heating when visitors are expected, it does not look so attractive a deal.

I have a feeling that things are looking up with Christophe's involvement, but there is obviously room for improvement. As things are it would seem that a bit of cashing-in is taking place, and the arrow disappears. It would be good to see it reinstated on the basis of more favourable reports.

> **WIMEREUX** 62930 Pas-de-Calais.
> 6.5 km N of Boulogne
> **M** Tues., Fri.

Once upon a time, when white flannels were *de rigueur* seaside gear for the gentlemen, and parasols and shady hats for the ladies - and I do mean gentlemen and ladies - Wimereux was *the* place to go for a naughty (but nice) weekend. A breath of sea air, a stroll along the promenade, and a delicious dinner of food unheard of back home was a very pleasant little escape. Abroad but not too far abroad. The Atlantic Hotel dominated the sea front then, as it does today.

With Boulogne suffering from a shortage of hotels and a surfeit of traffic, it makes good sense to head along the coast road and stay in Wimereux. The little town retains its sleepy old-fashioned air, even if the main through road is usually too congested for agreeable shopping. More tranquil is the Tuesday morning market by the river, which gave its name to the town

Given fair weather it is still very agreeable to stroll along the wide *digue,* where children pedal furiously, mothers push buggies and stout, elderly couples take their constitutionals. There's a wide and wonderful beach to explore when the tide recedes and none at all when it is high. If that coincides with a strong wind, the waves pound against the seawall and kids play dodge-the-spray along the prom. A wall of boulders keeps the seawater in a permanent pool for those disinclined to walk the considerable distance to the water when the tide is at it's lowest. I enjoy the town in winter too, when I have to share the whole expanse of beach with only with a few muffled figures and the prom is populated by a poodle-walkers wrapped up in furs.

NEW ➤ Hotel Atlantic and Restaurant La Liègeoise (HR)M
Digue de Mer (0)3.21.32.41.01; fax (0)3.21.87.46.17 R cl. Sun. p.m. HR cl. Feb.

It was a very good day for the little resort when Alain Delpierre decided to sell his restaurant in Boulogne and put all his eggs in the Wimereux basket. The legendary Atlantic was looking sad and shabby before he set about restoring it to the standard of its heyday. Now the Art Deco façade gleams with paint, cream, peach and blue; a focus that the town can be proud of is intact.

There are surprisingly few hotels or restaurants capitalising on sea views in the Pas-de-Calais. Without doubt the Atlantic has the prime site along the whole Côte d'Opale It makes the most of them. A seat by the panoramic windows of the restaurant Liègeoise makes you feel you could be on an ocean liner, cresting the waves. This, understandably, is not only my favourite restaurant, but that of a good many locals, looking for a treat or a business extravaganza, so make sure you book. The staff are as friendly as their boss and Laurent, the *sommelier,* is a supremo in his profession.

Not surprisingly, fish is the star turn on the menus. The 115f version (not weekends) features Alain's home-smoked salmon, fish *'selon l'arrivage du jour',* and dessert. For 170f you could choose six oysters or fresh crab with a shellfish sauce, followed by roast monkfish with mushrooms and Basmati rice, but there are carnivore alternatives - *magret* or fillet of beef for example. On the *carte* a sole cooked with *langoustines* costs 140f or turbot on a bed of spinach and leeks 140f. You don't come here for gastronomic fireworks, but rather for the freshest fish cooked simply to perfection.

Downstairs is a more modest *brasserie* which spills out onto the wide terrace in fine weather. Blue and white canvas director's chairs spell out the marine theme, windbreaker glass screens extend the season. This has to be the most agreeable outdoor eating in the area. Or drinking for that matter, since this is also a bar/*salon de thé.* Seafood and salads are the fare, and it is perfectly acceptable to order just a platter of oysters - a dozen *fines* cost 80f, or 12 *langoustines* with the kind of mayonnaise that begs to be mopped up with some home-made bread (70f). If you have the afternoon to spare the *plâteau de fruits de mer* at 195f should take care of that nicely.

This is primarily a restaurant with rooms, rather than a hotel with food, but the Delpierres have decorated all ten bedrooms, each in a different colour, and hung co-ordinating flowery curtains, laid new carpets and installed modern bath/shower rooms. Decisions have to be made - a larger room facing the side, or a smaller one with sea-view. They all cost 450f. As the cooking is so good here, 430f per person *demi-pension* would be a good choice.

Ask before you book if there are any special offers - *forfaits* - going. Alain often arranges out-of-season-bargains.

It would be hard to find shortcomings with the new-style Atlantic - sea views, fine cooking, comfortable rooms, and best of all an exceptionally warm welcome from Alain and Beatrice Delpierre. Arrowed on all counts.

Otherwise:
Paul et Virginie (HR)S
18 rue Ge. De Gaulle (0)3.21.32.42.12; fax (0)3.21.87.65.85 Cl.14/12-19/1 Cl. Sun. p.m.

A century or so ago Les Mauriciens was the most impressive house in Wimereux. Now its stables have been converted into a small two-star hotel by the lady who once lived in the big house. Many readers have been impressed by her friendliness (and ability to speak good English). The bedrooms are small and simple, their degree of smallness and simplicity being reflected in the price range of 190-400f. Dinner is an optional extra, with Madame only too willing to point out the other dining possibilities in the town. Given fair weather, breakfast served in the cobbled courtyard makes a good start to the day.

Here is the report of a discerning and experienced correspondent:

"Nice here. My room was low-end of 2-star, on the small side, uncharming fluorescent strip lights, nothing-special furniture with a handle missing from one sliding door of the wardrobe, but warm and really more than adequate. With shower and wc it cost 280f. Dinner was rather good. I chose the 139f menu but the 90f one looked fine too. I had gorgeous mussels in paprika sauce, conger eel with saffron sauce, melt-in-the-mouth tarte tatin. Recorded music of course, at first pop, not loud but still too loud, but later quieter Mantovani-ish meandering which could at least be ignored. A proper breakfast i.e. neither butter not jams in packets cost 36f". Ron Smyth.

NEW ➤ **La Goëlette** (Ch'd)M
13 Digue de Mer (0)3.21.32.62.44

Turn right from l'Atlantic along the prom and dive behind the beach huts to find this 1930s villa, freshly painted in cream and blue, How pleasing it is, incidentally, to see a building like this, constructed in the little resort's prime, put to good contemporary use and not pulled down to make way for apartment blocks, as in Le Touquet. Encouragingly, the signs are that Wimereux has learned that character is not a commodity that can be introduced instantaneously, and its older buildings are one of its greatest assets.

The delightful owner, Mary Avot, describes herself as *celibataire* (spinster). Her parents helped her buy the tall narrow house a couple of years ago and her father has contributed to the conversion into a B&B, which had opened only a few months before my visit and, without any advertisement except word of mouth is already fully booked for weekends and holidays.

Four charming bedrooms are furnished with chic restraint - bare polished wooden floors, antique pine furniture and lack of fussiness giving a Scandinavian look. The two front rooms are undoubtedly the ones to go for; 400f buys a fabulous view directly out to sea. The two rear rooms are pretty nice too, at 350f, but overlook roofs rather than waves. All four have luxurious bathrooms and smart bed-linen.

Breakfast lives up to the high standard, at present served in the front room; Mary was decorating the rear downstairs room to provide a bar and sitting area.

I owe the discovery of this gem to a kind reader, who sums up the situation:

"We have discovered a fantastic place to stay. It has been opened recently by a charming young French lady, Mary Avot, who has supervised the decoration of this 1930s house to its original standard. The house faces the sea and is right on the esplanade. We were given a room facing Wimereux's beach on the first floor, with pine furniture, huge windows and we felt we were on a boat for a cruise." Patricia Marlborough.

▶ L'Epicure (R)M
1 rue de la Gare (0)3.21.82.21.83; fax (0)3.21.33.53.20 Cl. Wed.; Sun. p.m. Christmas holidays

As you approach Wimereux from Boulogne, the freshly-painted Epicure stands out on the corner of the road. It's tiny, inside (just 16 covers) and out, pretty as a picture in fresh peachy tones.

The youthful chef-*patron*, Philippe Carée, composes his menu each day with whatever is freshest and best from the market, particularly the fish market. He is gaining in confidence and is not afraid to keep it simple. His pastry - always the mark of a skilful chef - is worth saving space for. Service with a smile. Menus start at a bargain 125f, and the carafe wine is better than adequate.

An arrow repeated - if anything he has got even better than when it was first awarded.

Le Centre (HR)S
78 rue Carnot (0)3.21.32.41.08; fax (0)3.21.33.82.48. R. cl Sun. p.m o.o.s. and Mon.

One of those archetypally French hotels that have been in the centre of the little town as long as anyone can remember, with the nice Boulanger family at the helm. The food makes no concession to fashion fads and is as resolutely substantial and traditional as anyone nostalgic for unfussy, seasonal fare could wish for. Better perhaps in winter than when the sunshine beckons, always packed, dark and intimate with the cheerfulness coming from the chatter of French families who know what they like and know too that they will find it here. Mary Avot (see La Goëlette) says that it is the favourite Wimereux restaurant of all her clients, who find it *'adorable'* *'romantique'* and *'vivant'*.

Menus start at 99f (e.g. *moules marinières, lapin en gelée maison, crème brulée,* then for 170f you could choose *coquille St. Jacques, pavé de boeuf,* cheeses and *profiteroles. Plats du Jours* could be steak *tartare* at 75f, *confit de canard,* 68.50f or *moules en casserole* 65f. An *omelette aux champignons* at 42.50f would make an excellent lunch served with good frites.

It is for the food that you would choose Le Centre but there are 25 rooms, 295f with bath or shower. Ask for one at the rear, overlooking the courtyard, rather than those on the main road. Parking available.

Hotel du Centre

NEW Cap Nord (R)S
Digue de Mer

A new brasserie on the promenade run by Jean-Marc and his sister Catherine Boulanger, with Catherine in charge. On days when sitting outside is not a good idea, even with the glass windshields, it is no hardship to retreat into the interior; the décor here is bright and cheerful, adopting a Scandinavian-look open-plan. A large galleon-shaped bar adds considerable character. With a family dedicated to good food it is not surprising that Catherine knows a thing or two about cooking and presentation. While the *brasserie carte* enables customers to eat exactly what they fancy throughout the day, the main menu concentrates on local produce, especially fish, with the chef delighted to show off his specialities. Prices for three courses run from 55f to 130f.

In fact there is truly something here for everyone - breakfast by the sea, afternoon *pâtisserie, apéritifs,* full Monty. In summer there is a special light menu with lots of salads and in winter the kind of satisfying calorific fare, like *raclette, choucroute* and *fondue, 'pour rendre les soirées d'hiver encore plus conviviales'* to quote Jean-Marc.

A very welcome addition to the Wimereux scene.

Otherwise:
NEW La Cardabelle (R)S
116 rue Carnot (0)3.21.87.64.05.0

Another new face for Wimereux. On the main street opposite l'Epicure, a pretty little restaurant with rustic décor featuring stalls with straw roofs, check tablecloths, specialising in *pâtés*, grills and pies. Simple menus at 65, 85 and 120f. Reports welcome.

One other Wimereux bonus is an excellent wine shop, **Mille Vignes** at 90 rue Carnot (0)3.21.32.60.13, run by Nick Sweet. He has a wide, well-chosen range of wines on offer, from superb *vins fins* to *vin de table*. Every bottle we have bought from him has been spot on. Infinitely more pleasurable to buy here, benefiting from friendly helpful advice, than to fight your way through the supermarkets.

WIMILLE 62200 Pas-de-Calais.
2 km SE of Wimereux

Take the D233 that leaves Wimereux by the river and dives under the bridge. Stick with it till you see a church ahead, turn right and the Relais is on the left-hand corner. No hardship if you get lost - the surrounding countryside is particularly attractive and well worth exploring.

➤ **La Brocante** (R)L-M
2 rue Ledinghen (0)3.21.83.19.31; fax (0)3.21.87.29.71 Cl. Sun. p.m.; Mon.
When the respected Gault et Millau guide looked for a chef to represent the best regional cooking in the North of France, it was to Jean-Francois Laurent of La Brocante that they turned, awarding him 16 points out of a theoretically possible 20. He is a one-off in the region - more innovative than any other. If your idea of a good meal is steak with a daring touch of béarnaise, head elsewhere.

Le Relais de la Brocante.

He has been cooking for 12 years now in the untouristy situation of a sleepy village centre, in the former presbytery next to the church. It later became a canteen for the local school and then an antique shop - hence the name Jean-Francois chose for his restaurant - La Brocante.

The old building has been converted to give a feeling of intimacy and cosiness to counter the severity of the cold stone walls. Fresh flowers, polished antiques, a grandfather clock, deep leather armchairs all help to dissipate any restaurant formality. And it's tiny - so book.

Jean-François' enthusiasm for ingredients that have spent the least possible time between farm/sea and his kitchen encourages him to cycle round the neighbourhood searching out likely suppliers. His passion is researching old recipes and re-creating them with regard to today's tastebuds. He could not have chosen to live in a more favoured region. The Boulogne fish is some of the best in France and the countryside is rich and fertile. Whatever he fails to find growing there, he cultivates himself in his *potager.*

Combining unlikely ingredients is another signature theme. From Licques, famous for its poultry, he chooses a plump guinea fowl and adds to the casserole a secret ingredient that you know is there but can't quite put your finger on. Coffee. Just a grain or two to add that *je ne sais quoi.* Licquorice is another taste-teaser - he grates a shred or two of the root into one or two appropriate desserts, and only the true gourmet would know what it was that gave the extra punch. His star turn I sampled on my last visit - *galette de kipper aux oignons, fleur de thym et jus de poule.* In other words a kipper cake. The base of thin potato roundels is neatly arranged in circles, the onions are cooked in local beer, flavoured with thyme and alternated with the kipper flakes, and the chicken *jus* is pepped up with just a touch of... coffee.

Menus start at 160f.

Not for everyone, but a quite exceptional chef, and arrowed accordingly.

Otherwise:

NEW La Bonne Idée (R)S

68 rue de l'Aiglon (0)3.21.31.49.36 Open every lunch time and Fri., Sat. and Sun. p.m.

Can't wait to try this one myself. It has been highly recommended and sounds just my kind of place. Madame Yvette Coquerelle is the *patronne*-chef and dishes up '*cuisine familiale*', in other words good nosh, good helpings, no menu but just what she feels like cooking that day, with an emphasis on local dishes. Splendid recipe. There are only 25 covers and you must book. Great atmosphere I'm told. Tell me more.

WIRWIGNES Pas-de-Calais.
12 km SE of Boulogne on the D341

Mémère Harlé (R)S

Route de Dèsvres (0)3.21.87.34.87 open only for Sunday lunch

Drive through the Forêt de Boulogne and on the corner of a crossroads stands an establishment that has changed little since 1919. Here is the legend of Granny Harlé:

"Once upon a time, in a small village deep in the Boulonnais countryside, with a name difficult to pronounce - Wirwignes - there was an admirable woman, an honest Christian and an excellent cook, who made the best Tarte au Papin in the whole area. A marvellous tart with thick sides as golden as a halo, as creamy as the milk of springtime and with the perfume of a girl from the islands. People would travel to this place just to come for a taste of this tart whose pastry captured the smell of the different woods burned in the oven while cooking the casing and whose cream, made from the very best milk, had the creaminess of a smile from His Eminence."

Yes, well. The amazing thing is that Guy Louchez and his wife still serve the best Tarte au Papin in the whole area, made from the original recipe. Not a lot else has changed either. The dining room is as pretty as an old picture, with mauve periwinkle tiles. The menu formula is exactly as it always has been - soup, tongue, garden vegetables, roast leg of lamb, gratin of potatoes, flageolet beans, cheeses from Philippe Olivier and of course the famous tart, cooked on a wood fire as always.

This feast costs 120f and is served for Sunday lunch only on reservation. Predictably the place is packed.

WISSANT Pas-de-Calais 62179.
17 km S of Calais
M Wed.

In a superb position between the two sheltering arms of the two Caps, Blanc and Gris, Wissant has arguably the finest beach of all the fine beaches of this coastline. It would be a finicky child indeed who was not enchanted by the choice of sand, wet or dry, rocks, pools, and puddles. Sand yachts provide extra animation. Great for walkers too, with wonderful cliff-edge paths in both directions.

Unusually, the centre of Wissant is not the beach but some way back, around a distinctive hotel, the black and white Normandy, where there are seats for conversation and plenty of drinking opportunities. This is where to find:

NEW Le Vivier (HR)S-M
pl. de l'Eglise (0)3.21.35.93.61; fax (0)3.21.82.10.99

This gets the 'new' label because, although it has appeared briefly in FE before, there have been considerable changes and it is now a hotel as well as a restaurant. Two hotels in fact, under the same management. Le Vivier 1. is in the centre of the village; Le Vivier 2, brand new, is in the rue Victor Hugo, same telephone number. The latter has views over the bay, and all rooms have garden, terrace or balcony, baths or showers, all for 380f.

The original Vivier is easy to spot because of the old fishing boat full of flowers outside its doors. Here the rooms are light and airy and good sized, at the same price, but without the view. There is a little garden at the back. The pleasant restaurant downstairs predictably majors on fish, but there is a good range of meat and poultry dishes too, with fresh local produce used throughout. Menus from 87f, sole - 92f.

With friendly, helpful proprietors, who will arrange transport to stations or ferries, this would be a good choice for a family holiday, especially as there are kitchenettes provided in some rooms in the new building. Lock up garages are another asset, and there are special weekly rates throughout the year.

Wines and spirits by John Doxat

Bonne cuisine et bons vins, c'est le paradis sur terre.
(Good cooking and good wines, that is earthly paradise.)

King Henri IV

OUTLINE OF FRENCH WINE REGIONS

Bordeaux
Divided into a score of districts, and sub-divided into very
many *communes* (parishes). The big district names are
Médoc, St Emilion, Pomerol, Graves and Sauternes. Prices
for the great reds (châteaux Pétrus, Mouton-Rothschild,
etc.) or the finest sweet whites (especially the miraculous
Yquem) have become stratospheric. Yet château in itself
means little and the classification of various rankings of
châteaux is not easily understood. Some tiny vineyards
are entitled to be called château, which has led to disputes
about what have been dubbed 'phantom châteaux'.
Visitors are advised, unless wine-wise, to stick to the
simpler designations.

Bourgogne (Burgundy)
Topographically a large region, stretching from Chablis
(on the east end of the Loire), noted for its steely dry
whites, to Lyons. It is particularly associated with fairly
powerful red wines and very dry whites, which tend to
acidity except for the costlier styles. Almost to Bordeaux
excesses, the prices for really top Burgundies have gone
through the roof. For value, stick to simpler local wines.
   Technically Burgundies, but often separately listed, are
the Beaujolais wines. The young red Beaujolais (not
necessarily the over-publicised *nouveau*) are delicious,
mildly chilled. There are several rather neglected
Beaujolais wines (Moulin-à-Vent, Morgon, St Amour, for
instance) that improve for several years: they represent
good value as a rule. The Mâconnais and Chalonnais also
produce sound Burgundies (red and white) that are usually
priced within reason.

Rhône
Continuation south of Burgundy. The Rhône is particularly
associated with very robust reds, notably Châteauneuf-du-
Pape; also Tavel, to my mind the finest of all still *rosé*

wines. Lirac *rosé* is nearly as good. Hermitage and
Gigondas are names to respect for reds, whites and *rosés*.
Rhône has well earned its modern reputation – no longer
Burgundy's poorer brother. From the extreme south
comes the newly 'smart' dessert *vin doux naturel*, ultra-
sweet Muscat des Beaumes-de-Venise, once despised by
British wine-drinkers. There are fashions in wine just like
anything else.

Alsace
Producer of attractive, light white wines, mostly medium-
dry, widely used as carafe wines in middle-range French
restaurants. Alsace wines are not greatly appreciated
overseas and thus remain comparatively inexpensive for
their quality; they are well placed to compete with popular
German varieties. Alsace wines are designated by grape –
principally Sylvaner for lightest styles, the widespread and
reliable Riesling for a large part of the total, and
Gerwürtztraminer for slightly fruitier wines.

Loire
Prolific producer of very reliable, if rarely great, white
wines, notably Muscadet, Sancerre, Anjou (its *rosé* is
famous), Vouvray (sparkling and semi-sparkling), and
Saumur (particularly its 'champagne styles'). Touraine
makes excellent whites and also reds of some distinction
Bourgueil and Chinon. It used to be widely believed – a
rumour put out by rivals? – that Loire wines 'did not
travel': nonsense. They are a successful export.

Champagne
So important is Champagne that, alone of French wines, it
carries no AC: its name is sufficient guarantee. (It shares
this distinction with the brandies Cognac and Armagnac.)
Vintage Champagnes from the *grandes marques* – a
limited number of 'great brands' – tend to be as expensive
in France as in Britain. You can find unknown brands of
high quality (often off-shoots of *grandes marques*) at
attractive prices, especially in the Champagne country
itself. However, you need information to discover these,
and there are true Champagnes for the home market that
are *doux* (sweet) or *demi-sec* (medium sweet) that are
pleasing to few non-French tastes. Champagne is very
closely controlled as to region, quantities, grape types,
and is made only by secondary fermentation in the bottle.
From 1993, it is prohibited (under EEC law) to state that
other wines are made by the 'champagne method' – even
if they are.

Minor regions, very briefly

Jura – Virtually unknown outside France. Try local speciality wines such as *vin jaune* if in the region.

Jurançon – Remote area; sound, unimportant white wines, sweet styles being, the better.

Cahors – Noted for its powerful *vin de pays* 'black wine', darkest red made.

Gaillac – Little known; once celebrated for dessert wines.

Savoy – Good enough table wines for local consumption. Best product of the region is delicious Chambéry vermouth: as an aperitif, do try the well distributed Chambéryzette, a unique vermouth with a hint of wild strawberries.

Bergerac – Attractive basic reds; also sweet Monbazillac, relished in France but not easily obtained outside: aged examples can be superb.

Provence – Large wine region of immense antiquity. Many and varied *vins de pays* of little distinction, usually on the sweet side, inexpensive and totally drinkable.

Midi – Stretches from Marseilles to the Spanish border. Outstandingly prolific contributor to the 'EEC wine lake' and producer of some 80 per cent of French *vins de table*, white and red. Sweet whites dominate, and there is major production of *vins doux naturels* (fortified sugary wines).

Corsica – Roughish wines of more antiquity than breeding, but by all means drink local reds – and try the wine-based aperitif Cap Corse – if visiting this remarkable island.

Paris – Yes, there is a vineyard – in Montmartre! Don't ask for a bottle: the tiny production is sold by auction, for charity, to rich collectors of curiosities.

HINTS ON SPIRITS

The great French spirit is brandy. Cognac, commercially the leader, must come from the closely controlled region of that name. Of various quality designations, the commonest is VSOP (very special old pale): it will be a cognac worth drinking neat. Remember, *champagne* in a cognac connotation has absolutely no connection with the wine. It is a topographical term, *grande champagne* being the most prestigious cognac area: *fine champagne* is a blend of brandy from the two top cognac sub-divisions.

Armagnac has become better known lately outside France, and rightly so. As a brandy it has a much longer

WINES AND SPIRITS BY JOHN DOXAT

history than cognac: some connoisseurs rate old armagnac (the quality designations are roughly similar) above cognac.

Be cautious of French brandy without a cognac or armagnac title, regardless of how many meaningless 'stars' the label carries or even the magic word 'Napoleon' (which has no legal significance).

Little appreciated in Britain is the splendid 'apple brandy', Calvados, mainly associated with Normandy but also made in Brittany and the Marne. The best is *Calvados du Pays d'Auge*. Do taste well-aged Calvados, but avoid any suspiciously cheap.

Contrary to popular belief, true Calvados is not distilled from cider – but an inferior imitation is: French cider (cidre) is excellent.

Though most French proprietary aperitifs, like Dubonnet, are fairly low in alcohol, the extremely popular Pernod/Ricard *pastis*-style brands are highly spirituous. *Eau-de-vie* is the generic term for all spirits, but colloquially tends to refer to local, often rough, distillates. Exceptions are the better *alcools blancs* (white spirits), which are not inexpensive, made from fresh fruits and not sweetened as *crèmes* are.

Bringing Back Those Bottles

When thinking of what to bring back from France in the way of alcoholic beverages, apart from considerations of weight and bulk conditioned by your mode of travel, there are a few other matters to bear in mind. Within the theoretically unlimited import for personal consumption of products which have paid any national taxes in the country of origin ('duty free' is a separate subject), there are manifest practical as well as some semi-official restrictions.

In wine to choose sensibly is not inevitably to go for the least expensive. Unless you envisage having to entertain a lot of relatives, beware the very cheapest of French table wines! Though France produces many of the world's greatest, her prolific vineyards also make wines to which no British supermarket would allocate shelf-space. Quality does count along with value. Primarily what you are saving by purchasing in France is the comparatively high excise duties imposed in Britain against the minimal ones in France. However, the British tax is just the same on a bottle of the most ordinary *vin ordinaire* as on the rarest of vintage claret. When it comes to the latter, buying fine vintage wines in France does not automatically mean obtaining a bargain, unless you are an expert. There are not that many specialist wine merchants in France, a commerce in which Britain excels.

To summarise: it is undoubtedly sound, middle range wines that are the most sensible buy.

If you like those famous liqueurs, such as Bénédictine, Chartreuse, the versatile Cointreau, which are so expensive in Britain, shop around for them: prices seem to vary markedly.

I have briefly dealt elsewhere with French spirits. If you are buying Scotch whisky, gin or vodka, you may find unfamiliar names and labels offering apparent bargains. None will harm you but some may have low, even unpleasant, taste characteristics. It is worth paying a trifle more for well-known brands, especially de-luxe styles. Though they are little sold in Britain, former French colonies distill several excellent types of rum (*rhum*).

I deem it a good idea to make an outline list of intended purchases, after deciding what you can carry and how much you wish to spend. As to wines, do you want mainly red, or only white, or what proportion of both types? Can you afford champagne? Best to buy that in visiting the region where you should have the opportunity to taste and possibly find a bargain. What about other sparklers? What do you require in dessert wines, vermouths, liqueurs, spirits? Does your list work out at more cases (12 bottles) than you can easily transport? A conspicuously overloaded vehicle may be stopped by police as a traffic hazard. Now you have a list of sorts. What about cost? For essential comparisons, I would put against each item the maximum (per bottle) I would be prepared to pay in Britain. Certainly carry a pocket calculator so, as you examine potential purchases, you can easily work out what you are saving.

Condensed glossary
of French wine and ancillary terms

Alsace – See Wine Regions.

Abricotine – Generic apricot liqueur: look for known brands.

Alcool blanc – Spirit distilled from various fruits (not wine); not fruit-flavoured cordials.

Aligoté – Light dry Burgundy.

Anis – Aniseed, much flavoured in Pernod-type aperitifs.

Anjou – See Loire (Wine Regions).

Aperitif – Literally 'opener': any drink taken as an appetiser.

Appellation (d'origine) Contrôlée – or AC wine, whose label will give you a good deal of information, will usually be costlier – but not necessarily better – than one that is a VDQS 'designated (regional) wine of superior quality'. A newer, marginally lesser category is VQPRD: 'quality wine from a specified district'. Hundreds of wines bear AC descriptions: you require knowledge and/or a wine guide to find your way around. The intention of the AC laws was to protect consumers and ensure wine was not falsely labelled – and also to prevent over-production. Only wines of reasonable standards should achieve AC status: new ones (some rather suspect) are being regularly admitted to the list.

Armagnac – See Hints on Spirits.

Barsac – Very sweet Sauternes of varying quality.

Basserau – A bit of an oddity: sparkling red Burgundy.

Beaumes-de-Venise – Well-known *vin doux naturel*; see Provence (Minor Regions).

Beaune – Famed red Burgundy; costly.

Bergerac – Sound red wine from south-west France.

Blanc de Blancs – White wine from white grapes alone. Sometimes confers extra quality but by no means always. White wine made from black grapes (the skins removed before fermentation) is *Blanc de Noirs* – Carries no special quality connotation in itself.

Bordeaux – See Wine Regions.

Bourgeuil – Reliable red Loire wine.

Bourgogne – Burgundy; see Wine Regions.

Brut – Very dry; description particularly applicable to best sparkling wines.

Brut Sauvage – Dry to the point of displeasing acidness to most palates; very rare though a few good wines carry the description.

Cabernet – Noble grape, especially Cabernet-Sauvignon for excellent, if not absolutely top grade, red wines.

Cacao – Cocoa; basis of a popular *crème*.

Calvados – See Hints on Spirits.

Cassis – Blackcurrant; notably in *crème de cassis* (see Kir).

Cave – Cellar.

Cépage – Indicates grape variety; e.g. *Cépage* Cabernet-Sauvignon.

Chablis – See Burgundy (Wine Regions). Fine Chablis are expensive.

Chai – Ground-level storehouse, wholly employed in Cognac and sometimes in Bordeaux and other districts.

Champagne – See Wine Regions. Also specially note *Méthode Traditionelle* below.

Château(x) – See Wine Regions (Bordeaux).

Châteaneuf-du-Pape – Best known of powerful Rhône red wines.

Chenin-blanc – Grape variety associated with many fine Loire wines.

Clairet – Unimportant Bordeaux wine, its distinction being probable origin of English word Claret.

Clos – Mainly a Burgundian term for vineyard formerly (rarely now) enclosed by a wall.

Cognac – See Hints on Spirits.

Corbières – Usually a sound south of France red wine.

Côte – Indicates vineyard on a hillside; no quality connotation necessarily.

Côteau(x) – Much the same as above.

Crème – Many sweet, sometimes sickly, mildly alcoholic cordials with many local specialities. Nearer to true liqueurs are top makes of *crème de menthe* and *crème de Grand Marnier* (q.v.). See also Cassis.

Crémant – Sparkling wine with strong but rather brief effervescence.

Cru – Literally 'growth'; somewhat complicated and occasionally misleading term: e.g. *grand cru* may be only grower's estimation; *cru classé* just means the wine is officially recognised, but *grand cru classé* is most likely to be something special.

Cuve close – Literally 'sealed vat'. Describes production of sparkling wines by bulk as opposed to individual bottle fermentation. Can produce satisfactory wines and certainly much superior to cheap carbonated styles.

Cuvée – Should mean unblended wine from single vat, but *cuvée spéciale* may not be particularly special: only taste will tell.

Demi-sec – Linguistically misleading, as it does not mean 'half-dry' but 'medium sweet'.

Domaine – Broadly, Burgundian equivalent to Bordeaux *château*.

Doux – Very sweet.

Eau-de-vie – Generic term for all distilled spirits but usually only applied in practice to roughish *marc* (q.v.) and the like.

Entre-deux-Mers – Undistinguished but fairly popular white Bordeaux.

Frappé – Drink served with crushed ice; viz. *crème de menthe frappé*.

Fleurie – One of several superior Beaujolais wines.

Glacé – Drink chilled by immersion of bottle in ice or in refrigerator, as distinct from *frappé* above.

Goût – Taste; also colloquial term in some regions for local *eau-de-vie* (q.v.).

Grand Marnier – Distinguished orange-flavoured liqueur. See also *crème*.

Haut – 'High'. It indicates upper part of wine district, not necessarily the best, though Haut-Médoc produces much better wines than other areas.

Hermitage – Several excellent Rhône red wines carry this title.

Izarra – Ancient Armagnac-based liqueur much favoured by its Basque originators.

Juliénas – Notable Beaujolais wine.

Kir – Well-chilled dry white wine (should be *Bourgogne Aligoté*) plus teaspoon of *crème de cassis* (q.v.). Made with champagne (or good dry sparkling wine) it is Kir Royale.

Liqueur – From old *liqueur de dessert*, denoting post-prandial digestive. Always very sweet. 'Liqueur' has become misused as indication of superior quality: to speak of 'liqueur cognac' is contradictory – yet some very fine true liqueurs are based on cognac!

Litre – 1.7 pints; 5 litres equals 1.1 gallons.

Loire – See Wine Regions.

Méthode Traditionelle – Most widely used description of superior sparkling wine made as is champagne, by fermentation in bottle, now that any labelling association such as 'champagne method' is banned.

Marc – Mostly coarse distillations from wine residue with strong local popularity. A few *marcs* ('mar') – *de Champagne, de Bourgogne* especially – have achieved a certain cult status.

Marque – Brand or company name.

Meurseult – Splendid white Burgundy for those who can afford it.

Minervoise – Respectable southern red wine: can be good value as are many such.

Mise – As in *mise en bouteilles au château* ('château-bottled', or ... *dans nos caves* ('in our cellars') and variations.

Montrachet – Very fine white Burgundy.

Moulin-à-Vent – One of the rather special Beaujolais wines.

Muscadet – Arguably the most popular light dry Loire white wines.

Muscat – Though used for some dry whites, this grape is mainly associated with succulent dessert-style wines.

Nouveau – New wine, for drinking fresh; particularly associated with now tiring vogue for *Beaujolais Nouveau*.

Pastis – General term for powerful anis/liquorice aperitifs originally evolved to replace banned *absinthe* and particularly associated with Marseilles area through great firm of Ricard.

Pétillant – Gently, naturally effervescent.

Pineau – Unfermented grape juice lightly fortified with grape spirit; attractive aperitif widely made in France and under-appreciated abroad.

Pouilly-Fuissé – Dry white Burgundy (Macon); sometimes over-valued.

Pouilly-Fumé – Easily confused with above; a very dry fine Loire white.

Porto – Port wine: usually lighter in France than the type preferred in Britain and popular, chilled, as an aperitif.

Primeur – More or less the same as *nouveau*, but more often used for fine vintage wine sold *en primeur* for laying down to mature.

Rosé – 'Pink wine', best made by allowing temporary contact of juice and black grapes during fermentation; also by mixing red and white wine.

Sauvignon – Notable white grape; see also *Cabernet*.

Sec – 'Dry', but a wine so marked will be sweetish, even very sweet. *Extra Sec* may actually mean on the dry side.

Sirop – Syrup; e.g. sugar-syrup used in mixed drinks, also some flavoured proprietory non-alcoholic cordials.

Supérieur(e) – Much the same as *Haut* (q.v.) except in VDQS.

VQRPD. – See AC above.

Vin de Xeres – Sherry ('vin de 'ereth').

Glossary of cooking terms and dishes

(It would take another book to list comprehensively French cooking terms and dishes, but here are the ones most likely to be encountered.)

Aigre-doux	bittersweet
Aiguillette	thin slice (*aiguille* – needle)
Aile	wing
Aioli	garlic mayonnaise
Allemande (à l')	German style, i.e.: with sausages and sauerkraut
Amuse-gueules	appetisers
Anglaise (à l')	plain boiled. *Crème Anglaise* – egg and cream sauce
Andouille	large uncooked sausage, served cold after boiling
Andouillettes	ditto but made from smaller intestines, usually served hot after grilling
Anis	aniseed
Argenteuil	with asparagus
Assiette Anglaise	plate of cold meats
Baba au rhum	yeast-based sponge macerated in rum
Baguette	long, thin loaf
Ballotine	boned, stuffed and rolled meat or poultry, usually cold
Béarnaise	sauce made from egg yolks, butter, tarragon, wine, shallots
Beurre blanc	sauce from Nantes, with butter, reduction of shallot-flavoured vinegar or wine
Béchamel	white sauce flavoured with infusion of herbs
Beignets	fritters
Bercy	sauce with white wine and shallots
Beurre noir	browned butter
Bigarade	with oranges
Billy By	mussel soup
Bisque	creamy shellfish soup
Blanquette	stew with thick, white creamy sauce, usually veal
Boeuf à la mode	braised beef
Bombe	ice-cream mould
Bonne femme	with root vegetables
Bordelais	Bordeaux-style, with red or white wine, marrowbone fat
Bouchée	mouthful, e.g. vol-au-vent
Boudin	sausage, white or black
Bourride	thick fish-soup
Braisé	braised

Brandade (de morue	dried salt-cod pounded into a mousse
Broche	spit
Brochette	skewer
Brouillade	stew, using oil
Brouillé	scrambled
Brûlé	burnt, e.g. *crème brûlée*
Campagne	country style
Cannelle	cinnamon
Carbonnade	braised in beer
Cardinal	red-coloured sauce, e.g. with lobster, or in *pâtisserie* with redcurrant
Cassolette or *cassoulette*	small pan
Cassoulet	rich stew with goose, pork and haricot beans
Cervelas	pork garlic sausage
Cervelles	brains
Chantilly	whipped sweetened cream
Charcuterie	cold pork-butcher's meats
Charlotte	mould, as dessert lined with sponge-fingers, as savoury lined with vegetable
Chasseur	with mushrooms, shallots, wine
Chausson	pastry turnover
Chemise	covering, i.e. pastry
Chiffonade	thinly-cut, e.g. lettuce
Choron	tomato Béarnaise
Choucroute	Alsatian stew with sauerkraut and sausages
Civet	stew
Clafoutis	batter dessert, usually with cherries
Clamart	with peas
Cocotte	covered casserole
Cocque (à la)	e.g. *oeufs* – boiled eggs
Compôte	cooked fruit
Concassé	e.g. *tomates concassées* – skinned, chopped, juice extracted
Confit	preserved
Confiture	jam
Consommé	clear soup
Cou	neck
Coulis	juice, purée (of vegetables or fruit)

Court-bouillon	aromatic liquor for cooking meat, fish, vegetables
Couscous	N. African dish with millet, chicken, vegetable variations
Crapaudine	involving fowl, particularly pigeon, trussed
Crécy	with carrots
Crème pâtissière	thick custard filling
Crêpe	pancake
Crépinette	little flat sausage, encased in caul
Croque-Monsieur	toasted cheese-and-ham sandwich
Croustade	pastry or baked bread shell
Croûte	pastry crust
Croûton	cube of fried or toasted bread
Cru	raw
Crudités	raw vegetables
Demi-glâce	basic brown sauce
Doria	with cucumber
Émincé	thinly sliced
Étuvé	stewed, e.g. vegetables in butter
Entremets	sweets
Farci	stuffed
Fines herbes	parsley, thyme, bayleaf
Feuilleté	leaves of flaky pastry
Flamande	Flemish style, with beer
Flambé	flamed in spirit
Flamiche	flan
Florentine	with spinach
Flûte	thinnest bread loaf
Foie gras	goose liver
Fondu	melted
Fond (d'artichaut)	heart (of artichoke)
Forestière	with mushrooms, bacon and potatoes
Four (au)	baked in the oven
Fourré	stuffed, usually sweets
Fricandeau	veal, usually topside
Frais, fraîche	fresh and cool
Frangipane	almond-cream pâtisserie
Fricadelle	Swedish meat ball
Fricassé	(usually of veal) in creamy sauce
Frit	fried
Frites	chips
Friture	assorted small fish, fried in batter
Froid	cold
Fumé	smoked
Galantine	loaf-shaped chopped meat, fish or vegetable, set in natural jelly

Galette	Breton pancake, flat cake
Garbure	thick country soup
Garni	garnished, usually with vegetables
Gaufre	waffle
Gelée	aspic
Gésier	gizzard
Gibier	game
Gigot	leg
Glacé	iced
Gougère	choux pastry, large base
Goujons	fried strips, usually of fish
Graine	seed
Gratin	baked dish of vegetables cooked in cream and eggs
Gratinée	browned under grill
Grecque (à la)	cold vegetables served in oil
Grenadin	nugget of meat, usually of veal
Grenouilles	frogs; cuisses de grenouille – frogs' legs
Grillé	grilled
Gros sel	coarse salt
Hachis	minced or chopped
Haricot	slow cooked stew
Hochepot	hotpot
Hollandaise	sauce with egg, butter, lemon
Hongroise	Hungarian, i.e. spiced with paprika
Hors-d'oeuvre	assorted starters
Huile	oil
Île flottante	floating island – soft meringue on egg-custard sauce
Indienne	Indian, i.e. with hot spices
Jambon	ham
Jardinière	from the garden, i.e. with vegetables
Jarret	shin, e.g. jarret de veau
Julienne	matchstick vegetables
Jus	natural juice
Lait	milk
Langue	tongue
Lard	bacon
Longe	loin
Macédoine	diced fruits or vegetables
Madeleine	small sponge cake
Magret	breast (of duck)
Maïs	sweetcorn
Maître d'hôtel	sauce with butter, lemon, parsley
Marchand de vin	sauce with red wine, shallots
Marengo	sauce with tomatoes, olive oil, white wine

Marinière	seamens' style e.g. *moules marinière* (mussels in white wine)
Marmite	deep casserole
Matelote	fish stew, e.g. of eel
Médaillon	round slice
Melange	mixture
Meunière	sauce with butter, lemon
Miel	honey
Mille-feuille	flaky pastry, (lit. 1,000 leaves)
Mirepoix	cubed carrot, onion etc. used for sauces
Moëlle	beef marrow
Mornay	cheese sauce
Mouclade	mussel stew
Mousseline	Hollandaise sauce, lightened with egg whites
Moutarde	mustard
Nage (à la)	poached in flavoured liquor (fish)
Nature	plain
Navarin (d'agneau)	stew of lamb with spring vegetables
Noisette	nut-brown, burned butter
Noix de veau	nut (leg) of veal
Normande	Normandy style, i.e. with cream, apple, cider, Calvados
Nouilles	noodles
Onglet	beef cut from flank
Os	bone
Paillettes	straws (of pastry)
Panaché	mixed
Panade	flour crust
Papillote (en)	cooked in paper case
Parmentier	with potatoes
Pâté	paste, of meat or fish
Pâte	pastry
Pâté brisée	rich short-crust pastry
Pâtisserie	pastries
Paupiettes	paper-thinslice
Pavé	thick slice
Paysan	country style
Périgueux	with truffles
Persillade	chopped parsley and garlic topping
Petits fours	tiny cakes, sweetmeats
Petit pain	bread roll
Piperade	peppers, onions, tomatoes in scrambled egg
Poché	poached
Poêlé	fried
Poitrine	breast
Poivre	pepper
Pommade	paste
Potage	thick soup

Pot-au-four	broth with meat and vegetables
Potée	country soup with cabbage
Pralines	caramelised almonds
Primeurs	young veg
Printanier (printanière)	garnished with early vegetables
Profiteroles	choux paslry balls
Provençale	with garlic, tomatoes, olive oil, peppers
Pureé	mashed and sieved
Quenelle	pounded fish or meat bound with egg, poached
Queue	tail
Quiche	pastry flan, e.g. *quiche Lorraine* – egg, bacon, cream
Râble	saddle, e.g. *râble de lièvre*
Ragoût	stew
Ramequin	little pot
Râpé	grated
Ratatouille	Provençale stew of onions, garlic, peppers, tomatoes
Ravigote	highly seasoned white sauce
Rémoulade	mayonnaise with gherkins, capers, herbs and shallots
Rillettes	potted shredded meat, usually fat pork or goose
Riz	rice
Robert	sauce with mustard, vinegar, onion
Roquefort	ewe's milk blue cheese
Rossini	garnished with foie gras and truffle
Rôti	roast
Rouelle	nugget
Rouille	hot garlicky sauce for *soupe de poisson*
Roulade	roll
Roux	sauce base – flour and butter
Sabayon	sweet fluffy sauce, with eggs and wine
Safran	saffron
Sagou	sago
St-Germain	with peas
Salade niçoise	with tunny, anchovies, tomatoes, beans, black olives
Salé	salted
Salmis	dish of game or fowl, with red wine
Sang	blood
Santé	lit. healthy, i.e. with spinach and potato
Salpicon	meat, fowl, vegetables, chopped fine, bound with sauce and used as fillings

Saucisse	fresh sausage	*Thé*	tea
Saucisson	dried sausage	*Tiède*	luke warm
Sauté	cooked in fat in open pan	*Timbale*	steamed mould
Sauvage	wild	*Tisane*	infusion
Savarin	ring of yeast-sponge, soaked in syrup and liquor	*Tourte*	pie
		Tranche	thick slice
Sel	salt	*Truffes*	truffles
Selle	saddle	*Tuile*	tile, i.e. thin biscuit
Selon	according to, e.g. *selon grosseur* (according to size)		
		Vacherin	meringue confection
Smitane	with sour cream, white wine, onion	*Vallée d'Auge*	with cream, apple, Calvados
		Vapeur (au)	steamed
Soissons	with dried white beans	*Velouté*	white sauce, bouillon-flavoured
Sorbet	water ice		
Soubise	with creamed onions	*Véronique*	with grapes
Soufflé	puffed, i.e. mixed with egg white and baked	*Vert(e)*	green, e.g. *sauce verte*, with herbs
Sucre	sugar (*sucré* – sugared)	*Vessie*	pig's bladder
Suprême	fillet of poultry breast or fish	*Vichysoisse*	chilled creamy leek and potato soup
Tartare	raw minced beef, flavoured with onions etc. and bound with raw egg	*Vierge*	prime olive oil
		Vinaigre	vinegar (lit. bitter wine)
		Vinaigrette	wine vinegar and oil dressing
Tartare (sauce)	mayonnaise with capers, herbs, onions	*Volaille*	poultry
		Vol-au-vent	puff-pastry case
Tarte Tatin	upside down apple pie		
Terrine	pottery dish/baked minced, chopped meat, veg., chicken, fish or fruit	*Xérès*	sherry
		Yaourt	yoghurt

FISH – Les Poissons, SHELLFISH – Les Coquillages

Alose	shad	*Daurade*	sea bream
Anchois	anchovy	*Écrevisse*	crayfish
Anguille	eel	*Éperlan*	smelt
Araignée de mer	spider crab	*Espadon*	swordfish
		Étrille	baby crab
Bar	sea bass	*Favouille*	spider crab
Barbue	brill	*Flétan*	halibut
Baudroie	monkfish, anglerfish	*Fruits de mer*	seafood
Belon	oyster – flat shelled	*Grondin*	red gurnet
Bigorneau	winkle	*Hareng*	herring
Blanchaille	whitebait	*Homard*	lobster
Brochet	pike	*Huître*	oyster
Cabillaud	cod	*Julienne*	ling
Calamar	squid	*Laitance*	soft herring-roe
Carpe	carp	*Lamproie*	lamprey
Carrelet	plaice	*Langouste*	spring lobster, or crawfish
Chapon de mer	scorpion fish	*Langoustine*	Dublin Bay prawn
Claire	oyster	*Lieu*	ling
Coquille St-Jacques	scallop	*Limand*	lemon sole
		Lotte de mer	monkfish
Crabe	crab	*Loup de mer*	sea bass
Crevette grise	shrimp	*Maquereau*	mackerel
Crevette rose	prawn	*Merlan*	whiting

Morue	salt cod	*St-Pierre*	John Dory
Moule	mussel	*Sandre*	zander
Mulet	grey mullet	*Saumon*	salmon
Ombre	grayling	*Saumonette*	rock salmon
Oursin	sea urchin	*Seiche*	squid
Palourde	clam	*Sole*	sole
Pétoncle	small scallop	*Soupion*	inkfish
Plie	plaice	*Thon*	tunny
Portugaise	oyster	*Tortue*	turtle
Poulpe	octopus	*Torteau*	large crab
Praire	oyster	*Truite*	trout
Raie	skate	*Turbot*	turbot
Rascasse	scorpion-fish	*Turbotin*	chicken turbot
Rouget	red mullet		

FRUITS – Les Fruits, VEGETABLES – Les Légumes, NUTS – Les Noix

HERBS – Les Herbes, SPICES – Les Épices

Ail	garlic	*Courgette*	courgette
Algue	seaweed	*Cresson*	watercress
Amande	almond	*Échalote*	shallot
Ananas	pineapple	*Endive*	chicory
Aneth	dill	*Épinard*	spinach
Abricot	apricot	*Escarole*	salad leaves
Arachide	peanut	*Estragon*	tarragon
Artichaut	globe artichoke	*Fenouil*	fennel
Asperge	asparagus	*Fève*	broad bean
Avocat	avocado	*Flageolet*	dried bean
Banane	banana	*Fraise*	strawberry
Basilic	basil	*Framboise*	raspberry
Betterave	beetroot	*Genièvre*	juniper
Blette	Swiss chard	*Gingembre*	ginger
Brugnon	nectarine	*Girofle*	clove
Cassis	blackcurrant	*Girolle*	edible fungus
Céléri	celery	*Grenade*	pomegranate
Céléri-rave	celeriac	*Griotte*	bitter red cherry
Cêpe	edible fungus	*Groseille*	gooseberry
Cerfeuil	chervil	*Groseille noire*	blackcurrant
Cerise	cherry	*Groseille rouge*	redcurrant
Champignon	mushroom	*Haricot*	dried white bean
Chanterelle	edible fungus	*Haricot vert*	French bean
Châtaigne	chestnut	*Laitue*	lettuce
Chicorée	endive	*Mandarine*	tangerine, mandarin
Chou	cabbage	*Mangetout*	sugar pea
Chou-fleur	cauliflower	*Marron*	chestnut
Choux de Bruxelles	Brussels sprouts	*Menthe*	mint
		Mirabelle	tiny gold plum
Ciboulette	chive	*Morille*	dark brown crinkly edible fungus
Citron	lemon		
Citron vert	lime	*Mûre*	blackberry
Coing	quince	*Muscade*	nutmeg
Concombre	cucumber	*Myrtille*	bilberry, blueberry
Coriandre	coriander	*Navet*	turnip
Cornichon	gherkin	*Noisette*	hazelnut
Courge	pumpkin	*Oignon*	onion

Oseille	sorrel	*Pomme*	apple
Palmier	palm	*Pomme de terre*	potato
Pamplemousse	grapefruit	*Prune*	plum
Panais	parsnip	*Pruneau*	prune
Passe-Pierre	seaweed	*Quetsch*	small dark plum
Pastèque	water melon	*Radis*	radish
Peche	peach	*Raifort*	horseradish
Persil	parsley	*Raisin*	grape
Petit pois	pea	*Reine Claude*	greengage
Piment doux	sweet pepper	*Romarin*	rosemary
Pissenlit	dandelion	*Safran*	saffron
Pistache	pistachio	*Salsifis*	salsify
Pleurote	edible fungi	*Thym*	thyme
Poire	pear	*Tilleul*	lime blossom
Poireau	leek	*Tomate*	tomato
Poivre	pepper	*Topinambour*	Jerusalem artichoke
Poivron	green, red and yellow peppers	*Truffe*	truffle

MEAT – Les Viandes

Le Boeuf	Beef	*Le Porc*	Pork
Charolais	is the best	*Jambon*	ham
Chateaubriand	double fillet steak	*Jambon cru*	raw smoked ham
Contrefilet	sirloin	*Porcelet*	suckling pig
Entrecôte	rib steak		
Faux Filet	sirloin steak	*Le Veau*	Veal
Filet	fillet	*Escalope*	thin slice cut from fillet
L'Agneau	Lamb	*Les Abats*	Offal
Pré-Salé	is the best	*Foie*	liver
Carré	neck cutlets	*Foie gras*	goose liver
Côte	chump chop	*Cervelles*	brains
Epaule	shoulder	*Langue*	tongue
Gigot	leg	*Ris*	sweetbreads
		Rognons	kidneys
		Tripes	tripe

POULTRY – Volaille, GAME – Gibier

Abatis	giblets	*Lièvre*	hare
Bécasse	woodcock	*Oie*	goose
Bécassine	snipe	*Perdreau*	partridge
Caille	quail	*Pigeon*	pigeon
Canard	duck	*Pintade*	guineafowl
Caneton	duckling	*Pluvier*	plover
Chapon	capon	*Poularde*	chicken (boiling)
Chevreuil	roe deer	*Poulet*	chicken (roasting)
Dinde	young hen turkey	*Poussin*	spring chicken
Dindon	turkey	*Sanglier*	wild boar
Dindonneau	young turkey	*Sarcelle*	teal
Faisan	pheasant	*Venaison*	venison
Grive	thrush		